Since the publication of his *Introduction to Theoretical Linguistics* (1968), Sir John Lyons has been one of the most important and internationally renowned contributors to the study of linguistics. In a career which has spanned several decades, he has addressed himself to a broad range of issues of fundamental importance and is particularly noted for his seminal two-volume work, *Semantics* (1977). The present volume, which is edited with an introduction by F.R. Palmer, gathers together a collection of essays by distinguished scholars on topics related to Lyons' work. In a concluding essay, Lyons responds to the contributors and reflects on the intellectual underpinning of his own work.

T0370905

Grammar and meaning

Grammar and meaning

Essays in honour of
SIR JOHN LYONS

Edited by

F.R. Palmer
Professor Emeritus, University of Reading

CAMBRIDGE
UNIVERSITY PRESS

CAMBRIDGE UNIVERSITY PRESS
Cambridge, New York, Melbourne, Madrid, Cape Town, Singapore, São Paulo

Cambridge University Press
The Edinburgh Building, Cambridge CB2 8RU, UK

Published in the United States of America by Cambridge University Press, New York

www.cambridge.org
Information on this title: www.cambridge.org/9780521462211

First published 1995
Reprinted 1996
This digitally printed version 2008

A catalogue record for this publication is available from the British Library

Library of Congress Cataloguing in Publication data
Grammar and meaning: essays in honour of Sir John Lyons / edited by
F.R. Palmer
    p.   cm.
Includes index.
ISBN 0 521 46221 5 (hardback)
1. Grammar, Comparative and general. 2. Semantics. I. Lyons,
John, 1932– . II. Palmer, F.R. (Frank Robert)
P201.G675   1995
415–dc20   94-45099   CIP

ISBN 978-0-521-46221-1 hardback
ISBN 978-0-521-05477-5 paperback

Contents

viii   Contents

Contributors

JOHN ANDERSON
Professor of English Language, University of Edinburgh

BERNARD COMRIE
Professor of Linguistics, University of Southern California

R. M. W. DIXON
Professor of Linguistics, Australian National University

GERALD GAZDAR
Professor of Computational Linguistics, University of Sussex

RUTH M. KEMPSON
Professor of Linguistics, School of Oriental and African Studies, University of London

ADAM KILGARRIFF
Information Technology Research Institute, University of Brighton

ADRIENNE LEHRER
Professor of Linguistics, University of Arizona

KEITH LEHRER
Professor of Philosophy, University of Arizona

STEPHEN C. LEVINSON
Director of the Max Planck Institute for Psycholinguistics, Nijmegen, The Netherlands

PETER MATTHEWS
Professor of Linguistics, University of Cambridge

JIM MILLER
Lecturer in Linguistics, University of Edinburgh

F.R. PALMER
Emeritus Professor of Linguistics, University of Reading

PETER TRUDGILL
Professor of English Language and Linguistics, University of Lausanne

Foreword

F. R. PALMER

A Festschrift for John Lyons is long overdue. He is, without question, one of the most outstanding and internationally famed linguists of the present time, with a distinguished career as Lecturer in the Universities of London and Cambridge, as Professor in the Universities of Edinburgh and of Sussex and now as Master of Trinity Hall Cambridge. He has lectured widely and has published (and is still publishing) many important books and articles. He has deservedly received many honours and awards, including five honorary doctorates and, most significantly, a knighthood 'for services to the study of linguistics'. As yet, however, no volume has been published in his honour. That omission is now to be rectified.

There are, I believe, two requirements of a good Festschrift. The first is that it should have a clearly recognisable theme, and one, moreover, that is associated with the person in whose honour it is published. The second is that the contributions should be made by scholars who have been closely connected as colleagues, students or friends. I have, I hope, as editor, succeeded in satisfying both of these requirements. The choice of the theme was easy enough. John Lyons has worked mainly in the field of semantics, and is probably best known for his magnificent two-volume *Semantics* (1977), which is, I believe, the most comprehensive scholarly work on a single topic in linguistics that has ever been published. But he has also been interested in grammar, and in the relationship between grammar and semantics, as can be seen in (among others) his earlier, but no less scholarly, *Introduction to Theoretical Linguistics* (1968); for that reason the theme of 'Grammar and semantics' came readily to mind. The choice of contributors was a little more difficult, since the aim was to approach the theme from as many directions as possible and there was, in the end, the agonising task of deciding who should be left out. Inevitably there will be some who will be disappointed that, in spite of their close associations with him, they have not been asked to offer a paper.

xi

There are also two slightly unusual aspects of this volume. The first is that I am, perhaps, an unusual choice for editor. Editors of Festschrifts are usually junior colleagues or ex-students of the person honoured, but I am ten years older than John and entered the discipline some years before he did. Yet I agreed to take on this task partly because no fewer than three colleagues, from three different universities and acting quite independently, asked me to do so, but, more importantly, because of both my very long-standing friendship with him and my very great respect for him. The second unusual aspect is that he himself was asked to make a contribution to the volume. There were several reasons for this. One was that it seemed impossible to keep it a secret (though, admittedly, the secrecy of Fest-schrifts is usually breached). Rather more important was the fact that I wished that he should have some part in the choice of contributors, both because I felt that it was right that he should be personally involved in advising which of his friends and colleagues should be invited and because I was sure that he would greatly assist me in judging the kind of contribution each of them might make. Most important of all, however, is the fact that I knew that a paper from him would be seen as a most valuable contribution to the volume. What I had hoped for was a partly autobiographical account of his thinking, together with a restatement of his views and some critical comments on the other papers. I was not disappointed.

This contribution has provided me with an added bonus as editor. A long preface discussing the individual papers would now be both superfluous and presumptuous, particularly in view of the fact that my general theoretical approach to semantics and, indeed, to linguistics in general is very close to his. I could not have so clearly related the works of the various contributors to his own work as skilfully as he has done, and it would have been inappropriate for me, as mere editor, to make critical and telling remarks of the kind that are to be found in his paper.

Yet it may be useful to anticipate here his statement concerning what he considers to be the issues that are the most relevant to the topics discussed in this volume (p. 229): Is the grammatical (and phonological) structure of natural languages determined by meaning (and, if so, how and to what degree)? Is semantics a separate level of analysis on a par with grammar and phonology? Is the structure (grammatical, phonological, semantic) which linguists claim to be describing really part of the language or is it an artefact of their theoretical and methodological decisions? The extent, however, to which the various papers directly tackle these issues varies. The two most directly concerned are those of Matthews and Kilgarriff & Gazdar, who specifically discuss problems of levels, while the papers of Comrie and

Dixon are concerned with the meanings of grammatical categories (though with rather different views on the relationship between grammar and semantics). The contributions of Trudgill and Miller are more concerned with grammar (the first primarily descriptive, dealing with an instance of grammaticalization, the second concerned with the theoretical issue of sentence vs. clause). Those of Kempson and Lehrer & Lehrer deal with semantic theory, but even these are shown in the Lyons paper to be relevant to the basic issues. The reader who wishes to know what the volume is about and how it relates to the work of John Lyons should read his contribution first, though there will be a considerable advantage in looking at it again, especially for the critical comments, when the other papers are being read.

A Festschrift is intended to honour a distinguished academic career, but not to signal the end of it. We look forward to many more valuable contributions to scholarship from John Lyons in the future.

Polysemous relations

ADAM KILGARRIFF AND GERALD GAZDAR

1 Introduction

In the section of Lyons' *Semantics* that deals with the distinction between homonymy and polysemy, he notes that a major criterion 'is unrelatedness vs. relatedness of meaning . . . indeed, it is arguable that it is the only synchronically relevant consideration' (1977: 551). However, he goes on to argue that all attempts 'to explicate the notion of relatedness of meaning in terms of a componential analysis of the senses of lexemes . . . have so far failed' (1977: 552–3). Although Lyons is sympathetic to a treatment of the lexicon that seeks to maximise polysemy at the expense of homonymy, he does not himself go on in that book to reconstruct the notion of relatedness of meaning that such a treatment requires.

Discussing polysemy some nine years earlier, Lyons was a little more explicit about what might be required: 'Various . . . types of "extension" or "transference" of meaning were recognized by the Greek grammarians, and have passed into traditional works on rhetoric, logic, and semantics. Meanings that are more or less closely "related" in accordance with such principles are not traditionally regarded as being sufficiently different to justify the recognition of distinct words' (1968: 406). Metaphorical extension is the only kind of extension explicitly discussed in connection with polysemy in *Introduction to Theoretical Linguistics* although it is clear from the quotation just given that it was not the only one that Lyons had in mind. It is surprising, therefore, to find the following passage in a later work: 'it is metaphorical extension . . . that is at issue when one refers to the related meanings of polysemous lexemes. There are, of course, other kinds of relatedness of meaning, which are irrelevant in this connection' (1981: 47).

The opening lines of the entry for *silk* in Flexner (1987: 1780) read as follows:

> *silk* (silk), *n*. 1. the soft lustrous fiber obtained as a filament from the cocoon of the silkworm. 2. thread made from this fiber. 3. cloth made from this fiber. 4. a garment of this cloth.

If the notion of polysemy is to earn its keep, then it must surely be applicable to such a set of senses. And yet the relation between a meaning denoting a fibre and a meaning denoting a thread made from that fibre, or that between a meaning denoting a cloth and a meaning denoting a garment made from that cloth, is surely that of metonymy rather than metaphorical extension. Our concern in this chapter, however, is not to explore the range of polysemous relations that dictionaries attest to, but rather to attend to their systematic and partial regularity. If a relation holds for *silk* then it may well also hold for *cotton*. And if a relation holds for *silk*, *cotton* and *wool*, then it probably also holds for less familiar words like *guanaco*.

Our topic is thus what Apresjan calls 'regular polysemy' (1974). He distinguishes cases of polysemy where the same relationship holds between the senses for two or more polysemous words from those where the relationship is particular to a single word. He points to a similarity between relations of regular polysemy and those of derivational morphology and proceeds to catalogue the regular polysemous relations of Russian. But he does not explore the formal structure of the regularities, nor does he address their exception-prone character. And he does not consider how such relations might be called into service as part of an account of lexical structure. Apresjan's phrase, 'regular polysemy', is potentially misleading in a couple of respects. Firstly, by a standard Gricean inference, use of the phrase implies that there might be a category of 'irregular polysemy'. However, it seems to us that, once we have a fully developed theory of subregularity, it is unlikely that a distinction between 'irregular polysemy' and 'homonymy' would serve any purpose in a synchronic description of the lexicon. Secondly, the phrase fails to convey the problematic subregular character of the relations involved. Our thesis is that 'regular polysemy', while often less regular than lexical syntax or inflectional morphology, is, like them, subregular and is appropriately described using the same formal machinery. Arguably, polysemy is simply null derivation.

Until very recently, and with odd exceptions, polysemous relations have received little attention in the literature on the lexicon. We suspect that this neglect has a lot to do with the fact that linguists have not had plausible machinery for dealing with subregular phenomena. That situation has changed over the last few years in the wake of the development of a number of lexical description languages by computational linguists and their application to, *inter alia*, the representation of polysemy (see Kilgarriff (1992) and Copestake (1993) for full discussion and references to the literature). In this chapter we will use the lexical representation language DATR to represent polysemous relations such as those evidenced in the extract from the *Random House Dictionary* cited above. In section 2, we provide an informal introduction to the DATR language and, in section 3, we go on to define a lexicon fragment that illustrates how DATR can be used to express the kind of subregular generalisations that are pervasive over lexical senses.

2 Lexical representation

Evans & Gazdar (1989a, 1989b) give formal presentations of a semantics, and a theory of inference, for DATR, a lexical knowledge representation language. The goal of the DATR work was to define (and implement) a simple language that (i) has the necessary expressive power to encode the lexical entries presupposed by contemporary work in the unification grammar tradition, (ii) can express all the evident generalisations about the information implicit in those entries, (iii) embodies an explicit theory of inference, (iv) is readily implementable, and (v) has an explicit declarative semantics. DATR defines networks allowing multiple default inheritance of information through links typed by attribute paths. This typing provides the basis for a 'most specific path wins' default inheritance principle. The language is functional, that is, it defines a mapping which assigns unique values to node attribute-path pairs. Recovery of these values is deterministic – no search is involved.

In addition to punctuation, DATR contains two kinds of primitive object: nodes, which, by convention, are always marked with an initial capital letter, and atoms, which appear in lower case. When atoms appear between angle brackets they are referred to as attributes, and sequences of attributes are known as paths. Atoms that appear elsewhere are called values. DATR theories (in the logician's sense of theory – a set of axioms from which theorems may be derived) consist of a set of equations.[1] Every DATR equation has a pair of a node and a path as its left-hand side (LHS). The simplest kind of DATR equation simply has zero or more values on the RHS.

        Node:Path==Values.

Here are some examples:

        ENTITY:<collocates>==.
        FIBRE:<genus>==fibre.

Jersey:<alt garment collocates>==football.
Felt:<made-of>==matted fibre.

The first example says, unsurprisingly, that the set of collocates associated with the E NTITY node is empty; the second that the genus attribute for the FIBRE node has the value fibre; the third that the collocates list for the alternant garment sense of the Jersey lexeme consists of football; and the fourth that the made-of attribute for the lexeme Felt equates to the two-element value sequence matted fibre.[2] (Sequences of) values are the principal 'results' of a DATR theory: the typical operation involves proving a theorem that will provide the value sequence associated with a given node/path pair.

More generally, the RHS of equations can be values, inheritance descriptors (quoted or unquoted) or (possibly empty) sequences of values and/or descriptors. Inheritance descriptors specify where the required values can be inherited from, and sequences allow arbitrary lists of atoms to be built as values. Inheritance descriptors come in several forms with two dimensions of variation. The unquoted/quoted distinction specifies whether the inheritance context is local (the most recent context employed) or global (in simple cases, the initial context employed). Once the context is established, the descriptor specifies a new node, a new path or both to be used to determine the inherited value. We will give examples of most of the syntactic possibilities below.

A second type of simple DATR equation uses a node/path pair as its inheritance descriptor and thus has the following form,

Node1:Path1==Node2:Path2.

which says that the value of Path1 at Node1 is to be found by getting the value of Path2 at Node2. A variant of this second DATR statement type uses a Node as an inheritance descriptor,

Node1:Path==Node2.

but this can be seen as simply an abbreviation for

Node1:Path==Node2:Path.

And such a statement tells us that the value of Path at Node1 is to be sought at Node2. Here are some examples of this frequently used statement type:

Flax:<>==CROP.
CROP:<>==PLANT.

```
PLANT:<>==ENTITY.
Canvas:<alternants>==ARTEFACT .
```

Here, the first three statements tell us that the lexeme Flax inherits values from corresponding paths at the CROP node; that CROP inherits values from PLANT and that the latter inherits from ENTITY. The final example says that the value for the <alternants> path of the lexeme Canvas is to be sought from the corresponding path at the ARTEFACT node.

Another type of simple DATR equation uses a path as an inheritance descriptor and has the form

```
Node:Path1==Path2.
```

which can be seen as no more than an abbreviation for

```
Node:Path1==Node:Path2.
```

and this says that the value of Path1 at Node is to be sought by finding the value of Path2 at Node.

```
ENTITY:<alt genus word>==<word>.
```

This example can be glossed as saying that the value for the <alt genus word> path at the ENTITY node is to be obtained by finding the value for the attribute word at the same node.

A third type of DATR equation turns out to be invaluable in DATR analyses, but is conceptually rather different from the equation types that we have just introduced. It uses a quoted path as the inheritance descriptor and looks like this.

```
Node:Path1=="Path".
```

Its interpretation involves a global reference to the node from which one's query originated – at the risk of oversimplification, we can paraphrase it as saying that the value of Path1 at Node is whatever the value of Path2 is at the original query node. The following is a characteristic example of the use of this quoted path form:

```
YARN:<made-of>=="<source>".
```

This says, in effect, that yarns are made of whatever substance is identified as the value of the source attribute at the node from which the query originated. If we had said,

```
YARN:<made-of>==<source>.
```

then we would most likely get no value at all, since this is just equivalent to

YARN:<made-of>==YARN:<source>.

and <source> is unlikely to be defined at the (abstract) YARN node, nor, in the absence of a global reference mechanism, could it be usefully defined so as to return exactly the source of whatever particular lexeme we happened to be interested in.

There are two other basic DATR equation types, which use quoted nodes and quoted node/path pairs as their descriptors:

Node1:Path=="Node2".
Node1:Path1=="Node2:Path2".

Their semantics is subtle and, although our treatment of the flax/linen relation makes use of an instance of the latter, they will not be discussed further here.

One further aspect of DATR is illustrated in the fragment that we present in section 3. This is the possibility of having sequences of values and/or inheritance descriptors on the right-hand side of equations. Thus all of the following are perfectly legal, along with an infinity of others:

Node1:Path1==Value1.
Node1:Path1==Value1 Path2.
Node1:Path1==Path2 Value1.
Node1:Path1==Value1 Node2.
Node1:Path1==Node2 Value1.
Node1:Path1==Value1 Value2.
Node1:Path1==Value1 "Path2".
Node1:Path1==Node2:Path2 Value1.
Node1:Path1=="Path3" Value1 Node2:Path2.
Node1:Path1==Node2:Path2 Value1 "Path3" Value2.

Here are some concrete examples taken from the fragment with which the present chapter deals.

PLANT:<collocates>==grow ENTITY.
Cotton:<alt fibre collocates>==wool FIBRE:<collocates>.
YARN:<made-of>=="<source>" fibre.
CROP:<alternants>==fibre seed PLANT.

These behave as the notation would lead you to expect – instead of getting atomic values from them, one gets value sequences.

Now that we have presented the syntax of the DATR language, we will turn briefly to a couple of key rules of inference that apply in the language. The first rule implements local inheritance, and uses the following additional metanotational device: the expression $E0\{E2/E1\}$ denotes the result of substituting $E2$ for all occurrences of $E1$ in $E0$.

(LOC) Node2:Path2==A.
       Node1:Path1==B.

─────────────────────────

       Node1:Path1==B{A/Node2:Path2}.

Rule LOC says that if we have a theorem Node1:Path1==B., where B contains Node2:Path2 as a subexpression, and we also have a theorem Node2:Path2==A., then we can derive a theorem in which all occurrences of Node2:Path2 in B are replaced by A. In the simplest case, this means that we can interpret a statement of the form

       Node1:Path1==Node2:Path2.

as an inheritance specification meaning 'the value of Path1 at Node1 is inherited from Path2 at Node2'. So, for example, from:

       Flax:<word>==flax.
       Linen:<source>==Flax:<word>.

one can infer:

       Linen:<source>==flax.

LOC can also handle inheritance for node and path descriptors, in view of the following, already noted, equivalences:

       Node1:Path1==Node2.   *is equivalent to*
       Node1:Path1==Node2:Path1.

       Node1:Path==Path2.   *is equivalent to*
       Node1:Path1==Node1:Path2.

Rule LOC implements a local notion of inheritance in the sense that the new node or path specifications are interpreted in the current local context. The second inference rule considered here implements a non-local notion of inheritance: quoted paths specify paths which are to be interpreted in the context of the node in which the original query was made (the global context), rather than the current context.[3]

(GLO) Node1:Path2==Value.
       Node1:Path1==A.

─────────────────────────

       Node1:Path1==A{Value/"Path2"}.

To see how the operation of the GLO rule differs from LOC, consider the following theory:

> YARN:
>   <source>==undefined
>   <made-of>==<source>.
>
> Linen:
>   <source>==flax
>   <made-of>==YARN.

The intention here is that the YARN node expresses the generalisation that yarns are made of whatever the source material is for the instance of yarn involved. But the theory as stated fails to express this intention since we can derive the following unwanted theorem:

> Linen:
>   <made-of>==undefined.

To achieve the desired result, we must modify the theory as follows:

> YARN:
>   <source>==undefined
>   <made-of>=="<source>".
>
> Linen:
>   <source>==flax
>   <made-of>==YARN.

With this change, the GLO inference rule allows us to derive the theorem we want:

> Linen:
>   <made-of>==flax.

The proof is as follows:

> 1 Linen:(made-of)==YARN.   <given>
> 2 YARN:(made-of)=="<source>".   <given>
> 3 Linen:(made-of)=="<source>". <LOC on 1 and 2>
> 4 Linen:(source)==flax.   <given>
> 5 Linen:(made-of)==flax.   <GLO on 3 and 4>

For completeness, we state below the only other inference rule that is relevant to the fragment in this chapter, but we will not discuss it.

> (QNP) Node2:Path2==Value.
>   Node1:Path1==A.
>   ───────────────────────
>   Node1:Path1==A{Value/"Node2:Path2"}.

In addition to the conventional inference described above, DATR has a non-monotonic notion of inference by default: each equation about some node/path combination implicitly determines additional equations about all the extensions to the path at that node for which no more specific equation exists in the theory.

To characterise this notion of default inference, we need some auxiliary definitions. The expression Path1^Path2 denotes the path formed by concatenating the two paths. And we say that Path3 is an extension of Path1 if and only if there is a Path2 such that Path3=Path1^Path 2, and that Path3 is a strict extension of Path1 if and only if Path2 is non-empty. We also use the ^ operator to denote extension of all the paths in a DATR equation, as in the following examples:

If	S	is	N:<a>==v.
then	S^<bc>	is	N:<a b c>==v.
If	S	is	N1:<a>==N2:<bc>.
then	S^<bc>	is	N1:<a b c>==N2:<b c b c>.
If	S	is	N1:<a>=="<>".
then	S^<bc>	is	N1:<a b c>=="<b c>".

Given an equation S, we define the root of S to be the node/path expression appearing to the left of the equality in S (e.g. the root of Node:Path== Value. is Node:Path). Given a set of equations T, a Node and a Path, we say Node:Path is specified in T if and only if T contains an equation S whose root is Node:Path.

Let Node1:Path1 and Node1:Path2 be such that Node1:Path1 is specified in T. We say Node1:Path2 is connected to Node1:Path1 (relative to T) if and only if:

1 Path2 is an extension of Path1;
2 there is no strict extension Path3 of Path1 of which Path2 is an extension such that Node1:Path3 is specified in T.

So Node1:Path2 is connected to Node1:Path1 if and only if Path1 is the maximal subpath of Path2 that is specified (with Node1) in T.

Given a set of equations T, we define the path closure of T to be:

{S^Q | S is an equation in T, with root Node:Path, and
Node:Path^Q is connected to Node:Path}

It is clear from these definitions that any Node:Path is connected to itself and thus that T is always a subset of the path closure of T. The path closure contains all those theorems which can be inferred by default from T. The operation of path closure is non-monotonic: if we add more equations to our original theory, some of our derived equations may cease to be true. The two forms of inference in DATR are combined by taking the path closure of a theory first, and then applying the inference rules to the result.

To illustrate path closure, consider the following example theory:

```
CROP:
  <>==PLANT
  <syntax>==MASS-NOUN:<>
  <alt fibre>==FIBRE:<>.

Cotton:
  <>==CROP
  <word>==cotton.
```

We can infer by default the following theorems, among others:

```
CROP:
  <genus>==PLANT:<genus>
  <made-of>==PLANT:<made-of>
  <artefact>==PLANT:<artefact>
  <collocates>==PLANT:<collocates>
  <syntax cat>==MASS-NOUN:<cat>
  <syntax count>==MASS-NOUN:<count>
  <syntax concrete>==MASS-NOUN:<concrete>
  <alt fibre alt yarn>==FIBRE:<alt yarn>
  <alt fibre alt yarn alt fabric>==FIBRE:<alt yarn alt fabric>.

Cotton:
  <word form>==cotton
  <genus>==CROP:<genus>
  <word root form>==cotton
  <made-of>==CROP:<made-of>
  <artefact>==CROP:<artefact>
  <collocates>==CROP:<collocates>
  <syntax cat>==CROP:<syntax cat>
  <syntax count>==CROP:<syntax count>
  <syntax concrete>==CROP:<syntax concrete>
  <alt fibre alt yarn>==CROP:<alt fibre alt yarn>
  <alt fibre alt yarn alt fabric>==CROP:<alt fibre alt yarn alt
    fabric>.
```

Note the way in which equations that have paths on their RHS are also extended by the subpath used to extend the LHS. This characteristic of the DATR language plays a crucial role in our treatment of alternant meanings in the rest of this chapter.

3 Representing polysemy

In the fragment presented below, information about both the word and its denotation is accessed through a node in an inheritance network associated with the word. We refer to these eponymous nodes as *lexemes*. Thus a query regarding the syntax of the word *silk*, and a query asking what type of thing silk is, will both be made at the same node. There are many kinds of information about denotations which have consequences for words: for example, the kind of thing a word denotes determines, at least by default, the alternations that it will participate in; and, in many languages, the type of denotation determines the default noun class or gender for a word. There is thus much to be gained from holding the two types of information together. The matter receives a fuller discussion in Kilgarriff (1992). Below, we proceed on the basis that linguistic and encyclopedic information should inhabit the same representation scheme.

Our example fragment of lexical semantics embodies the taxonomy shown in figure 1.1. This taxonomy gets encoded in DATR as follows:

```
ARTEFACT:<>==ENTITY.
PLANT:<>==ENTITY.
FIBRE:<>==ENTITY.
CROP:<>==PLANT.
YARN:<>==ARTEFACT.
FABRIC:<>==ARTEFACT.
GARMENT:<>==ARTEFACT.
Cotton:<>==CROP.
Flax:<>==CROP.
Silk:<>==FIBRE.
Wool:<>==FIBRE.
Nylon:<>==FIBRE.
Linen:<>==YARN.
Felt:<>==FABRIC.
Canvas:<>FABRIC.
Jersey:<>==FABRIC.
Suit:<>==GARMENT.
```

To that basic structure, we wish to add generalisations about fibre, yarn, fabric and garment senses. Once we have established that *silk*, say, is being used in its fabric sense, we wish to treat the word as we would *canvas* or *felt*. We need to distinguish secondary senses from primary ones in such a way that the paths for accessing information about them are different. We do this by prefixing the path with alt (for alternation). There might be several alternations, so we identify the alternation by the path element following

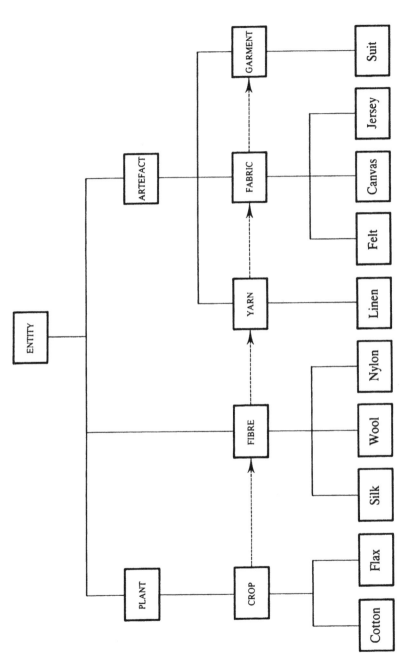

Figure 1.1 Taxonomy with alternations indicated

alt, for which we shall use the genus terms of the alternative senses. Let us also now add some flesh to the bare bones of the taxonomy, and state some genus terms, word values (i.e. the word associated with the node), and collocates at various low-level nodes, and other information whose role will become clearer as we proceed.

```
ENTITY:
  <word)=="<word>"
  <collocates>==
  <artefact>==no
  <made-of>==itself.

ARTEFACT:
  <>==ENTITY
  <artefact>==yes.

FIBRE:
  <>==ENTITY
  <genus>==fibre
  <collocates>==spin ENTITY
  <alt yarn>==YARN:<>.

Silk:
  <>==FIBRE
  <word>==silk
  <source>==insect
  <collocates>==worm FIBRE
  <alt yarn alt fabric collocates>==fine FABRIC:<collocates>.

YARN:
  <>==ARTEFACT
  <genus>==yarn
  <collocates>==stitch weave ARTEFACT
  <alt fabric>==FABRIC:<>.

FABRIC:
  <>==ARTEFACT
  <genus>==fabric
  <collocates>==cut sew ARTEFACT.
```

Now, if we query the fragment to obtain a value for

> Silk:<genus>

the value is fibre, whereas for

> Silk:<alt yarn genus>

the <alt yarn> path prefix diverts the inheritance (via FIBRE) to YARN. The effect of the empty path on the right-hand side of the equation

FIBRE:<alt yarn>==YARN:<>.

is to direct the inheritance to the YARN node with the path prefix replaced by the null path. In this case, that leaves the path <genus>, which is evaluated at YARN to give yarn. This prefix stripping yields the desired results in that, once we have specified that we have the yarn sense of a fibre word, the analysis behaves as if the primary sense were a yarn sense.

The axioms involving collocates exploit DATR sequences. The evaluation of sequences is such that each sequence member is treated as if it were alone on the RHS of the equation, is evaluated, and the value is placed back in the sequence. If we wish to find the collocates of the primary fibre sense of *silk*, we need to evaluate.

Silk:<collocates>

At the Silk node, we find an equation for which the LHS matches, and the RHS is specified as a sequence. The first element of the sequence is an atom, worm, so that becomes the first element of the sequence that is returned. The second element is not an atom, but a node, so for the remainder of the sequence we need to evaluate

FIBRE:<collocates>

which is again specified as a sequence. The first element, spin, is an atom and thus returned unchanged. The second element is a node, ENTITY. For the latter, <collocates> is given as the null sequence. We now have all the components of the sequence that forms the value for the original query. The empty sequence disappears and the value sequence returned is worm spin.

Alternation is rarely wholly regular and it is often necessary to overrule inherited values, or to add specifications that are not inherited to an inherited sense. This is easily done in DATR. The garment alternant sense of the fabric word *jersey* typically denotes not just any garment made of jersey, but rather one that covers the trunk of the wearer, hence:

Jersey:<alt garment differential >==covers trunk.

Likewise, the collocates of particular alternants may be very specific and not restricted to those one might inherit from the more general meaning category to which the alternant belongs:

Jersey:<alt garment collocates>==football GARMENT:<collo-
cates>.

In general, any number of further specifications may be added to an inherited sense in this way.

Alternation relations display transitivity. Just as words that denote fibres
may have alternant senses that denote yarns, so words that denote yarns
may have alternant senses that denote fabrics, as with the word *linen*:

YARN:
  <>==ARTEFACT
  <genus>==yarn
  <made-of>==“<source>” fibre
  <collocates>==stitch weave ARTEFACT
  <alt fabric>==FABRIC:<>.

Linen:
  <>==YARN
  <word>==linen
  <source>==flax
  <alt fabric alt garment collocates>==crumpled GARMENT:
    <collocates>.

FABRIC:
  <>==ARTEFACT
  <genus>==fabric
  <made-of>==“<word>” yarn
  <collocates>==cut sew ARTEFACT
  <alt garment>==GARMENT:<>.

From the fragment presented so far, we can prove DATR theorems such as
the following:

Linen:
  <word>==linen
  <genus>==yarn
  <artefact>==yes
  <made-of>==flax fibre
  <collocates>==stitch weave

  <alt fabric word>==linen
  <alt fabric genus>==fabric
  <alt fabric artefact>==yes
  <alt fabric made-of>==linen yarn
  <alt fabric collocates>==cut sew.

Transitivity becomes apparent when we reconsider a word like *silk*, which can denote a fibre, a yarn made from that fibre, or a fabric made from the yarn that is made of the fibre. In the approach developed here, the basic mechanism for transitive alternations is to use as many <alt x> prefixes (where x is the identifier for the alternation) as required. Thus, from the fragment presented so far, we can prove DATR theorems such as the following:

```
Silk:
    <word>==silk
    <genus>==fibre
    <artefact>==no
    <made-of>==itself
    <collocates>==worm spin

    <alt yarn word>==silk
    <alt yarn genus>==yarn
    <alt yarn artefact>==yes
    <alt yarn made-of>==insect fibre
    <alt yarn collocates>==stitch weave

    <alt yarn alt fabric word>==silk
    <alt yarn alt fabric genus>==fabric
    <alt yarn alt fabric artefact>==yes
    <alt yarn alt fabric made-of>==silk yarn
    <alt yarn alt fabric collocates>==fine cut sew.
```

A word like *cotton* has alternant senses that stretch all the way from the crop grown in the southern states of the USA through to the garments we are wearing, as the following examples attest:

> The children were harvesting the cotton. [CROP]
> Every gin was clogged with cotton. [FIBRE]
> He threaded the needle with black cotton. [YARN]
> I'll buy three metres of the red cotton, please. [FABRIC]
> We always wash the cottons separately. [GARMENT]

We can augment our fragment to allow all these senses of *cotton*:

```
GARMENT:
    <>==ARTEFACT
    <genus>==garment
    <made-of>=="<word>" fabric
    <collocates>==wear clean ARTEFACT.

PLANT:
```

```
    <>==ENTITY
    <genus>==plant
    <source>==vegetable
    <collocates>==grow ENTITY.

CROP:
    <>==PLANT
    <collocates>==seed sow harvest PLANT
    <alt seed>==SEED:<>
    <alt fibre>==FIBRE:<>.

Cotton:
    <>==CROP
    <word>==cotton
    <collocates>==field picking gin belt CROP
    <alt fibre collocates>==wool FIBRE:<collocates>
    <alt fibre alt yarn collocates>==mill YARN:<collocates>
    <alt fibre alt yarn alt fabric alt garment collocates>==cool
      GARMENT:<collocates>.
```

We can now prove a variety of theorems about the various alternant senses of *cotton*. Note, in particular, how the DATR treatment of the Cotton lexeme allows one to fine-tune the set of collocations associated with each sense.

```
Cotton:
    <word>==cotton
    <genus>==plant
    <artefact>==no
    <made-of>==itself
    <collocates>==field picking gin belt seed sow harvest grow

    <alt fibre word>==cotton
    <alt fibre genus>==fibre
    <alt fibre artefact>==no
    <alt fibre made-of>==itself
    <alt fibre collocates>==wool spin

    <alt fibre alt yarn word>==cotton
    <alt fibre alt yarn genus>==yarn
    <alt fibre alt yarn artefact>==yes
    <alt fibre alt yarn made-of>==cotton fibre
    <alt fibre alt yarn collocates>==mill stitch weave

    <alt fibre alt yarn alt fabric word>==cotton
    <alt fibre alt yarn alt fabric genus>==fabric
```

```
<alt fibre alt yarn alt fabric artefact>==yes
<alt fibre alt yarn alt fabric made-of>==cotton yarn
<alt fibre alt yarn alt fabric collocates>==cut sew.

<alt fibre alt yarn alt fabric alt garment word>==cotton
<alt fibre alt yarn alt fabric alt garment genus>==garment
<alt fibre alt yarn alt fabric alt garment artefact>==yes
<alt fibre alt yarn alt fabric alt garment made-of>==cotton
  fabric
<alt fibre alt yarn alt fabric alt garment collocates>==cool
  wear clean.
```

There may be any number of <alt x> prefixes, and a query may be redirected any number of times. There can be any number of alternations specified at nodes: CROP, for example, has two, one pointing to the FIBRE node and the other pointing to a SEED node (the latter omitted from the example fragment). Each alternation possibility redirects inheritance to another node and strips off the relevant <alt x> prefix. Thus, as the number of <alt x> prefixes grows, so the number of potential usage-types which the theory is describing for the word increases exponentially (in principle, if not in practice). All the alternations directly available to the primary sense of the word form a set of possibilities at depth 1 (thus fibre and seed are depth 1 alternants for crops). These, in turn, may lead to nodes at which further alternations are defined (e.g. yarn at FIBRE) and these form the set of possibilities at depth 2. And so on, recursively.

Suppose we now add another crop to our fragment:

```
Flax:
<>==CROP
<word>==flax
<collocates>==linseed CROP.
```

Unsurprisingly, we can immediately prove theorems like these:

```
Flax:
<word>==flax
<genus>==plant
<collocates>==linseed seed sow harvest grow

<alt fibre word>==flax
<alt fibre genus>==fibre
<alt fibre collocates>==spin.
```

Those results look plausible enough, but if we push into the depth 2 alternations then a problem emerges:

Flax:
    <alt fibre alt yarn word>==flax
    <alt fibre alt yarn genus>==yarn
    <alt fibre alt yarn collocates>==stitch weave.

The problem here is that the word flax is not used to refer to the yarn
derived from flax fibre. The alternation from crop senses to yarn senses has
exceptions, even if we restrict the notion of crop to 'fibre-producing crop'.
We have already seen how DATR permits idiosyncratic collocations to be
stipulated for remote alternants. It is no harder to use it to stipulate that
certain remote alternants are not available to a lexeme. The simplest way to
achieve this is illustrated in the revised definition for the Flax node shown
below (UNDEFINED is the name of a node that is not defined).

Flax:
    <>==CROP
    <word>==flax
    <collocates>==linseed CROP
    <alt fibre alt yarn>===UNDEFINED.

With the additional axiom, we lose all the problematic theorems that could
be inferred in its absence. However, in this particular case, we might want
instead to do something a bit more interesting:

Flax:
    <>==CROP
    <word>==flax
    <collocates>==linseed CROP
    <alt fibre alt yarn>=="Linen:<>".

Linen:
    <>==YARN
    <word>==linen
    <source>==Flax:<word>
    <alt fabric alt garment collocates>==crumpled GARMENT:
        <collocates>.

This version of the theory leads to almost the same set of theorems as our
original theory did:

Flax:
    <alt fibre alt yarn word>==linen
    <alt fibre alt yarn genus>==yarn
    <alt fibre alt yarn collocates>==stitch weave.

The crucial difference lies in the value of the word attribute of the depth 2 yarn alternant: in place of flax, we now find linen. We will not take a stand here on the question of whether one should say of *flax* that its yarn alternant is undefined or whether one should say that the alternant is defined and is exactly what you would expect it to be, except in that this particular alternant is written as *linen* not *flax*.[4] The latter approach is perfectly coherent in the context of a DATR lexicon although it takes us beyond the territory of polysemy as standardly construed.

Our use of an UNDEFINED node, above, is a way of eliminating alternants that do not exist. For depth 1 alternants, it may be that descriptive concision is better achieved by means of a positive specification of the applicable alternations. To this end, we introduce an attribute alternants whose value will be a list of the available alternants at the node.

```
ENTITY:
  <alternants>==.
CROP:
  <alternants>==fibre seed PLANT.
FIBRE:
  <alternants>==yarn ENTITY.
YARN:
  <alternants>==fabric ARTEFACT.
FABRIC:
  <alternants>==garment ARTEFACT.
Canvas:
  <alternants>==ARTEFACT.
```

The mechanism employed for alternants is exactly the same as that already employed for collocates: the RHS is given as zero or more alternant attributes followed by the name of a higher node from which further alternants may be sought. The ultimately general ENTITY node, unsurprisingly, has an empty set of alternants associated with it. The only interesting case in the list just given is that of *canvas*: the Canvas node is a daughter of the FABRIC node which, by default, leads to alternant garment senses in its daughters. But, by stipulating that Canvas alternants are to come from ARTEFACT rather than GARMENT, the default is bypassed.[5]

Our topic in this chapter has been polysemous relations and thus polysemy. But what are we to do when no subregular relation holds? Although we share Lyons' sympathy for maximal polysemy, a DATR lexicon is perfectly well able to represent homonymies.

```
Jersey1:
  <>==FABRIC
```

```
<word>==jersey
<made-of>==knitted yarn
<alt            garment            collocates>==football
GARMENT:<collocates>.
```

Jersey2:
```
<>==ISLAND
<word>==jersey
<alternants>==cattle ISLAND
<collocates>==tax Bergerac Channel ISLAND:<collocates>.
```

In a sense, however, our priorities have been the reverse of those of Lyons in his writings on homonymy and polysemy. For us, alternation relations and the formal explication of the notion of relatedness of lexical meaning form the primary object of study. Polysemy is simply the name for the sets of multiple senses that fall out from a theory of such relations: 'the only synchronically relevant consideration', as Lyons puts it. And that leaves homonymy as the name for whatever same-form/multiple-sense cases remain. What makes the study of polysemous relations difficult is the pervasive subregularity of the phenomenon. Our claim is that that subregularity is formally no different from the subregularity one finds in the lexical representation of syntax and morphology. DATR was developed on a testbed of lexical examples involving syntactic subcategorisation and inflectional morphology, but, as we hope to have shown, it offers a rather natural way of formalising polysemous relations also.

Appendix
EXAMPLE LEXICON FRAGMENT

```
ENTITY:
  <word>=="<word>"
  <made-of>==itself
  <alt $alt alt>==<alt>
  <alt $alt word>==<word>
  <alternants>==
  <collocates>==
  <artefact>==no
  <syntax>==NOUN:<>.
NOUN:
  <cat>==noun
  <count>==yes
  <concrete>==yes.
```

```
MASS-NOUN:
  <>==NOUN
  <count>==no.
ARTEFACT:
  <>==ENTITY
  <artefact>==yes.
PLANT:
  <>==ENTITY
  <genus>==plant
  <source>==vegetable
  <collocates>==grow ENTITY.
CROP:
  <>==PLANT
  <syntax>==MASS-NOUN:<>
  <collocates>==seed sow harvest PLANT
  <alt fibre>==FIBRE:<>
  <alt seed>==SEED:<>
  <alternants>==fibre seed PLANT.
Cotton:
  <>==CROP
  <word>==cotton
  <collocates>==field picking gin belt CROP
  <alt fibre collocates>==wool FIBRE:<collocates>
  <alt fibre alt yarn collocates>==mill YARN:<collocates>
  <alt fibre alt yarn alt fabric alt garment collocates>==cool
    GARMENT:<collocates>.
Flax:
  <>==CROP
  <word>==flax
  <collocates>==linseed CROP
  <alt fibre alt yarn>=="Linen:<>".
FIBRE:
  <>==ENTITY
  <genus>==fibre
  <syntax>==MASS-NOUN:<>
  <collocates>==spin ENTITY
  <alt yarn>==YARN:<>
  <alternants>==yarn ENTITY.
Silk:
  <>==FIBRE
  <word>==silk
  <source>==insect
  <collocates>==worm FIBRE
```

```
      <alt yarn alt fabric collocates>==fine
    FABRIC:<collocates>.
Wool:
    <>==FIBRE
    <word>==wool
    <source>==animal
    <collocates>==sheep shear fleece FIBRE
    <alt yarn alt fabric collocates>==warm
    FABRIC:<collocates>.
Nylon:
    <>==FIBRE
    <word>==nylon
    <artefact>==yes
    <source>==synthetic
    <alt yarn alt fabric alt garment collocates>==stocking
      GARMENT:<collocates>.
YARN:
    <>==ARTEFACT
    <genus>==yarn
    <syntax>==MASS-NOUN:<>
    <made-of>=="<source>" fibre
    <collocates>==stitch weave ARTEFACT
    <alt fabric>==FABRIC:<>
    <alternants>==fabric ARTEFACT.
Linen:
    <>==YARN
    <word>==linen
    <source>==Flax:<word>
    <alt fabric alt garment collocates>==crumpled
      GARMENT:<collocates>.
FABRIC:
    <>==ARTEFACT
    <genus>==fabric
    <syntax>==MASS-NOUN:<>
    <made-of>=="<word>" yarn
    <collocates>==cut sew ARTEFACT
    <alt garment>==GARMENT:<>
    <alternants>==garment ARTEFACT.
Felt:
    <>==FABRIC
    <word>==felt
    <made-of>==matted fibre
    <collocates>==hat FABRIC.
```

Canvas:
    <>==FABRIC
    <word>==canvas
    <made-of>==woven yarn
    <collocates>==sail tent painting boxing FABRIC.
    <alternants>==ARTEFACT
Jersey:
    <>==FABRIC
    <word>==jersey
    <made-of>==knitted yarn
    <alt garment collocates>==football
    GARMENT:<collocates>.
GARMENT:
    <>==ARTEFACT
    <genus>==garment
    <made-of>=="<word>" fabric
    <collocates>==wear clean ARTEFACT.
Suit:
    <>==GARMENT
    <word>==suit
    <made-of>==fabric
    <collocates>==grey business GARMENT.

NOTES

This chapter is a sequel to Kilgarriff (1995). We are grateful to Ann Copestake, Roger Evans and Lionel Moser for relevant conversations and to SERC for the grant to Kilgarriff during his doctoral research.

1 There is actually a formal distinction in DATR between two kinds of equation (notated with '==' and '=', respectively) but the discussion in this chapter will simply ignore this technical nicety.

2 Collocates are words that commonly occur as near neighbours of instances of the lexeme that have the specified sense. Our intended interpretation of collocates is the purely statistical one to be found in Church & Hanks (1989). However, the examples given for the example fragment in this chapter are entirely hypothetical – we have not done the empirical work that would be required to discover what the collocates *really* are.

3 The correct formulation of the rule of inference depends on the already noted distinction between two kinds of DATR equation, but we continue to ignore that technicality here.

4 An exactly analogous case occurs with the garment alternation for the fabric sense of *wool*: the relevant form is *woollen* or *woolly*, not *wool*. The same analytical alternatives are available.

5 Nothing in the fragment as presented in this chapter formally connects the value of the alternants attribute to the <alt x> machinery. In effect, alternants simply tells the user of the lexicon which <alt x> paths have meaningful values. It is not difficult to make a formal link between the two, within the DATR code, such that, for example, <alt x z> only has a defined value at node N just in case x is to be found on the RHS of the evaluation of N:<alternants>. And recursively for <alt x alt y z>, etc. But the technicalities of how one might do this are of no real relevance to the present study.

REFERENCES

Apresjan, Ju. D. (1974) Regular polysemy. *Linguistics* 142: 5–32.
Church, Kenneth & P. Hanks (1989) Word association norms, mutual information and lexicography. In *Twenty-seventh Annual Conference of the Association for Computational Linguistics*, 76–83.
Copestake, Ann (1993) The representation of lexical semantic information. DPhil. dissertation, University of Sussex.
Evans, Roger & Gerald Gazdar (1989a) Inference in DATR. *Fourth Conference of the European Chapter of the Association for Computational Linguistics*, 66–71.
   (1989b) The semantics of DATR. In Anthony G. Cohn (ed.). *Proceedings of the Seventh Conference of the Society for the Study of Artificial Intelligence and Simulation of Behaviour*, London: Pitman/Morgan Kaufmann, 79–87.
Flexner, Stuart Berg (1987) *The Random House Dictionary of the English Language*, 2nd edn, New York: Random House.
Kilgarriff, Adam (1992) Polysemy. DPhil. dissertation, University of Sussex.
   (1995) Inheriting polysemy. In Patrick Saint-Dizier & Evelyne Viegas (eds.) *Computational Lexical Semantics*, Cambridge University Press.
Lyons, John (1968) *Introduction to Theoretical Linguistics*, Cambridge University Press.
   (1977) *Semantics*, vol. II, Cambridge University Press.
   (1981) *Language, Meaning and Context*, London: Fontana.

2

Fields, networks and vectors

ADRIENNE LEHRER AND KEITH LEHRER

The traditions of semantics in linguistics and philosophy have overlapped somewhat in recent decades, but earlier trends and treatments in each discipline have dealt with rather different aspects of meaning. In this essay we hope to unite some of these different threads. It is a special pleasure to contribute to a volume in honour of Sir John Lyons, who has made major contributions to a theory of meaning.

In Lyons' early work (1963, 1968) the meaning of a word was conceived of as its place in the lexical network of the semantic field to which it belonged. A theory of reference – to hook up language and the world – is also a necessary part of the semantic enterprise. We wish to explore how theories of sense and reference can be related.

1 A word on terminology

The word *meaning* is used in many different ways, in both philosophy and linguistics. It has been used to describe extralinguistic relationships, that is, between an expression and something in the external world, and intra-linguistic relationships – between expressions within a language or between those in different languages. Given the ambiguity of the word *meaning*, we shall try to avoid using this word, instead employing *reference* or *denotation* for word–world connection, and *sense*, which Lyons has defined as the 'place in a system of relationships which it contracts with other words in the vocabulary' (Lyons, 1968: 427).[1]

2 Sense and reference

An adequate semantic theory of reference and sense must explain how reference is determined by a variety of factors which include sense as a

26

central determinant. Such a theory must account for widely recognised features of vagueness and indeterminacy. It must explicate the role of pragmatic determinants. It must accommodate the fact of semantic change. It must include an analysis of the influence of experts and the limits of their influence on reference and sense. It must contain as a salient feature an account of the connection between sense, the network relationships between words, and reference, the relationship between the word and the world. Finally, the theory should clarify how sense and reference combine to yield the interpretation of a word in idiolects and languages. We shall present a semantic theory which combines these various factors, a theory of the aggregation of vectors, to account for reference and sense.

3 Representing meaning

Some semantic theories, especially those offered by philosophers, have described the sense and/or reference of an expression by quoting and disquoting the same expression with minor grammatical amendments. Examples are the following: *dog* means 'dog', or *dog* refers to dogs, *Rover is a dog* is true if and only if Rover is a dog. Such descriptions of sense or reference leave the reader with the impression that they are uninformative. The problem is not that language must be used to explain the relationship between language and the world, though this feature may lead to paradox or linguistic provincialism. There is no escape from the need to use language to account for the relationship between language and the world. The triviality is, we suggest, the result of the fact that the disquoted use of the expression is one that exhibits a certain linguistic role (Sellars, 1963). Merely exhibiting an item that plays a linguistic role does not yield an informative account of that role. An informative scientific account of the linguistic role must go beyond merely exhibiting the item that plays a linguistic role to an explanation of the character of that role. A description of the network relationships of the word along with a variety of pragmatic features provides an essential part of the explanation.

4 Vectors

The metaphor of vectors and its application to language originated with Ziff (1972: 32) and was developed by K. Lehrer (1984). Ziff writes:

The factors that serve to determine what is said have something of the character of vectors and what is said can be thought of as something of a vector sum. To suggest that the factors that serve to determine what is said can be thought of as vectors is, of course, at once to suggest that they can be represented by directed line segments, that they can sensibly be thought of as forces having a magnitude, a direction in some sort of linguistic space and a sense in which the direction is proceeding. It is also to suggest that one factor can, as it were, serve to deflect another. And more importantly, it is also to suggest that these factors may be active and operative even though owing to the interactions of other factors their action and operation may not be readily apparent.

We feel that the metaphor of vectors is useful in our understanding of reference, since indeed many forces, including forces of different kinds, occur and interact in a complex way.[2] Some of these vectors have been widely discussed, for example, indirect and non-literal uses of language (Bach & Harnish, 1979) and indexicals; others have been discussed in some of the linguistics literature but less so in the philosophical writings on language, such as indeterminacy and semantic change.

5 Expressions where pragmatics is required for reference

It has been acknowledged that pragmatic principles are required to determine the truth value of sentences that contain indexicals (deictics) of all sorts, and this includes practically all sentences with the possible exception of eternal sentences like *Two plus two equals four*, where the present tense is analysed not as a deictic but as semantically tenseless.

Deictic expressions include pronouns, tense, determiners, adverbials like *here, there, now, then, yesterday, today* and verbs like *come, go, bring* and *take* (see Fillmore, 1971). Even the interpretation of deictics is not straightforward. Consider a personal pronoun like *we*, which is usually analysed as referring to the speaker and one or more additional individuals. Such an analysis is correct in (1):

(1) We went to the store.

But consider (2) and (3):

(2) Twenty thousand years ago we lived in caves, but now we live in houses.
(3) We Americans – not you and I personally – consume too much energy.

In (2), the second instance of *we* could, but need not, include the speaker, but the first instance certainly does not. In (3) *we* refers to some vague subset of Americans, and the sentence explicitly excludes the speaker without contradiction (see Kitagawa & Lehrer, 1990).

Place deictics like *here* can also be problematically vague, and can refer to a small precise area, a city, country, planet, universe and anything in between. Similar examples can be constructed with other indexicals. Those discussed by Saka (1991) include use of kin terms, as in:

(4) Where is Daddy?
(5) Mother called yesterday.

One has to know who the speaker is to determine the reference of *Daddy* or *Mother*.

Pragmatic factors are also required for vague predicates, like *bald*, and for the many scalar expressions that refer to norms (which shift with context). The reference for *a heavy wine* will depend on the class of wine, the norms for the class, the experience of the speaker and/or hearer and the other wines being compared. A similar list of conditions are applicable to *cool evening, tall tree, large animal*, etc. An interpretation will require indexing the relevant norms, contexts, participants, etc.

6 Value vectors

The truth conditions for sentences like *BV Cabernet Sauvignon 1989 is good* involve not only the specifications listed above but also preference of unspecified individuals (either the speaker or the wine connoisseur community or both). In the case of interpretation of many, possibly most, vague terms the unspecified and often controversial norms lead to variation from speaker to speaker and place to place (see A. Lehrer, 1983). Even words that are normally considered to be purely descriptive have values as a part of their sense, for example, *sour*: a person who liked a highly acidic wine would describe it as *tart*, whereas someone who disliked it would use *sour*.

Many words incorporate an evaluative element as a part of their sense. Consider the sentences in (6) and (7):

(6) a. Oliver North was a hero.
    b. Oliver North was a villain.
    c. Oliver North was a fool.
(7) a. The Contras were freedom fighters.
    b. The Contras were terrorists.

The statements in (6) and (7) were hotly debated in the 1980s, reflecting the political beliefs and ideologies of the speakers. An analysis like 'Contras were freedom fighters' is true if and only if Contras were freedom fighters does not help us at all with the truth conditions because it leaves the matter of the reference of *freedom fighter* unsettled.

However much people may disagree on the truth of the sentences in (6) and (7), there is much greater agreement on the sense of *hero* and *villain* or *freedom fighter* and *terrorist*.

7 Indeterminacy

Closely connected to the topic of vagueness is that of indeterminacy – the fact that word senses often have fuzzy boundaries.[3] As a result, it is often not clear how to apply a word to a thing, event, property, etc. Prototype theory was constructed to avoid this problem by concentrating on paradigm cases, not borderline ones. A. Lehrer explored this topic (1970, 1974), and many working lexical semanticists have in fact used something like optional features or components (Wierzbicka, 1985; Lipka, 1985) to handle this phenomenon. For example, a *glass* is a usually cylindrical container without a handle, intended for drinking from, and it is usually made of glass, but it can be made of other vitreous material and it can be of another shape, and it can be used for other purposes. In evaluating the truth of a sentence like *X is a glass*, where *X* is non-prototypical, we must make some decision on whether to extend the expression *glass* to a non-prototypical instance.

Colour terms have notoriously indeterminate borders, and a sentence like (8) provides an interesting case:

(8) Bing cherries are red.

People say things like (8), or at least they might infer this, because they say things like *cherries are red*. But it is more accurate to say:

(9) Bing cherries are maroon.

Sentences (8) and (9) are apparently incompatible, so either one of the sentences is incorrect, probably (8), or the use of *red* is contextually sensitive.[4] If people disagree about (8) and (9), we do not assume it to be a factual dispute about the colour of cherries but about the applicability of predicates.

8 Fixing reference by appealing to experts

One suggestion for fixing reference has been proposed by Putnam (1970, 1975). A part of Putnam's theory includes a sociological feature, whereby there is a division of labour that delegates to experts in a scientific field the authority to determine the reference of terms like *water, gold, lemon, tiger* and *cat*, not only in this world but in other possible worlds, like Twin Earth.[5]

Putnam (1975) is correct to emphasise the social factor, but the role he assigns to experts is oversimplified. Consider *arm* (the body part), which physicians define as the part of the body between the shoulder and elbow. This contrasts with the *forearm*, the part from the elbow to the wrist.[6] Although our consultants (mostly students and colleagues) are willing to delegate the correct use of some technical terms, like *arthritis* (an example from Burge, 1979), they are adamant in rejecting expert advice on *arm*. Their reaction is that physicians might have their own good reasons for such a lexical distinction, but it is irrelevant to the word's sense and use for others. If the majority of speakers reject the authority of experts for some cases, authority is not delegated to them. The influence of expertise depends on how much weight we give to their usage, and this is variable.

9 Fixing reference by appealing to possible worlds

Appeal to possible worlds has been used by Putnam and others to determine sense and reference beyond the actual world. The sense (intension) in such accounts is a function or rule that determines the reference or extension of a term in possible worlds beyond the actual world. The need for considering the extension in possible worlds results from the fact that it is obviously incorrect to identify the sense (intension) merely in the actual world. Such methods presuppose, however, that we can readily determine which worlds are possible. But can we? How weird can possible worlds be? The kinds of possible worlds that philosophers construct might just be too ordinary. We normally define *die* as an irreversible biological process, but we can imagine a world in which death is a reversible process. Is this difference a linguistic one involving the sense of *die* or a reflection of death in our world? Imagine a world in which it is normal to be schizophrenic and paranoic and where people believe that some inanimate objects, like chairs, want to kill them. For such a population, *chair* would have semantic and pragmatic components lacking in the sense of this word for us. In Kurt Vonnegut's world there are seven sexes, and so the sense of *sex* in his world must be considerably different from our sense.[7] Or imagine a world where things change so rapidly that the inhabitants lack a concept of things and speak like Quine's (1960) natives of stages instead. The pragmatic factors of fact and context in the actual world influence sense and reference in a way that transcends possible-world cogitation.

10 Semantic change

The causal theory of meaning, also referred to as the historical theory, holds that there is a baptismal event in which a name is given to a thing or class of things, and then transmitted to others via a causal or historical chain (Kripke, 1980). As a general theory of the origin of word meanings, this is rather fanciful. A language is transmitted from one generation to the next, of course, but not in the simple, linear way that the causal theory suggests.

One of the facts of language, however distressing to some language conservatives, is that language, including meaning (sense and reference), is constantly changing. Language change, including semantic change, is a traditional part of linguistics. Moreover, the relationship between linguistic variation (including sense variation) and change is taken for granted.[8] Some changes involve radical shifts, which at the time are considered errors, such as the application of *Madagascar*, the shift of sense of *bead* from 'prayer' to 'small round ball', and the shift of *sofa* from 'camel saddle' to 'furniture for sitting' (see Mercier, 1992a). Most shifts are more gradual, involving a widening or narrowing of sense or reference. Examples widely found in books of semantic change include the narrowing of *deer* from 'animal' to its current sense and the widening of the verb *sail* from 'go by sailing vessel' to 'go by any sea-going vessel' to 'transport through media other than water'.

Other semantic shifts create not only an extension or restriction of sense or reference, but more commonly, additional senses, sometimes metaphorical, sometimes not.[9] One of the problems with the causal theory is that it cannot account for these natural processes in a natural way (Mercier, 1992b). All such shifts are treated as deviations from the norm or mistakes.

Sometimes changes in sense or reference come about because of new discoveries or belief shifts, but there is no routine way in which these shifts occur. In the case of *atom*, where the word originally included the sense 'indivisible', physicists continued to refer to the same objects as *atoms* after the atom was split, but the sense of *atom* changed so as not to include 'indivisible'. If a synchronic account were to completely capture a speaker's understanding of the sense of an expression, a conjecture made in 1875 like *Someday the atom may be split* would have been completely unintelligible to a scientist who took indivisibility as a defining characteristic of atoms. In fact, a synchronic sense is pregnant with the potentiality of diachronic change, and the conjecture would have been understood.

Putnam (1975) has constructed a famous example in which cats turn out to be Martian spy robots, and he has predicted that a similar thing would happen: we would continue calling these furry creatures *cats*, but the sense of *cat* would change.[10]

A rather different outcome occurred in the case of *witch*. In the scientific and legal domains, the theory of witchcraft was rejected, and so the sense of *witch* ceased to have any reference. Some religious fundamentalists retain the belief that witches exist, but presumably the disagreement between such fundamentalists and scientists is not a matter of the sense of *witch* but of their existence. (*Witch* also has a metaphorical sense of 'wicked woman'.) Other outcomes might have been possible. It could have turned out that *witch* remained in the language for referring to individuals with certain personalities. In that case, the reference of *witch* might have remained, but the sense would have changed (similar to Putnam's Martian cats).

A still different outcome occurred in the case of *Indian*. European explorers who landed in the New World at first thought they had found India, and called the New World inhabitants *Indians* (or the equivalent in their native languages). Even when they discovered their mistake, they continued to use *Indian* for the New World inhabitants. But the word also continued to be used (in English, at least) with its old sense and reference as well, creating an ambiguity in the term. (A counterpart to Putnam's example would be a case in which only some cats, striped ones, turned out to be Martian spy robots.)

Another case would be where the sense and reference both change. For example, the noun *ship* at an earlier period of time referred only to sailing vessels and had that sense; but when steam ships were invented, *ship* was applied to them as well. The shift of sense needed to include steamships in the reference of *ship* depends on defining *ship* as 'large vessel for travelling across water'. Such changes in sense and reference are, we propose, most intelligible if sense and reference are matters of degree that change and shift in response to experience and discovery. The potentiality for change and indeterminacy are connected. If there were no potential for change, it would make more sense to look at synchronic relationships as fixed and fully determinate.

11 Semantic networks

One of Lyons' many contributions to semantics is that words and their senses do not exist as isolated elements – they are embedded in a set of rich lexical relationships of various sorts, and it is this set that constitutes the sense. One of these relationships is entailment, a relationship that both philosophical and linguistic traditions of semantics have investigated.

Examples from the literature include sentences like those in (10) and (11):

(10) X is a bachelor→X is an unmarried, adult, male.
(11) X is kissing Y→X is touching Y.

Cases of indeterminacy provide problems for analyticity, as do the objections raised by Quine, whose challenge of the analytic–synthetic distinction is well known. Putnam's example (1975), discussed above, has challenged the distinction by his popular example in (12):

(12) Cats are animals.

Also controversial are cases like (13):

(13) a. Tomatoes are vegetables.
     b. Tomatoes are fruits.

The examples in (13) illustrate a slightly different problem: namely, that classification is done for a variety of purposes. If edible plants are grouped for botanical taxonomic purposes, then (13b) is true; if for culinary purposes, then (13a) is true.[11] This means that there is a pragmatic factor that decides between botanical and culinary interests. Of course, one can simply assert that botanical interests are 'correct' and others are not, but this assertion is a bias and needs to be justified.[12]

A slightly different problem exists in (14), which most speakers would take to be true by definition. After all, something like (14) is likely to be used as part of a definition of *potato*:

(14) Potatoes are vegetables.

The problem with (14) is that *vegetable* (the relevant sense) is not a natural kind term like *animal*, but more akin to a culinary–functional class. Potatoes are usually considered vegetables, but they are nutritionally like grains in being starchy and relatively higher in calories than other vegetables, such as green beans and broccoli, and in this respect can be classified with rice and pasta. This makes the truth of (14) more complicated than an all-or-nothing matter.

Interestingly, the closest German equivalent to *vegetable* is *Gemüse*, and *Kartoffel* 'potato' is not categorised in its domain. Therefore, the translation of (14) as (15) would be rejected by German speakers (Lyons, 1963):

(15) Kartoffeln sind Gemüse.

Appealing to experts in these cases begs an important question: which experts – botanists or chefs? It is surely a philistine prejudice to insist that botanists should be given greater weight!

Although there is some indeterminacy and vagueness in these sense relations, mirroring that of reference, we hold that the sense relationships are in general more stable over time and from person to person than the reference relations. The following kinds of semantic entailments would not seem to be falsifiable by new discoveries; only a change of meaning (application and/or sense) would defeat them:

(16) If X is big in size, X is large (where the norm and context are indexed, as discussed above).
(17) If X is big in size, X is not small (also indexed).
(18) If X is scarlet, X is red.
(19) If X is a cannon, X is a weapon.
(20) If X kills Y, Y is dead.
(21) If X drops Y, Y falls.
(22) If X buys Z from Y, Y sells Z to X.
(23) Yellow is a colour.

In general, the relationship of antonymy, and entailments involving nominal kinds (e.g. artefacts, words like *bachelor*) and primary kinds (words like *yellow*, *sweet*, and similar perception expressions) have more stable network associations than (some) natural kind terms. It is hard to see how (23) could be falsified without a sense change of some sort, although it may be easy enough to construct scenarios involving such change.

Domains that are less stable, more subject to indeterminacy, individual variation and change, are found in many semantic fields, where there might be disagreements both on the reference and on the network relationships. Consider the various English words for the field of STREETS: *street*, *avenue*, *boulevard*, *lane*, *path*, *alley*, *road*, *freeway*, *highway*, *expressway* (plus others). A plausible analysis would postulate *street* as a superordinate for the set, but also allow it to contrast with the other words. (That is, the polysemy of *street* involves a general and a specific sense.) There would be partial overlap and partial synonymy for *street*, *avenue* and *boulevard*, and this set would contrast with *lane*, *path* and *alley*, which would also exhibit partial overlap and partial contrast. A third subset would include *road* as a superordinate for *highway*, *expressway* and *freeway*, terms that contrast in some localities and are synonymous in other places. However, other plausible analyses are possible, and we would expect speakers to disagree among themselves and change their minds, depending on what kinds of sentences, images and memories come to mind at the time they are making their judgments. However, even disagreements and inconsistencies are limited, and they can be pinpointed.

Change may come about as the individuals who name streets in new developments apply these terms in arbitrary and idiosyncratic ways, as they often do (Algeo, 1978; Lehrer, 1992). Or a change may come about as a result of a conversion from an ordinary term to a technical one. For example, city planners may draw up codes for traffic and parking that would involve precise definitions of *road*, *street*, *boulevard*, *avenue*, *lane* and *alley*.

12 Semantic fields

The semantic field is an important concept that Lyons introduced into the English-speaking linguistics community and a concept to which he made major contributions. In principle, we can invoke semantic networks without appealing to semantic fields; however, semantic fields play an important role in semantic analysis. Firstly, since most words are ambiguous, it is often simpler to deal with each of their senses in its own semantic domain. Secondly, fields provide an intermediate unit between the atomicity of single words and the whole of a vocabulary. Although a change in the sense of one word may have implications for other words, usually the effects are found only in that word's semantic field. (Kittay, 1992 develops this point.) A Putnam-like change in *cat* would affect *feline*, other hyponyms of *feline*, *animal*, and possibly other words, but it would not affect the sense or reference of *tulip*, *neutrino* or *avenue*. Thirdly, many words that have overlapping reference are embedded in different lexical networks, that is, in different semantic fields. One example would be *port* and *harbour*. Although these words can refer to the same object, *port* is embedded in a word field of entrances to a place, whereas *harbour* is embedded in a network of protection. *Womb* and *uterus* provide another example where the reference is the same but the networks are not coextensive. Emotive meaning, association and connotation have been reluctantly acknowledged as existing, but then ignored or relegated to pragmatics or literary studies. None the less, these factors play an important role in language sense and language use.

13 (How) Do we ever manage to communicate?

Given the indeterminacies and other problems that have been outlined above, it would seem that communication should be much more difficult than it apparently is.[13] At any time for a speech community there are conventions that fix reference, at least for prototypes, and there are network relations, many of which are highly stable. But even in cases of vagueness and indeterminacy there are conventions that permit mutual understanding.

14 A vector model of interpretation

Communication, which appears to occur with remarkable ease, depends on the shared interpretation of an expression by an articulate speaker and his or her engrossed listener. We shall now attempt to offer a theory of the interpretation of an expression, though we restrict our account to single words to start with the simplest case. There is a multiplicity of vectors that influence the interpretation of an expression. One of these is the place of the terms in a semantic network. A psychologically realistic account of the role of this factor in the interpretation of the expression must limit the extent of the network relations which contribute to the interpretation. The field theory of semantic relations specifies that limit: for example, anything referred to by the word *red* must be referred to by the word *coloured*. Within the framework of the computational theory of mind the position of an expression within a semantic network articulates the conceptual role of the expression. We are not necessarily advocating the computational theory of mind or conceptual role semantics; we simply observe that conceptual role semantics is based on intralinguistic relationships of the sort that the network theory articulates. Any such conceptual role semantics is going to have to limit the extent of such relationships determining the conceptual role, and field theory suggests the needed principle of localisation.

Another factor is the application of the word by previous speakers, as the causal theorists have insisted, but the ubiquity of linguistic change, the flux of usage which we have illustrated above, will undermine any simplistic theory of reference in terms of causality, however elegantly formulated in terms of ancestral relations. The present reference of an expression is influenced by more factors than an ancestral relationship to the original use of it. There is the importance of expertise in the use of some parts of the language, technical terms of science or art, as Reid (1785) and Putnam (1975) have insisted, but there are limits to our deference. We defer to lawyers and judges concerning the reference of the term *felony*, to philosophers concerning the term *epiphany* and, perhaps, to no one concerning the term *arm*. So, network relationships, causal relations and deferential relations are all factors in determining the reference of a term. That is part of our reason for claiming that pragmatics plays a large part in the determination of reference.

There is another part already suggested by the influence of a multiplicity of vectors: namely, that the various factors may all have some degree of influence, and the outcome must be the result of an aggregation of various degrees of influence. This suggests, therefore, that the factors are input vectors which interact to yield the output of reference. The output of reference is a vector that combines with an output vector of sense to yield interpretation.

15 Reference and vector aggregation: an informal account

We suggest a model of sense, reference and interpretation of a word as an aggregation of input vectors. There are various factors that influence sense and reference. These become the input vectors determining the sense or reference function of a word for an individual. The resulting sense or reference functions of individuals will then be regarded as vectors to be aggregated to determine a social or communal sense or reference function for the language. One typical form of aggregation is averaging a set of values to yield a significant average, for example, when one averages the heights of members of a population to determine the average height of a person in that population. Vector aggregation is in fact a form of averaging in which different weights are assigned to different vectors. Our proposal is that sense and reference, whether individual or social, are the result of assigning weights to various vectors of sense and reference and averaging.

Sense and reference thus conceived are averages of the relevant vectors in just the way that the average height of a person in a population is the average of the vectors constituting the heights of members of the population. The latter average is a simple average in which the height of each person is given the same weight, $1/n$, where n is the number of members of the population. A weighted average would be an average in which the heights of some people, adults perhaps, are given greater weight than the heights of others in computing the average height. The aggregation which yields sense and reference is a weighted average in which some vectors may be given greater weight than others to obtain the sense and reference functions of individuals. Moreover, some individual functions may be given greater weight than others, perhaps reflecting the relevance of expertise, to obtain the social or communal function.

When reference is the theoretical construct that interests us, the values of the construct should be quantitative, a matter of degree, to represent the widely accepted fact of the indeterminacy of reference (Quine, 1951; A. Lehrer, 1970, 1974; Zadeh, 1971). In fact, both semantic and referential relations are to some extent indeterminate, and, therefore, a quantitative account of sense and reference as matters of degree is adopted. (A formal account of the aggregation model of sense, reference and interpretation is contained in the appendix.)

The model leaves us with some residual theoretical problems in addition to the practical ones of specifying methods for ascertaining the values of various vectors and the weights for an individual to assign to those vectors. (Some suggestions are to be found in K. Lehrer and Wagner, 1980.) The primary problem concerns the acceptance of an account of reference specified in degrees rather than a simple *yes* or *no* format. Traditionally, an assignment function yielded a *yes* or *no* answer to the question of whether any object belonged to the reference of a term, indeed, any object in any possible world. We do not apologise for differing. The data suggest considerable indeterminacy. In some instances, it will be fully determinate that a term applies to a specific object, but there will be many indeterminate cases for most terms. We do not have a rule in our minds for determining whether or not every object in every possible world is part of the reference of every term, even when fully informed about the object. A satisfactory scientific account of the reference of words should, moreover, explain why the word refers to the objects it does, or has the degree of determinacy of referring to those objects, rather than simply positing the result without explanation.

A secondary objection might be that the aggregation is psychologically unrealistic. We do not, it might be objected, compute averages to determine the reference of a word. Indeed, we can perfectly well decide whether or not a word refers to an object without doing any arithmetic. Our reply to the objection begins by noticing that there is a great deal more indeterminacy about whether an object is referred to by a word than the objection suggests. The crux of our reply, however, is that the mathematical representation of a process within an individual does not imply that the individual reflectively carries out the computation. First of all, there are many unreflective and unconscious computations of the mind. Syntactic parsing is an example. Secondly, even if the process is not computational at all, the mathematical representation may be correct. The earth and moon do not compute the values of the laws of physics in order to conform to equations concerning gravitational attraction. Moreover, there is an argument based on neurophysiology to support vector aggregation as a model of human functioning (Churchland & Sejnowski, 1992). When you extend your arm to touch an object, the neurons conform to a model of vector aggregation to yield the resulting contact. We do not, of course, insist that our model of vector aggregation corresponds to neural aggregation, though it may, but suggest that anyone interested in a unified model of mind and language should be cheered by a model that tells us that the model of linguistic functioning recapitulates a plausible model of neural functioning.

15.1 Reference, networks and interpretation

How can we combine the theory of the vectors of reference with the theory of network roles in a unified explanation of interpretation? If communication occurs, then there must be some consensus or agreement in the way in which people use words. Were there none, my interpretation of what you say would be mistaken, and communication would fail. It is, however, notorious that people apply the same words differently, even among those living together, as domestic linguistic disputes reveal. Even such words as *sweet* and *dry* applied to wines are applied very differently by different speakers (A. Lehrer, 1983). Such disagreement is, of course, compatible with agreement in central cases, so that all might agree that sugar is sweet and pepper is not. One key to understanding communication is the greater agreement among speakers concerning the sense or semantic role of an expression in a linguistic network. The very people who disagree about whether a wine with zero sugar content and a marked fruity bouquet is sweet or dry will agree that if the wine is sweet, then it is not dry. Thus, our suggestion is that network role is a marked area of agreement. This may be, in part, due to an innate understanding of abstract linguistic structures, as work concerning semantic universals (Talmy, 1980; Jackendoff, 1990) suggests. These structures, for example, antonymy structure (Lehrer and Lehrer, 1982), may be innately understood and interpreted by the assignment of lexical items to the abstract positions in the structure.

15.2 A paradox of reference

Vectors of reference are influenced by the circumstances of an individual. These vectors include how a word is introduced to a person initially, which may be individualistic and perhaps idiosyncratic. The outcomes of individual aggregations of reference must be expected to differ. However, communication must incorporate interpretation of the referential intentions of the speaker, for understanding without such interpretation would be reduced to the understanding of linguistic relations between tokens without any understanding of what the tokens refer to. Communication would fail. We arrive at what might be considered a paradox of reference. The vectors of reference vary from individual to individual and yet they are

essential to the understanding of expressions. By contrast, network relations appear to be less variable, but an understanding of them is insufficient
for an understanding of a linguistic expression. What is required, therefore,
is an account of interpretation of expressions combining an understanding
of reference and network relations.

15.3 The individual and society: a dynamic duo

The solution to the paradox depends, first of all, on recognising the
dynamic processes, aggregation processes, whereby individuals come to
assign reference the way they do. The aggregation process described above
occurs over time, and one feature, the most heavily weighted factor for
some words, is the conviction of the individual concerning the way others
apply the word. The reason, therefore, that reading an expression into a
network carries a social determinant of reference with it is that the
aggregation of the individuals often gives dominant weight to what they
take to be the social assignment of reference. Of course, the soundness of
the conviction about how others apply the term will depend on the
information that an individual has about the linguistic behaviour and
intentions of others.

The social reference assignment is, on our account, an average of the
individual reference assignment and is, in this way, a fiction like the average
child born in 1991. One should not conclude, however, that there is no fact
of the matter concerning the social reference assignment. There is a fact of
the matter about the weight of the average baby born in 1991, for that is the
average weight of such babies. This means that an individual can have a
more or less correct view about the social reference assignment of members
of the group. Thus, an individual reference assignment can be more or less
idiosyncratic depending on the correctness of his or her conviction about
the social reference assignment and the weight that he or she gives to that
reference assignment in aggregating the vectors of reference.

The moral of the story is that there is a dynamic interaction between the
individuals and the linguistic community to which they belong. The
individuals aggregate what they take to be the social reference assignment.
The social reference assignment is itself an aggregate of individual reference
assignments. The dynamics of this interaction and aggregation generate
similarity between individual reference assignments and the social assignment. Given this similarity, interpretation of an expression in terms of the
position of the expression in a semantic network carries an understanding
of reference along with it. It is, however, important to notice that this

account of the interpretation of an expression allows for wide variation among different individuals in how they apply a single word and wide variation within individuals as well. On the theory we are offering, interpretation and communication vary greatly in the degree of mutual understanding among individuals concerning the reference of a word. They vary from almost exact coincidence to wide disagreement. That, we suggest, is the reality of our use and understanding of the language of others.

The underlying agreement in linguistic networks, though allowing of some variation as well, allows us to draw inferences upon which we agree and to resolve our referential disagreements as they become manifest. We need only re-adjust our convictions about the reference assignments of others and aggregate our improved information. The method of aggregation does not guarantee that we shall agree in our reference assignment, but, being an average of our assignments and those of others, it does provide a method for improving our agreement. That is all we need to carry on the business of linguistic communication and the various other businesses it serves. When we need exact referential agreement we know how to get it. Keep exchanging information and aggregating until the point of convergence clarifies. When we do not need exact referential agreement, communication proceeds comfortably without it.

What is most impressive about our language ability is that we can use and exploit the dynamics of meaning by negotiation and decision. We can stipulate a precise technical definition whenever we consider this necessary, a process that is always dynamic; we can talk about our disagreements in sense and reference and either adopt one usage or understand the usage of the others in a conversation. But successful negotiation is only possible if there is stability elsewhere in the system, since we use other words to define the words in question. We may rebuild the ship of language at sea, but we need a stable working place within the ship for our constructive efforts.

APPENDIX

Reference and vector aggregation

We shall propose a formal model which represents the various factors of reference as vectors and their resulting influence as the aggregation of the vectors. The simplest model of vector aggregation is the weighted averaging of vectors. Weighted averaging is a form of averaging in which the various factors averaged are given different weights, whereas simple averaging gives equal weight to the factors averaged. Notice immediately that the role of experts and the division of labour theory of reference, where not all people are equal in their influence on reference, is naturally amenable to weighted averaging. Different people might be assigned different weight depending on their expertise or our willingness to defer to their expertise concerning reference.

To give us a formal model, suppose that each member of a group assigned a degree of determinacy to the application of the term *felony* to a crime described in as much detail as one wished. Let there be one hundred people in a reference-determining group. We have values $r_i\langle\text{'f'},c\rangle = n$ for each of the individuals, where r_i is a reference function for person i who assigns value n as his or her degree of determinacy that the term 'f', *felony*, refers to the crime c. We can aggregate the values by assigning weights, w_i, to the various members of the group and multiplying to find a weighted average. For the sake of mathematical simplicity, suppose that the weights assigned to members of the group are in the interval of 0 and 1, that they sum to 1, and that the values of n assigned by individuals as their degree of determinacy are also in the interval of 0 and 1. (We assume nothing about the sum of the n values assigned by members of the group.)

We then obtain the value of reference determined by aggregating expertise, r_e, as follows:

E. $r_e\langle\text{'f'},c\rangle = w_1 r_1\langle\text{'f'},c\rangle + w_2 r_2\langle\text{'f'},c\rangle + \ldots + w_j r_j\langle\text{'f'},c\rangle.$

The value of $r_e\langle\text{'f'},c\rangle$ is an average and can be expected to fall between the extreme values of 0 and 1 but not coincide with those extreme values whenever the reference values of individuals differ. Thus, in many cases some degree of indeterminacy about the reference of a term should be expected, and that outcome seems empirically warranted.

The equation, E, which aggregates the reference functions of various individuals, can be re-interpreted and used to aggregate various factors influencing an individual instead of the influence of diverse individuals. We may think of the various functions r_1, r_2 and so forth to r_n as the results of determining the degree of determinacy of reference an individual would assign on the basis of various factors mentioned above. The various weights would be those that the individual assigns to those factors, and the resulting function, r_e, would be a reference function for an individual. The individual reference function is then renamed and used in the social aggregation, E. This aggregates the individual functions to extend the analysis beyond the individual or idiolect reference function to the social or communal reference function.

Combining sense and reference

Our formal account combines an interpretation function for a person consisting of a network component, the position, p, in a semantic field, f, and a reference function consisting of a range of application, a. Thus, we have two functions for interpreting a word, w. The first represents the position of the word in a semantic field and gives us the sense of the word.

$s\langle\text{'w'},p\rangle$

and the second represents the reference of the word

$$r\langle\text{'w'},a\rangle$$

Each of these functions is a quantitative value reflecting the degree of determinacy of the respective assignments. The greater determinacy of network relations will be reflected in higher values in some cases than the values of the reference function. In other cases, this order will be reversed. In the case of wine words, for example, we may be quite uncertain about the reference of wine descriptors while very certain of the semantic relations between them, but in the case of road descriptors we might be more certain of the reference of the descriptors than of the semantic relations between the words.

Empirically, there seems to be greater determinacy about sense than reference in languages and idiolects, but both have some degree of indeterminacy. We may expect the central role of sense in interpretation to be reflected in a higher degree of determinacy about the place of a word in a semantic field and the greater weight given to the sense function than the reference function in our interpretation function for a word. The central role of sense in interpretation is the result of the fact that the sense function is more stable and less sensitive to the shifting influence of pragmatic factors. Aggregation of reference plays itself out on the background of semantic fields of sense.

How can we combine the functions of sense and reference to obtain a unified interpretation of a word? There is, of course, the simple pair of functions,

$$\langle s\langle\text{'w'},p\rangle, r\langle\text{'w'},a\rangle\rangle$$

to which we could assign some degree of determinacy, perhaps a simple average of the values of sense and reference functions. That is, however, too simple a view. These two functions are themselves vectors of interpretation and might be given different weight. We may, in fact, explicate our claim about the greater determinacy of sense functions over reference functions in terms of the greater weight given to the sense function than the reference function in ascertaining the values of the interpretation function. Again, assuming that the weights applied to each are nonnegative and together sum to 1, we compute the value of the interpretation function as a weighted average. We use the weights w_s and w_r to average the values of sense s and reference r, to obtain the value of the interpretation function, i, as follows:

$$i\langle\text{'w'},s,r\rangle = s\langle\text{'w'},p\rangle w_s + r\langle\text{'w'},a\rangle w_r$$

The resulting function gives us the degree of determinacy of the interpretation of the word 'w' based on the degree of determinacy of the sense function and reference function for a word. The interpretation is an aggregation of the vectors of function and sense. The communal interpretation of a word is an aggregation of the individual interpretations. These in turn are influenced by the vectors of individual convictions about the communal interpretation. Sense and reference, personal and communal, interact as vectors that are activated by new information about language, the world and each other. Reference is the flux of pragmatic aggregation organised within a field of sense.

NOTES

We wish to thank Marga Reiner, Laura Waddell Ekstrom and Paul Saka for comments and suggestions on earlier drafts.

1 In some recent philosophical work, intralinguistic relationships (such as those among synonyms, antonyms, etc.) have been considered syntax (following Morris, 1946).

2 The spatial interpretation of vector theory suggested by Ziff is, however, inessential to mathematical representation of a subject matter in terms of vector theory. We shall employ vector theory in a more abstract way as the weighted average of initial values to compute an outcome rather than adopting the spatial representation of vectors suggested by Ziff.

3 Vagueness is one kind of indeterminacy. Predicates like *bald* are vague, but indeterminacy can result from other factors, such as the referential expressions discussed above.

4 For us *maroon* is a shade of purple, not red. However, if some speakers classify *maroon* as a shade of red, that is evidence for the indeterminacy we discuss.

5 Putnam claims that scientists would decide that Twin Earth's XYZ, which is perceptually and functionally equivalent to water, but atomically different, was not water. This is an interesting empirical prediction that could be false.

6 We came upon this example because a doctor friend chided us (and everyone else) for using *arm* incorrectly. Marga Reiner raises the question of whether *arm* is a natural kind term. The term 'natural kind' is somewhat vague, but law-cluster concepts appear to be natural kind terms. The medical use of *arm* is a law-cluster concept, according to our medical expert.

7 Vonnegut never explains how reproduction works: he says it is too complicated for humans to understand.

8 For example, see the paper by Lewandowska-Tomaszczyk (1985). Classic works on semantic change include Ullmann (1962), Stern (1931) and Williams (1975). Mercier (1992a, 1992b) has discussed semantic change in the context of philosophical semantics.

9 Saka (1992) points out the difficulties that truth-conditional semantics has in dealing with lexical ambiguity. Since ambiguity is the normal case of word sense, not a rare exception, this is indeed a serious problem. Metaphor, too, is a common linguistic phenomenon which truth-conditional semantics has so far had little to contribute to (see Goodman, 1968; A. Lehrer, 1974, 1983; Kittay, 1987). Nunberg (1979) discusses polysemy and the extension of referring expressions, but he does not deal with sense relationships.

10 Kripke (1980) and Putnam (1970) accept a position of essentialism with respect to rigid designators, which include natural kinds. So that if something is a cat, it must have certain biological properties (e.g. genetic material). Therefore, a cat must be an animal, where *animal* is also defined in terms of some biological properties. Whether the things we call *cats* are this (i.e. a natural kind) is an empirical matter.

11 *Vegetable* as a botanical term is used for the kingdom.
12 If tomatoes were always and only served with other fruits, for instance, only in fruit salads, or as a dessert, then (13b) would be accepted without question.
13 In fact, how well we do communicate is an empirical question. A. Lehrer's research (1983), as well as that of many others, suggests that miscommunication may be frequent.

REFERENCES

Algeo, J. (1978) From classic to classy: changing fashions in street names. *Names* 26: 80–95.

Bach, K. & R.M. Harnish (1979) *Linguistic Communication and Speech Acts*, Cambridge, MA: MIT Press.

Burge, T. (1979) Individualism and the mental. *Midwest Studies* 4: 73–121.

Churchland, P.S. & T.J. Sejnowski (1992) *The Computational Brain*, Cambridge, MA: MIT Press.

Fillmore, C.J. (1971) *Santa Cruz Lectures on Deixis*, Bloomington, IN: Indiana University Linguistics Club, 1975.

Goodman, N. (1968) *Languages of Art*, Indianapolis, IN: Bobbs Merrill.

Jackendoff, R. (1990) *Semantic Structures*, Cambridge, MA: MIT Press.

Kitagawa, C. and A. Lehrer (1990) Impersonal uses of personal pronouns. *Journal of Pragmatics* 14: 739–59.

Kittay, E.F. (1987) *Metaphor: its Cognitive Force and Linguistic Structure*, Oxford: Clarendon Press.
    (1992) Semantic fields and the individuation of content. In Lehrer & Kittay (eds.): 220–52.

Kripke, S. (1980) *Naming and Necessity*, Cambridge, MA: Harvard University Press.

Lehrer, A. (1970) Indeterminacy in semantic description. *Glossa* 4: 87–110.
    (1974) *Semantic Fields and Lexical Structure*, Amsterdam: North-Holland.
    (1983) *Wine and Conversation*, Bloomington: Indiana University Press.
    (1992) Names and naming: why we need fields and frames. In Lehrer & Kittay (eds.): 123–42.

Lehrer, A. & E.F. Kittay (eds.) (1992) *Frames, Fields, and Contrasts*, Hillsdale, NJ: Lawrence Erlbaum.

Lehrer, A. & K. Lehrer (1982) Antonymy. *Linguistics and Philosophy* 5: 483–501.

Lehrer, K. (1984) Coherence, consensus, and language. *Linguistics and Philosophy* 7: 43–55.

Lehrer, K. & C. Wagner (1980) *Rational Consensus in Science and Society*, Dordrecht: Reidel.

Lewandowska-Tomaszczyk, Barbara (1985) On semantic change in a dynamic model of language. In J. Fisiak (ed.) *Historical Semantics – Historical Word Formation*, Berlin: Mouton, 297–323.

Lipka, L. (1985) Inferential features in historical semantics. In J. Fisiak (ed.) *Historical Semantics – Historical Word Formation*, Berlin: Mouton, 339–54.

Lyons, J. (1963) *Structural Semantics*, Oxford: Blackwell.

(1968) *Introduction to Theoretical Linguistics*, Cambridge University Press.

(1977) *Semantics*, 2 vols., Cambridge University Press.

Mercier, A. (1992a) Normativism and the mental: a problem of language individuation. MS, Los Angeles.

(1992b) Linguistic competence, conventions, and authority: Individualism and anti-individualism in linguistics and philosophy. Unpublished PhD dissertation, UCLA.

Morris, C.W. (1946) *Signs, Language, and Behavior*, Englewood Cliffs, NJ: Prentice Hall.

Nunberg, G. (1979) *The Pragmatics of Reference*, Bloomington: Indiana University Linguistics Club.

Putnam, H. (1970) Is semantics possible? In H.E. Kiefer & M.K. Munitz (eds.) *Language, Belief, and Metaphysics*, Albany: State University of New York Press, 139–52. Reprinted in H. Putnam, (1975) *Mind, Language, and Reality*, Cambridge University Press, 139–52.

(1975) The meaning of 'meaning'. In *Mind, Language and Reality*, Cambridge University Press, 215–71.

Quine, W.V.O. (1951) Two dogmas of empiricism. *Philosophical Review* 60: 20–43.

(1960) *Word and Object*, Cambridge, MA: MIT Press.

Reid, T. (1785) *Essays on the Active Powers of Man*, Edinburgh.

Saka, P. (1991) Lexical decomposition in cognitive semantics. Unpublished PhD dissertation, University of Arizona, Tucson.

(1992) Ambiguity and truth-conditional semantics. MS, Berkeley, CA.

Sellars, W. (1963) *Science, Perception, and Reality*, New York: Humanities Press.

Stern, G. (1931) *Meaning and Change of Meaning*, reprinted Bloomington: Indiana University Press, 1964.

Talmy, L. (1980) Lexicalization patterns: semantic structure in lexical forms. In T. Shopen (ed.) *Language and Typology*, vol. III, New York: Cambridge University Press.

Ullmann, S. (1962) *Semantics*, Oxford: Blackwell.

Wierzbicka, A. (1985) *Lexicography and Conceptual Analysis*, Ann Arbor, MI: Karoma.

Williams, J.M. (1975) *Origins of the English Language*, New York: Free Press.

Zadeh, L. (1971) Quantitative fuzzy semantics. *Information Sciences* 3: 157.

Ziff, P. (1972) *Understanding Understanding*, Ithaca, NY: Cornell University Press.

3

Syntax, semantics, pragmatics

PETER MATTHEWS

The fields referred to in the title of this chapter have become part of the institutional structure of linguistics. Each has scholars who specialise in it, and advertisements for teaching posts will often specify expertise in one or more of them. The divisions between them are also reflected in the organisation of lecture courses and exam papers. But are they just an institutional convenience? Or do these terms refer to real distinctions?

Let us begin by reminding ourselves of their history. The term 'syntax' is far older than the others, and has been used by most linguists throughout this century to refer to a branch of grammar concerned with the construction of sentences. Since the 1940s that has often been taken to exclude the study of meaning; but it does not have to be so interpreted. For Bloomfield, for example, semantics was a 'phase' of linguistics whose task was to relate formal features to features of 'distinctive' or 'linguistic meaning' (1935: 74, 138, 141). But just as the units of Bloomfield's lexicon associated forms with meanings, so too did his units of grammar. Therefore their study was not separate from semantics, but part of it. Semantics as Bloomfield defined it was 'ordinarily divided' into grammar and lexicon (138), or 'equivalent to' the investigation of these fields (513, notes to section 5.1).

The separation of syntax from semantics is above all due to Bloomfield's followers, and their own successor Chomsky. Whatever his apparent or reported practice, the implication of Bloomfield's theory was that linguistic units are identified by pairing differences in form with differences in meaning. That was indeed the general view of structural linguists in the generation after Saussure. But for Harris especially distribution was the sole criterion (1951: 5). Syntactic units in particular were established by repeated substitutions of forms (Harris, 1946; 1951: ch. 16), without reference to meanings. For the early Chomsky, linguistic theory was again 'a completely formal discipline', in which the structure of language as 'an instrument or a tool' is studied 'with no explicit reference to the way in which this instrument is put to use' (1957: 103). In this spirit, his own theory of syntax was 'completely formal and non-semantic' (93). The 'correspondences between formal and semantic features' were then to be studied in 'a more general theory of language' of which a 'theory of linguistic form' is one part and a theory of meanings – that is, of the 'use of language' – is another (102).

Not every post-Bloomfieldian took precisely that view; nor did Chomsky from at the latest 1964 onwards. For Hockett, for example, the 'design of a language' included semantics as a 'peripheral' subsystem. As such, it associated grammatical units and the ways in which they are arranged with 'things and situations, or kinds of things and situations' (1958: 138); but it was separate from the 'grammatical system'. This was a 'central' subsystem, and it was at that level that the units and their arrangements were themselves identified (137). In what Chomsky later called his 'standard theory', the 'major components of a generative grammar' similarly included a 'semantic component' (1965: 16). But it was again distinct from the 'syntactic component'. The latter specified an 'infinite set of abstract formal objects', each corresponding to an 'interpretation' of a sentence. The semantic component then supplied this interpretation. For many of Chomsky's followers, it was also essential that syntactic rules should have what Katz & Postal called an 'independent syntactic justification' (1964: 157). This notion was derived from Chomsky's original account of 'linguistic theory', which in turn derived from Harris' criterion that the 'description of the language structure' (1951: 372) should be a compact account of distributions.

In short, the distinction between syntax and semantics arose from the post-Bloomfieldian doctrine that linguistic study should not merely 'start from the phonetic form and not from the meaning' (Bloomfield, 1935: 162), but should postpone an account of meanings until, as Hill put it, the 'description of sounds and their patternings . . . is done' (1958: 3). Morphemes were therefore identified in order to state 'the limitations of occurrence of linguistic elements over long stretches of speech' (Harris, 1951: 156), phrases in order to 'reduce the number of classes which we require when we state the composition of each utterance' (262), and so on. In the same spirit, transformations were posited because they led to a 'significant simplification' (thus, for instance, Chomsky, 1957: 41) of a grammar that generated strings of phonemes (13). 'Correlations' between a formal description and 'things', 'situations' or the way a language is 'put to use' belonged to a separate study.

What of the distinction between semantics and pragmatics? The term 'pragmatics' was invented, as is well known, by the semiotician Morris (1937, 1938); and until the early 1970s only a handful of linguists used it or referred to his ideas. They were explained in surveys by, for example, Ullmann (1962) or Nida (1964). But in America Hockett (1958) did not cite or discuss them. Nor did Chomsky (1957, 1965). Nor did Katz & Fodor (1963) or Katz & Postal (1964), in the first generativist accounts of the 'semantic component'.

Throughout this period, however, there was a distinction between what Bloomfield had called 'linguistic meaning' and the further meanings that a form might have when it was uttered. The linguistic meaning of a form was what was 'common to all the situations that call forth' its utterance (Bloomfield, 1935: 141). Thus, for the word *apple*, it would comprise 'the features which are common to all the objects of which English-speaking people use' this form. A sentence too was a linguistic form, and by implication it too had a linguistic meaning. As Chomsky put it near the end of the 1960s, its 'intrinsic meaning' was determined by the rules of a generative grammar (1972: 71). This grammar formed a speaker's 'linguistic competence', existing in abstraction from linguistic 'performance'. By implication, sentences when uttered would have other, non-intrinsic meanings, with which a study of linguistic competence was not concerned.

Our present distinction between semantics and pragmatics arose in response to the critique of that view in the years that followed. Both the critique and the response took varying forms; but by the middle of the 1970s Chomsky himself had restricted the rules of 'sentence grammar' to the assignment of 'logical forms' (1976: 104), and soon afterwards he talked of speakers having 'a system of "pragmatic competence"' which interacts with their 'grammatical competence' (1977: 3). Still in the middle of the decade, Kempson among others saw pragmatics as 'a theory of communication' (1975: 81) which belonged in essence to an account of performance (81, 206ff.). In either view, the response was to defend a 'semantic theory' that dealt with sentence meanings in abstraction from the context of utterance by proposing a 'pragmatic theory' which would supplement it.

This survey of the history has necessarily been brief. But it reminds us, in particular, that these divisions have their origin in successive attempts to limit the subject of linguistic enquiry. Harris and the Chomsky of the 1950s sought to restrict it, in the first instance, to an account of distributions. Syntax was accordingly the domain of rules that characterised the forms of sentences; semantics was a *terra incognita* that lay outside. Even when Katz & Fodor set out to explore it, their working definition was negative:

'Synchronic linguistic description minus grammar equals semantics' (1963: 172, title of section 3). In the 1960s the primary aim of linguistics was to give an account of linguistic competence. The ability to interpret sentences was part of that competence; but only in so far as it was independent of the context of utterance. When that restriction was in turn breached, what had lain beyond it was again conceived of as a new and separate field of study. For many, it too was defined negatively: 'Pragmatics', in a formula that was once quite common, 'equals meaning minus semantics.'

It does not follow that the divisions are bad; but each is a relic of a restriction that originally owed more to methodology than to fact. We must therefore look carefully at current definitions to see whether they make sense. What follows can be no more than a sketch; but it suggests that these are not coherent fields of investigation. The terms belong to a specific theory of meaning, which is indeed a relic of the history I have described.

Let us look first at definitions of 'semantics'. For many writers, it is simply a 'branch of linguistics devoted to the study of meaning in language' (Crystal, 1991: s.v.). That is also the scope of Lyons' *magnum opus* (1977); but, as a glance at the table of contents makes clear, it includes many topics that are elsewhere treated under 'syntax' and almost all that, at the time of writing, had been explored in 'pragmatics'. Is syntax then a subfield of semantics? That, as we have noted, was how Bloomfield saw it. Is pragmatics another subfield? In the entry on 'semantics' in the Oxford *Encyclopaedia*, it is said that, as the term is used 'nowadays', it 'usually comprehends pragmatics as well' (Allan, 1992: 395). We might then say that the term 'semantics' has two senses: semantics in a wide sense ('semantics$_1$') is the study of meaning; in a narrow sense ('semantics$_2$') it is what is left of semantics$_1$ when pragmatics, and, if syntax is included, syntax also, are subtracted from it.

If we take this line, there are three problems. First, we must give a coherent definition of 'syntax'. In the recent past, most scholars seem to have assumed that that is easy. Secondly, we must give a coherent definition of 'pragmatics'. This is a problem that Levinson addressed ten years ago (1983: 5–35), and few are likely to deny that it is difficult. Thirdly, we must show that, given these definitions, what remains is itself a coherent subfield.

Syntax, to return to Crystal's dictionary, is 'a traditional term for the study of the rules governing the way words are combined to form sentences in a language' (1991: s.v.). Crystal points out that this definition distinguishes syntax from morphology, but he says nothing about its relation to semantics. Nor does the Oxford *Encyclopaedia*. It has indeed no general entry under 'syntax'; nor under 'grammar', of which syntax is part. But many textbooks give the impression that the study of syntax is one thing, and the study of meaning – whether semantics₁ or semantics₂ – is another. They also give the impression that there is a hierarchy of levels. Fromkin & Rodman, for example, deal first with phonetics; then phonology; then morphology; then syntax; then, finally, semantics (1988: Part 2 = chs. 2–6). They say in one place that semantics is concerned with 'the ways in which sounds and meanings are related'; but this is by implication to be distinguished from 'how words may be combined into phrases and sentences' (24).

Fromkin & Rodman's introduction first appeared in 1974; like many such books, it is conservative, and its organisation reflects the earlier post-Bloomfieldian view of levels as successive phases of investigation. But the fencing off of syntax from semantics was by then controversial, and has since been widely disregarded. There are whole schools of linguists who would expect a grammar to be 'on semantic principles': thus, for example, the title of Dixon's recent 'new approach' to English (1991). Many who once rejected such a concept have now modified their views. Chomsky, for example, was for some twenty years a strong defender of what had been in origin a distributionalist thesis of the autonomy of syntax. But by the mid-1980s he was saying clearly that the syntax of words might be in part a function of their meanings. In what he called 'core grammmar' or 'core language', syntactic rules of the kind he had originally proposed were now 'virtually eliminated' (1986: 86). The basic structure of a sentence is instead a 'projection' of the lexical entry for a verb. This will have to specify its 'categorial selection' – for example, that *persuade* requires as its complements a noun phrase and a subordinate sentence. But that will in turn follow from its 'semantic selection'. Thus *persuade* semantically selects 'a goal and a proposition' (87).

This general view of syntax is not new. It is there in essence in the *Syntax* of Apollonius Dyscolus, which is the earliest treatment we have. But the reason why it has been rediscovered is that, by the mid-1970s, it had become clear to generative grammarians that 'syntactic' and 'semantic' rules could often do effectively the same job. Take, for example, the agreement in *these books*. A common solution in the 1960s was to copy a feature of plurality from the noun to the demonstrative. This was technically a syntactic transformation; it was obligatory, and in that way *this books* was excluded. But an alternative is to say that, if a demonstrative determines a noun, the phrase is semantically uninterpretable unless both have the same number. *These* is in itself plural; *books* is also plural; therefore, as an ancient grammarian would have said, the two are congruent and can stand together in this construction. But *this* and *books* are not congruent. Therefore *this books* is excluded, this time by a rule that for the generativists was technically one of semantics.

Which account is right? There is no easy answer if we persist in distinguishing levels in the way they were still conceived in the mid-1960s. On the one hand, a phrase like *this books* breaks a rule. No grammatical sentence can contain it; so, if the object of 'syntax' is to separate what is grammatical from what is ungrammatical, that rule must be part of it. On the other hand, it is well known that in other constructions there is often notional agreement. Therefore the rules cannot be complete unless the meanings of individual words and phrases are taken into account.

By the mid-1970s, Chomsky himself was stressing that there is no *a priori* division between facts of syntax and facts of semantics. There are simply facts, and we have to work out how they should be explained. But why should the forms of explanation be presented as separate? Until the 1940s, it had been generally assumed that syntax was concerned with meaning. For Bloomfield, as we have seen, it was one sub-branch of the semantic phase of linguistics. This view had been rejected by one school of linguists in North America, and their division between distribution and meaning had been taken over unchanged in the earliest work on generative grammar. But the preoccupations which had led them to make it were long dead. Syntax, we can still say, is the study of 'how words may be combined into sentences'. But their combinability reflects in part their meanings; therefore syntactic relations are in part semantic relations. Although they do not always make it explicit, that is the view which many syntacticians do seem, in reality, to have returned to.

There are, however, other aspects of meaning that are not part of syntax. In particular, there are plainly other aspects of word meaning. Might these then be one object of 'semantics' in the narrow sense – what we have called 'semantics₂'? What else might then belong to it?

Let us return to the Oxford *Encyclopaedia*. As we have seen, 'semantics' itself is defined in a wide sense ('semantics₁'). But 'some people', we are told, 'restrict the term . . . to the study of sense and sense relations' (Allan, 1992: 395). The implication, then, is that 'semantics₁' (the study of meaning) equals the study of sense and sense relations ('semantics₂') plus pragmatics. That in turn is 'the context-dependent assignment of meaning to language expressions' when used. The entry on 'pragmatics' is by a different contributor; but it too says that pragmatics 'involves the context-dependent aspects of meaning'. These aspects, it adds, 'are systematically abstracted away from in the pure semantics of logical form' (Horn, 1992: 260). The implication is that at least some branch of what we are calling 'semantics$_2$' is concerned with 'logical form'.

What do we mean by the terms that enter into such accounts? The term 'context-dependent' is less technical than the others, and may well seem the best starting point. Pragmatics, once more, deals with what is context-dependent; semantics$_2$, it might be suggested, deals with what is left. But there is a sense in which all aspects of meaning are context-dependent. What I mean by the speech I utter depends on my own background: that I am a speaker of English, of a certain form of English, with a certain range of vocabulary, certain intellectual and other interests, certain beliefs and prejudices, and so on. What my hearers get from it depends in turn on how well their backgrounds match mine: for example, if they do not know English they will get very little. All this is part of the 'context' of my utterances.

A natural rejoinder is that when we talk of 'context' we exclude everything that has to do with the language system that is in use. But in that case it is not clear that these formulations offer any positive definition of 'pragmatics'. It seems that we must first say what belongs to the language system. Evidently, some candidates are anything to do with 'sense and sense relations' or with 'logical form'. Pragmatics will then deal with 'context-dependent aspects of meaning' – but that means simply 'aspects of meaning' – that do not belong to it.

What then is meant by 'sense' and 'logical form'? The latter term was introduced by Chomsky in the mid-1970s: it referred, he said, to 'those aspects of semantic representation that are strictly determined by grammar, abstracted from other cognitive systems' (1977: 5). Elsewhere in the Oxford *Encyclopaedia*, it is said to be one 'major case of a grammatically relevant semantic representation' (Grimshaw, 1992: 81; s.v. 'grammatical meaning'). But although this is clearly a candidate for our account of a language system, Chomsky's later usage implies that it is part of syntax. By the time this article in the *Encyclopaedia* was drafted, he had already talked in several places of 'LF' as a 'syntactic level' (1981: 335; 1986: 84). This is natural, once we admit that syntax is itself concerned with aspects of meaning and not just with distribution.

If that is right, we are left with 'sense and sense relations'. In general usage, the term 'sense' refers to a 'system of linguistic relationships . . . which a lexical item contracts with other lexical items' (Crystal, 1991: s.v.). These relationships are called 'sense relations'. But according to Allan in the Oxford *Encyclopaedia*, we can also talk of 'the senses of phrases and sentences'. These are 'computed from the senses of their constituents', the 'most primitive chunks of meaning' being in the dictionary (1992: 395). So, 'semantics$_2$' would be the study of relations of meaning among these 'primitive chunks' and the ways in which the 'senses' of larger 'chunks' are computed.

This view of semantics has been familiar for thirty years, since the proposal of Katz & Fodor (1963). But when that was made, it was assumed that syntax was not concerned with meaning. It was also assumed that 'synchronic linguistic description', in the words of a formula cited earlier, consisted simply of 'grammar', in the sense that Chomsky had originally proposed, plus semantics as so conceived. Linguistics was not concerned with any study of semantics (our 'semantics$_1$') that went beyond their dictionary and their 'projection rules'. But if those assumptions are abandoned, the definition as I have given it is neither clear nor universally accepted. On the one hand, syntax too will involve relations of meaning among lexical items. If collocations are sense relations – as they are according to Crystal's dictionary – so are relations of 'selection' or valency; if synonymy is a sense relation, so is that of having the same valency. On the other hand, pragmatics is often said to include what Grice (1975: 44f.) called 'conventional implicatures'. Take the example *She was poor but honest*. In such an account, the speaker 'asserts' no more than 'a simple conjunction', merely 'suggesting' that there is a 'contrast between poverty and honesty' (Horn, 1992: 262). But the difference between *She was poor but honest* and *She was poor and honest* is surely one of 'sense'.

One problem, then, is to distinguish the 'sense relations' that belong to syntax from those that would belong only to 'semantics$_2$'. For example, it might be a fact of syntax that *persuade* has a valency like those of *order* or *ask*; but a fact of 'semantics', in the narrow sense, that *I asked him to leave* and *I persuaded him to leave* have different 'senses'. But the difficulty is precisely that the meanings of words cannot be partitioned in that way. On the one hand, we cannot describe meaning independently of distribution, and then say that distributions follow from it. For we know that there are differences of valency that cannot be so explained. On the other hand, we cannot say that valency is separate either from meaning or from 'other aspects' of meaning. It is part of the meaning of *hit* that it takes a goal or direct object, and this is intimately bound up with the kinds of action that *hit* describes. The true distinction is the old one, which seems to have re-appeared in Chomsky's writings over the past decade. On the one hand, there is the lexicon, and on the other there is syntax, which is in part a 'projection' of part of it.

The other problem is the one against which so many scholars have batted their heads, of distinguishing 'semantics' and 'pragmatics'. Broadly speaking, they have tried to make this distinction in two ways, often implying that they are equivalent. In one definition, semantics is concerned with aspects of meaning that belong, as we said earlier, to the language system; in the other, it is concerned with 'truth conditions'. That is, in particular, how it was most often seen in the 1970s, when the term 'pragmatics' first came into general use.

In one view, then, we have to say what belongs to 'the language system'. Evidently, the lexicon belongs to it. So, by implication, do the semantic relations in syntax that are a projection of it, and the ways in which they are realised formally. But do 'semantic representations' of sentences also belong to it? The problem, of course, is how they can be identified.

One answer is simply that they are compositional. Take, for example, the sentence *Did he leave?* We know the meanings of *he* and *leave*; the latter includes its valency, from which, in addition, we know the syntactic – that is, the semantic – relation in which the verb and pronoun stand. The language system will also distinguish sentence types – declarative, interrogative (realised here with the aid of the auxiliary), and so on. The semantic representation of a sentence is then an amalgam of these various kinds of 'primitive' meanings.

In this account, the assertion that sentence meanings are compositional is not, as is often claimed, a hypothesis. They are simply so by definition. But when Katz & Fodor first sought to explicate this principle, they had supposed that the scope of 'semantics' could be determined independently: for example, a semantic theory had to account for 'nonsyntactic ambiguity' (1963: 175). So too did those who first appealed to truth conditions. The basic assumption, in the words of yet another contribution to the Oxford *Encyclopaedia*, is that, 'in essence, the meaning of a sentence is equivalent to the conditions under which that sentence is true' (Cresswell, 1992: 404). It might be claimed, then, that this gives us an independent criterion. On the one hand, we can determine, for any sentence, what these conditions are. On the other hand, we can determine the meanings of words, constructions and so on. We then propose, as a hypothesis, that the truth conditions are a function of 'more primitive' meanings.

This view of sentence meaning has been widely criticised, and it would be pointless to repeat everything that has been said. But one basic problem concerns the criterion for truth. Take, for example, the sentence *He came in and took off his hat.* The meaning of *and* was one of Grice's original examples (1975), and what we have been told, repeatedly, is that although this sentence would normally be understood to refer to a sequence of actions, that is simply an 'implicature'. For it to be true, then, it is sufficient that the person referred to did, in whatever order, two things: (a) come in, (b) take off his hat. But suppose that I, as a speaker, say that this is wrong. I will say that the assertion is, in fact, false if he first took off his hat and then came in. Conversely, I will say that *He took off his hat and came in* is false if he came in first and then took off his hat. The implication is that, in the view of someone who divides semantics from pragmatics in this way, I am misguided. But why am I misguided?

It is difficult to put arguments in other scholars' mouths; but one possible answer is that we are not concerned with 'truth' as perceived by a lay speaker. Our primary concern is to establish truth conditions which are the projection, onto the sentences of a language, of the calculus of truth values in a system of logic. So, in one such system, there is a simple logical connector (&), and the conjunction *and* can be put in correspondence with it. We must, of course, ask if there is an alternative system of logic which, when projected onto English, gives a better account of the meaning of *and*. But it is evident that there is none. We must also show that, on the basis of this account, we can explain, partly by other means, the ways in which sentences with *and* are used and understood. That, it is claimed, is what Grice did.

This is an honest answer, and the only immediate objection to it is that it is not clear why we should suppose that languages are at heart projections of logical systems. But there is perhaps a variant answer, which does not rest on that assumption. Take, for example, the sentence *He was tired and he was hungry*. This can mean, and would ordinarily be taken to mean, that he was tired and hungry at the same time. Therefore it cannot be part of its truth conditions that he must have been hungry later. We then have two alternatives. We can say that *and*, or co-ordination with *and*, is ambiguous. In one case, the truth conditions require a sequence, in the other not. Alternatively, we again reject my judgment of *He came in and took off his hat*. In particular, it will be noted that I did not say that it would be false if he did both things at once. On that evidence, we insist that sequence cannot be essential to its truth.

The problem with this answer is that it would once again reduce the meanings of sentences to those of words and constructions. We look at different sentences in which a word *w*, or a construction with *w*, appears. We try to find what is common to their meanings: is a feature of sequence, for example, common to all sentences with *and*? Sometimes we will fail to discover such a feature; in that case the construction is ambiguous, or *w* is itself a homonym. Alternatively, we may succeed. But in either case the truth conditions are in part a function of whatever common meanings (whether of *w*, or of each of two homonymous *w*s, and so on) we have established.

In particular, there is no reason why the argument should be taken to support a theory based on truth conditions. The difference between *and* and *or* can be reduced to such conditions: in the honest answer, it is a projection of the difference between & and, say, ∨ . In the account derived from Grice, the difference between *and* and *but* cannot be: it has to be treated in terms of 'conventional' implicatures. But why should these different treatments matter? Our basic strategy is to establish a meaning common to the sentences of which any of these words forms part. Some can then be described in terms of truth conditions; but others cannot. Why should those that can be privileged?

It will be clear now that, apart from lingering references to truth conditions, we have effectively returned to Bloomfield's theory of the 1930s. Semantics will deal with 'linguistic meanings', with the features that a form or construction always has. Pragmatics will then study the further meanings that a sentence has for specific individuals in specific contexts of utterance. But Bloomfield made clear that his theory was founded on an assumption. It was, he said, 'the fundamental assumption of linguistics' (1935: 78, 144), and it implied precisely that 'each linguistic form has a constant and specific meaning' (145). Moreover, he knew very well that it would on occasion prove false.

So, surely, do we. We talk, for example, of an interrogative construction, as in *Can you help us?* But we know that such sentences have no 'constant and specific meaning'. Sometimes they are questions, sometimes requests, sometimes offers, and so on. Often there is 'hedging', so that an utterance can be taken in more than one of these ways. We therefore talk instead of what we call 'literal meaning'. 'Literally', we say, such sentences are always questions; when that is not what they in fact are, pragmatics must again take over. But that rests on the assumption that, even where there is no meaning common to all uses of a form or a construction, we must still draw some distinction between what is in our hypothesis essential and what is merely accidental. So, we say that the essential role of interrogatives is to form questions. Our reason, presumably, is that, having formally identified the construction, we find that a majority of interrogatives are only, or at least typically, used in that way. We then say that sentences like *Can you help us?*, even if they are generally or always either requests or 'hedged' requests, nevertheless are essentially questions.

For the currency of such treatments, see again the Oxford *Encyclopaedia* (Horn, 1992: 260). But why should the basic assumption be made? For Bloomfield, the reason was clear enough: he did not think that the study of language was possible without it. From him and other structuralists it passed into the tradition. But do we still believe that it is methodologically necessary? If not, why do we believe that it is right?

Unless that question can be answered, it is not clear, at least to this writer, why the institutionalised division between semantics and pragmatics should be retained. Nor is it clear to me, from our earlier arguments, why we should retain the institutionalised division between semantics and syntax. It may have occurred to some readers that, for example, 'categorial selection' is in principle different from 'semantic selection'. The former has to do with relations among formal units: thus by formal criteria we establish such units as noun phrases, and rules such as that by which *hit* requires a noun phrase as its complement. Only the latter has to do with meaning. Therefore all we were saying is that semantic relations can be described in such a way that relations in syntax can be predicted from them.

But why are they 'in principle' different? On the face of it the principle is the old one of the 1940s and 1950s, that distributions and meanings must be studied separately. But that was again adopted for methodological reasons, which were, moreover, peculiar to a specific school. One again asks why we should persist with it.

REFERENCES

Allan, K. (1992) Semantics: an overview. In Bright (ed.), vol. III: 395–9.

Bloomfield, L. (1935) *Language*, London: Allen and Unwin.

Bright, W. (ed.) (1992) *International Encyclopaedia of Linguistics*, 4 vols., New York: Oxford University Press.

Chomsky, N. (1957) *Syntactic Structures*, The Hague: Mouton.

(1965) *Aspects of the Theory of Syntax*, Cambridge, MA: MIT Press.

(1972) *Language and Mind*, enlarged edn, New York: Harcourt Brace Jovanovich.

(1976) *Reflections on Language*, London: Maurice Temple Smith.

(1977) *Essays on Form and Interpretation*, New York: North-Holland.

(1981) *Lectures on Government and Binding*, Dordrecht: Foris.

(1986) *Knowledge of Language*. New York: Praeger.

Cresswell, M.J. (1992) Truth-conditional and model-theoretic semantics. In Bright (ed.), vol. III: 404–6.

Crystal, D. (1991) *A Dictionary of Linguistics and Phonetics*, 3rd edn, Oxford: Blackwell.

Dixon, R.M.W. (1991) *A New Approach to English Grammar, on Semantic Principles*, Oxford: Clarendon Press.

Fromkin, V. & R. Rodman (1988) *An Introduction to Language*, 4th edn, New York: Holt, Rinehart and Winston.

Grice, H.P. (1975) Logic and conversation. In P. Cole & J.L. Morgan (eds.) *Syntax and Semantics*, vol. III: *Speech Acts*, New York: Academic Press, 41–58.

Grimshaw, J. (1992) Grammatical meaning. In Bright (ed.), vol. II: 81–3.

Harris, Z.S. (1946) From morpheme to utterance. *Language* 22: 142–53.

(1951) *Methods in Structural Linguistics*, University of Chicago Press.

Hill, A.A. (1958) *Introduction to Linguistic Structures*, New York: Harcourt Brace.

Hockett, C.F. (1958) *A Course in Modern Linguistics*, New York: Macmillan.

Horn, L.R. (1992) Pragmatics, implicature, and presupposition. In Bright (ed.), vol. III: 260–6.

Katz, J.J. & J.A. Fodor (1963) The structure of a semantic theory. *Language* 39: 170–210.

Katz, J.J. & P.M. Postal (1964) *An Integrated Theory of Linguistic Descriptions*, Cambridge, MA: MIT Press.

Kempson, R.M. (1975) *Presupposition and the Delimitation of Semantics*, Cambridge University Press.

Levinson, S.C. (1983) *Pragmatics*, Cambridge University Press.

Lyons, J. (1977) *Semantics*, 2 vols., Cambridge University Press.

Morris, C.W. (1937) *Logical Positivism, Pragmatism, and Scientific Empiricism*, Paris: Hermann.

(1938) *Foundations of the Theory of Signs*. Reprinted in *Writings on the General Theory of Signs*, The Hague: Mouton, 1971, 13–71.

Nida, E.A. (1964) *Toward a Science of Translating*, Leiden: Brill.

Ullmann, S. (1962) *Semantics*, Oxford: Blackwell.

4

Natural-language interpretation as labelled natural deduction

RUTH M. KEMPSON

It is uncontroversial that an account of semantics for natural language must provide an explanation of the information intrinsic to natural-language expressions. The assumption that such a semantics for natural language involves reconstructing the information natural-language strings convey about the non-linguistic objects they are used to describe has held sway now for some twenty years since Lewis (1972) poured scorn on the representational view of meaning then current – that of Katz (1972). However, this approach to natural-language content is far from unproblematic; and in this chapter I argue for a return to a representational approach. I advocate a proof-theoretic account of interpretation in which natural-language expressions are seen as providing the encoded input to a process of interpretation which builds structure via a process of deduction. The information an individual expression conveys is information about how to build structured configurations which constitute the interpretation of the string in which the expression is contained. The structures that result from this process are linked labelled databases set within a logic framework defining inference over complex databases. In section 1, I set out problems for the classical form of the truth-theoretic paradigm originally advocated by Montague (1974), arguing that we need both a concept of content which underdetermines truth-theoretic content for individual expressions and a process of interpretation for strings which involves structure building. In section 2, I set out a model of utterance interpretation meeting these requirements. In section 3, we see how ellipsis data problematic for standard truth-theoretic assumptions fall out from this model. Finally, in section 4, I draw out the consequences of adopting such a structural view of natural-language content – both for the nature of natural-language semantics and for syntax.

1 The problem of ambiguity

A major problem for truth-theoretic accounts of meaning is the prediction of multiple ambiguity across the board for a wide range of different expressions. First, and most familiar, there is an array of different kinds of interpretation assigned to pronominal expressions, labelled variously as indexical pronouns (which refer to some entity directly without apparent dependence), bound-variable pronouns, discourse coreference (Reinhart, 1983b, 1986), E-type pronouns (Evans, 1980; Heim, 1990) donkey-type pronouns (Kamp, 1984), lazy pronouns (Karttunen, 1968; Cooper, 1979). All these except indexical uses share the property that the interpretation of the pronoun is determined by some form of linkage with an antecedent, but the type of linkage varies, as does the type of content:

(1) John came in. He was sick.
(2) Every student worries that she is going to fail.
(3) Joan worries that she's going to fail.
(4) Only a few students entered the exam, but they were confident they would pass.
(5) Every student who entered for an exam, passed it.
(6) Every student who puts her cheque in the building society is more sensible that the student who puts it in her current account.

With model-theoretic assumptions underpinning the concept of linguistic content, the full set of pronominal uses is non-unitary (there is a voluminous literature on the degree to which the heterogeneity of this phenomenon can be reduced; for a representative sample, see Cooper, 1979; Kamp, 1984; Kempson, 1988; Heim, 1990; Chierchia, 1992).

This proliferation of ambiguities is, however, far from local to pronominal anaphora. All anaphoric expressions depend for their interpretation on some concept of context of utterance giving rise to a range of truth-theoretically discrete types of meaning. Examples (7)–(16) display an array of VP, nominal and demonstrative anaphoric dependencies, having in common only this property of dependency on their immediate surrounding context for assignment of some interpretation:

(7) John likes Mary, but I don't.
(8) Everyone worries about their logic paper, except Marcello, who never does.
(9) John kissed everyone that Sue didn't.
(10) Don't.

(11) Most students like maths, but I know at least one who does not.
(12) One will do.
(13) Jo telephoned a journalist every time Sue interviewed one.
(14) That man is a nuisance.
(15) She made a cake for John and that bastard never thanked her.
(16) Every time she had a coke, she knew that later that week, she'd have a headache.

The phenomenon is not even restricted to anaphoric processes. It applies to tense construal (Partee, 1984a), to the construal of indefinite NPs, to the interpretation of adjectives (Klein, 1980), adverbs (Stump, 1985), and so on. Indeed natural-language expressions, both simple and complex, are invariably construed relative to some unfolding concept of context, a problem which is widely recognised. We seem faced with a multiplicity of ambiguities far beyond what any lexical sources of ambiguity would lead us to expect.

Even granting some defined concept of context, we seem to be losing sight of the intuitions about natural-language expressions we are seeking to model. According to standard assumptions, we know there is no longer a single answer to the question 'What is a pronoun?': the answer is 'There are at least two types of pronoun – bound-variable pronouns and those established through discourse coreference.' There is no longer a single answer to the question 'What is a reflexive pronoun?' either. We answer, 'There are true reflexives, logophoric reflexives, emphatic reflexives . . .' To the question 'What is an indefinite NP?' we answer, 'There are ordinary indefinites and there are generics. There are also specific indefinites . . .' To the question 'What is a demonstrative?' at least, one might think that there is a clearcut answer: 'They require a demonstration, a pointing' (see Kaplan, 1979). But not a bit of it; such analyses have swept aside such examples as (15) and (16). Then there are the tenses. 'What is present tense?' 'Well, it's present or generic.' The list goes on and on. We might take this as demonstration of the diversity of natural-language expressions. But notice what we no longer have: we no longer have an account of what it means for something to be a pronominal, what it means for something to be a reflexive, what it means to be a demonstrative. And so on, right through the list. We have lost sight of the information conveyed by an expression in virtue of its being a pronominal, in virtue of its being a demonstrative, an indefinite, etc. But the concept of information to be associated with an expression is what we agreed as a starting point was the heart of any semantic explication.

1.1 The interaction of syntactic constraints and pragmatic processes: bound-variable anaphora

The problem of context-dependence is widely recognised, and has been the subject of much work throughout the 1980s (see Barwise & Perry, 1983; Kamp, 1984; and subsequent work in the Situation Semantics and Discourse Representation Theory paradigms). Despite the volume of literature in this area, its tie-up with this degree of ambiguity is not widely granted. Indeed a common response is to restrict attention to pronominal anaphoric processes, and retort (following Reinhart, 1983a) that such diversity splits neatly into two, those interpretations subject to configurational restriction and hence internal to the grammar, and those interpretations which are not, and are therefore outside the remit of grammar-internal explanation. The most well known such distinction is between so-called bound-variable anaphora and discourse coreference, only the former being seen as grammar-internal. The latter is taken to be a heterogeneous bunch of pragmatic phenomena.

This dichotomy, however, cannot be sustained – even for the anaphora phenomena for which this distinction is pertinent. The reason is this: for every anaphoric linkage, howsoever established, there is a corresponding bound-variable analogue. No matter how uncontentiously discourse-based a phenomenon is, it can interact with supposed syntactic constraints on interpretation. In particular there are anaphoric linkages demonstrating two major central cognitive activities:

1 Logical deduction:
  (17) Joan isn't so anti-private practice as not to have any private patients, but she's always complaining that they treat her as a servant.
2 Retrieval from memory of contingently known information associated with specified objects:
  (18) The fridge is broken. The door needs mending.

Establishing the anaphoric linkage in (17) involves a step of double-negation elimination; establishing the anaphoric linkage in (18) involves making a link in virtue of the knowledge that fridges have doors. Both processes are central to any account of human reasoning of the most general sort, and are not properties of the language faculty itself. But these examples have straightforward analogues in which the pronominal linkage involves central cognitive processes while yet licensing a bound-variable interpretation.

(19) Everyone of my friends who isn't so anti-private practice as not to have any private patients is complaining that they treat her as a servant.

(20) Every fridge needs the door mending.

The availability of such readings cannot be seen as a simple syntactic matter for which the grammar – without access to the inferential processes – dictates the syntactic environments within which such interpretations are licensed:[1] the availability of such interpretations is subject not merely to the existence of the requisite configuration, but also to how intervening operators are inferentially manipulated. In (19), the hearer is required to manipulate the double-negation rule of deduction '¬¬P ≡ P', in that form, to establish 'P' – in (19) 'P' being that 'x ranging over my friends has private patients'. In (21), with one negation, no such inferential step is licensed: the only interpretation is one in which the negation includes the construal of the indefinite within its scope and no suitable interpretation for the pronoun *they* as (indirectly) dependent on *every friend of mine . . .* can be constructed:

(21) Everyone of my friends who doesn't have any private patients is complaining that they misuse her time.

One might attempt the retort that the phenomenon does not involve steps of inference but rather movement of the relevant indefinite operator out of the scope of two negations in (19) as in (22), with (22′) schematically displaying the required movement:

(22) Every teacher who doesn't like a student gives her an A in compensation.

(22′) ∀x, x teacher ∃y, y student (¬ (x like y) → Q)

But leaving on one side the well-known problem of what form the value of the pronominal in the consequent (here given as Q) should take, this move will not do. It is essential that *any* in (19), as in (17), remain within the scope of the second negative in order to be licensed, as a negative-polarity *any*. Treating it as either a universal or an existential and moved out of the scope of negation to yield configurations analogous to either (1) or (2) yields the wrong interpretation:

1 ∀x ∀y ¬¬ (x have y) → Q
2 ∀x ∃y ¬¬ (x have y) → Q

The double-negation environment in (19) does not involve the assertion that 'for all ordered pairs x a friend, y a private patient such that it not be the case that x not-have y, it is the case that Q'. Nor does it involve the assertion that 'for all entities x a friend such that there is some private patient y of whom it not be the case that x not have y, it is the case that Q'. The only route to the right interpretation is to retain *any patient in situ* as having a narrow-scope existential interpretation, a proposition for which it not being the case that it is false is implied to be true. Indeed the force of the phrase *not so X as to not P* is to induce the step of deduction '¬¬P ≡ P'. Furthermore the step must be in that syntactic form: in order to establish an antecedent for the pronoun in 'Q', we need an assertion equivalent in form to '∃y x have y'. Recovering by a semantic mode of inference some unstructured set of worlds in which the proposition is true does not in and of itself provide the necessary structure. Only the syntactic form of inference will do. We cannot say that, '¬¬P' being simply identical semantically to 'P', the problem reduces to mere donkey-type anaphora, as the interpretation of (19) depends on the construal of the construction as a complex assertion about the degree to which the friends in question are anti-private practice, an assertion which involves a step of double-negation elimination as a subpart, and invites additional inferences by contrast about ways in which the friends in question are anti-private practice.

Analogous attempts to defuse the force of the injection of extra information recovered from general memory stores may be attempted (e.g. Partee, 1989), but also rebutted. We have to grant the interaction of configurational constraints on anaphoric dependency and processes of general reasoning. Granting this, the data (17)–(20) pose us with a number of alternatives, which – if we retain standard assumptions about syntax – leaves only one option free of inconsistency. It appears that the output of such general cognitive processes has to be checked against a syntactic restriction on interpretation, an interaction precluded by all standard theories of syntax. We could take these data as evidence that the encapsulation of the language faculty simply be abandoned *in toto* and allow free interaction of processes internal to the language faculty and central cognitive processes. Since this would involve jettisoning all possibility of characterising properties specific to language, this alternative is not acceptable. Notice, however, that the alternative of invoking the ambiguity of bound-variable anaphora and discourse coreference as a means of dividing off grammar-internal processes from general cognitive processes is not a viable option. To postulate ambiguity here is no help – the grammar-internal phenomenon still involves interaction with the relevant central cognitive processes. Yet to stipulate double-negation elimination or bridging cross-reference as a grammar-internal phenomenon is to incorporate central cognitive processes into the grammar, and this too involves reneging on all possibility of maintaining a distinction between what is the encoded input provided by some language module and general cognitive processes. Our only recourse seems to be to grant the underdeterminacy of all anaphoric expressions, allow the phenomenon of anaphoric dependence to be characterised as part of the pragmatic process of assigning interpretation to utterances, and characterise the constraint on bound-variable interpretations in like manner to the disjointness requirement on pronominal anaphora (principle B) as a filter on licit choices of anaphoric dependence made as part of this pragmatic process.

1.2 The interaction of syntactic constraints and pragmatic processes: island constraints and ellipsis

Exploring this last route gives us a much more syntactic view of content, already indicated by the syntactic form of inference required in examples such as (19). We appear to need to define concepts of locality, c-command, etc, over configurations licensed both by grammar-internal processes and by general cognitive processes. There is evidence that this is the right direction in which to look for a solution – though ultimately it will force us to revise our assumptions about the nature of syntax. As a syntactic view of utterance interpretation would lead us to expect, elliptical processes both display the underdeterminacy of natural-language expressions *vis-à-vis* the interpretation assigned to them even more dramatically than anaphora, and yet are subject to the so-called 'island' constraints familiar as grammar-internal constraints (see Morgan, 1973). It is this phenomenon which is puzzling from standard assumptions, for it appears to preclude semantic explanation (Dalrymple, Shieber & Pereira, 1991). The data are as follows. Bare argument fragments can be interpreted in context as expressing whole propositions, reconstructing complex propositional structure from some antecedent source:

(23) Joan wants Sue to visit Bill in hospital. And Mary too.

The elliptical *And Mary too*, which can be uttered by some other speaker, can be reconstructed either as 'Mary wants Sue to visit Bill in hospital', or 'Joan wants Mary to visit Bill in hospital', or as 'Joan wants Sue to visit Mary in hospital.' The same process is available when the antecedent clause contains fully tensed subordinate clauses as in (24), for which the fragment can be construed as a substitution for *Mary* as well as for *John*:

(24) John believes that Mary only likes sugar-free cakes. Sue too.

However, just as *wh*-questions cannot license binding of the *wh*-expression into a relative clause, so these fragments cannot be reconstructed as replacing some expression inside a relative clause:

(25) Joan visited the woman who likes Bill, in hospital. And Mary too.

The fragment in (25) can be construed as 'Mary visited the woman who likes Bill in hospital', and as 'Joan visited Mary in hospital.' But it cannot be interpreted as 'Joan visited the woman who likes Mary, in hospital.' This island-constraint phenomenon is generally taken as definitive of a grammatical phenomenon. Yet there is independent reason to consider that the interpretation of fragments is a pragmatic process (*contra* Reinhart, 1991), sensitive to general on-line constraints on utterance interpretation – just as is anaphora. First, it occurs across speakers:

(26) A: John's coming to the party.
     B: But not Mary?

Secondly, the fragment must not only follow the clause on which it depends for interpretation, but must follow it most nearly, as its closest sister:

(27) *Mary too and Bill hit John.
(28) Jo wrote to *The Times* and Sue went to see the editor. And Mary too.

Mary too in (28) cannot mean 'Mary wrote to *The Times*', despite the fact that *Jo wrote to the Times* is just as much a sister of *Mary too* as is *Sue went to see the editor*. Further, the sisterhood restriction is uniformly maintained except in cases in which the predicates only indicate the speaker's attitude towards what he is saying with the result that the main relevance inheres in the (pair of) subordinate clauses:

(29) I'm sure Kinnock will be returned, but I think not Hattersley.

Notice that an analysis of *I think* as some superimposed 'attitudinal disjunct', to preserve a sisterhood restriction, will not give the right results here. The second conjunct of (29) on this view should mean either (29′) or (29″):

(29′) I think I'm not sure that Hattersley will be returned.
(29″) I think I'm sure that Hattersley will not be returned.

depending on whether the conjunction is taken to be matrix conjunction with *not Hattersley* sister to *I'm sure Kinnock will be returned* (29′), or subordinate to the main predicate *I'm sure that*, with *not Hattersley* sister to *Kinnock will be returned*, with *I think* as an indication of attitude to be added after the computation of an interpretation for the remainder (29″). But it bears neither of these interpretations. *I think* has to be construed as replacing the initial matrix predicate *I'm sure*. An analysis in terms of a strict sisterhood condition on s-structure configurations would make the wrong predictions for (29).

Such fragments cannot in any case be assumed to involve reconstruction solely off the surface string (or s-structure configuration). The fragment may be reconstructed off some other elliptical structure, itself requiring some reconstructed interpretation as in (30):

> (30) A: Will you check the mistakes in our paper?
>   B: If I notice them. And the typing errors too.

B's utterance is perfectly acceptable, involving as it does reconstruction of the fragment *the typing errors* from what B has said immediately previously. But the form of this is a floating *if* clause, and not itself what B assumes A will use to reconstruct the fragment. What B presumes A will use is what she has recovered from that *if*-clause, viz. 'that A will check the mistakes in their paper'. But this is only recovered by a process of reasoning in context – hence pragmatically.

A further indication that this reconstruction is a pragmatic process is a restriction of parallelism on the fragment dictating that it be interpreted in like manner to the antecedent conjunct. This is a restriction sustained only up to inconsistency rather than invariably (as a blind syntactic restriction would). Thus

> (31) The men were all hungry and most of the women too.

does not mean that 'most of the women were all hungry'. However, this does not indicate syntactic optionality of the floated quantifying expression *all* since

> (32) The men were all hungry and the women too.

must mean that 'all the women were hungry'. We thus make the preliminary step of deducing that fragments, like pronouns, indefinites, tense and the rest, provide a (seriously) underdetermined input to a process of reasoning which takes such encoded input and reasons with other information on line to assign the fragment some intended interpretation. The significance of this conclusion is that it forces us to model utterance interpretation as a structure-building process, sensitive to the very same restrictions which are familiar from accounts of natural-language syntax. And hence we arrive at the interim conclusion that processes of interpretation need to be just as syntactic as the configurations familiar from syntactic theory.

Before attempting to model this process, we should reflect how faithfully the ideas correspond to current thinking in pragmatics. This view directly reflects claims of Relevance theory (Sperber & Wilson, 1986). The Relevance-theoretic view is that all cognitive processing by a human agent involves constructing representations from some input stimulus, those representations being part of a central cognitive system of representations for which inference is syntactically defined (see also Fodor, 1983). A characteristic property of natural-language expressions, however, is that they underdetermine the interpretation assigned to them; and part of the hearer's task is to decide what enrichment to choose by way of a full interpretation. Her choice is constrained by the simultaneous need to economise on cognitive effort while optimising the amount of inferential benefit in a way commensurate with matching the intentions of the speaker. This, the principle of relevance, is the central claim of Relevance theory. For our concerns here, the principal substance lies in the presumption of a structure-building process of interpretation: both the underdetermined input and the assigned output are assumed to be representations in some inferential system.

2 Utterance interpretation as labelled deductive reasoning

We now seek to model this inferential task within a labelled deductive system (LDS). We shall get there in several steps. We introduce:

1 the notion of types as propositions;
2 the concept of labelled formulae;
3 the concept of labelling as a control on how an inference structure is built up through a proof;
4 the use of variables in the labels;
5 relating concepts of local and non-local reasoning;
6 the concept of linked labelled databases.

We are assuming the hearer takes the words in sequence, and builds an interpretation from them by a process of reasoning. Some of these words provide the building blocks for the interpretation process, others provide instructions on how to complete the reasoning task. We assume that stored in the lexicon for each lexical item is a specification of its contribution to utterance interpretation. In the simple cases, this takes the form of a pair – a conceptual expression, and a specification of its logical type (expressed as in Montague semantics in terms of the two primitives:

e, an individual denoting expression

t, a truth-bearing entity

and combinatorial functions on these). A verb such as *love*, for example, expresses the two-place relation 'love', an expression of logical type '⟨e,⟨e,t⟩⟩'. Expressing its combinatorial potential directly, we can paraphrase this information as the instruction that 'if a category of type e is provided to combine with "love", then if a second category of type e is also provided, the result will be a proposition of type t'. We reflect this informal indication of the verb's combinatorial potential directly by presenting the type specification as a labelled premise in a conditional logic, with the verb's type being the proposition and the corresponding logical expression a matching label for that type. Here 'love' labels the type-as-proposition 'e→(e→t)'. With *John* entered in the lexicon as 'John:e' according to a general format 'α:t' to be read as 'α labels t', and *Mary* as 'Mary:e' we will then be able to present the processing of the interpretation of *John loves Mary* as the construction of a database containing three premises, 'John-e', 'loves:e→(e→t)', 'Mary:e', from which with two steps of →Elimination we build 'love (Mary)(John):t'.

The rule of →Elimination on which such combinatorial projection depends is defined to apply to 'declarative units' – pairs of label-plus-formula:

$$\frac{\begin{array}{l} α{:}P \\ β{:}P{\to}Q \end{array}}{β(α){:}Q}$$

The definition of rules of inference in terms of declarative units is part of a labelled deductive system (Gabbay, forthcoming). In this system, a logic is defined in terms of a logical language together with an associated algebra of labels: the labels reflect not merely what information the steps of reasoning rest on, but how those steps combine. They thus reflect the flow of information through a proof structure, and can be used as a meta-restriction on the proof steps to impose extra restrictions on that process without distorting the simplicity of the logical language itself.

This presentation of types as premises in a conditional logic assumes an isomorphism between the lambda-calculus and conditional (intuitionistic) logic. This Curry–Howard isomorphism (used in several applications of Parsing as Deduction – see Pereira, 1991; van Benthem, 1986) licenses a formalism in which types are treated as propositions, the lambda-calculus expression providing an interpretation for its corresponding formula. Here we use it to represent the combinatorial projection of lexical specifications of content as steps of natural deduction in the task of establishing some conclusion 'a' labelling 't', where 'a' is a composite label based on the words presented.

The application of such LDS assumptions in the area of natural-language understanding enables us to view the labels themselves as guaranteeing the order in which the premises apply. We use the notion of labels to define the concept of subject directly on the proof structure, annotating the first entry in the database as 'to be used last in some minimal chain of →Elimination leading to a conclusion of the form "a:t"', an annotation of the premise which is projected from the verb itself as part of the information encoded in the lexicon.

With the simple sentence *John loves Mary*, we can now see just how building a structured configuration can be seen as a systematic goal-directed task of natural deduction leading from the given input to a conclusion whereby the hearer works out what proposition the speaker has expressed to her by deduction over the types, the accumulation of the labels telling her what that proposition is. We have three words, *John*, *loves*, *Mary*, yielding from the lexicon three premises:

> John:e
> love:e→(e→t)
> Mary:e

With the extra annotation projected by the verb itself, two steps of Modus Ponens will lead to the proposition:

> love(Mary)(John):t

The database as presented so far is displayed in figure 4.1.

Figure 4.1

> *Goal* {w_i:x, w_j:y,. . .} ⊢ f(w_i, w_j, . . .):t
> Johne:e 'to be used last'
> love:e→(e→t)
> Mary:e
>
> deducing
>
> love(Mary):e→t
> love(Mary)(John):t

To complete it, all we have to add is the assumption that such sets of declarative units are themselves also labelled as fixed at a certain point in a flow of time, and that the verb projects this information too. In this case, the database is fixed as in a flow of time including some time of evaluation (see figure 4.2).

Figure 4.2

Goal $\{w_i{:}x, w_j{:}y, \ldots\} \vdash f(w_i, w_j, \ldots){:}t$
$s_1, s_1 \supset s_{NOW}$
John:e 'to be used last'
love:$e \rightarrow (e \rightarrow t)$
Mary:e

deducing

love(Mary):$e \rightarrow t$
love(Mary)(John):t

Notice how for every step of Modus Ponens taken, the information in the labels builds up, recording the assumptions used and their mode of combination, the resulting conclusion a well-formed formula of a predicate logic labelling the logical type 't'. So we obtain our first modelling of utterance interpretation as a reasoning task taking as input the information the words provide, and yielding as output a structured configuration over which inference can be syntactically defined.

2.1 Anaphora and variables in the labels

Such a sentence as this displays no obvious underdeterminacy, but the phenomenon of anaphora can be reconstructed, with its underdetermining input, and dependency established in context, as a process of natural deduction. An initiating assumption of some meta-variable over labels is entered as the premise lexically associated with the pronoun, an assumption which is discharged by instantiation from some information independently recoverable from the inference structure already presented:

(33) John loves Mary. She loves him.

We display the proof-theoretic process of interpretation in figure 4.3.

Figure 4.3

> *Goal* $\{w_i{:}x, w_j{:}y, \ldots\} \vdash f(w_i, w_j \ldots){:}t$
> $s_1, s_1 \supset s_{NOW}$
> John:e
> love:$e \to (e \to t)$
> Mary:e
> love(Mary):$e \to t$ Modus Ponens
> love(Mary)(John):t   Modus Ponens

> *Goal* $\{w_i{:}x, w_j{:}y, \ldots\} \vdash f(w_i, w_j \ldots){:}t$
> $s_1, s_1 \supset s_{NOW}$
> u:e   condition: $\theta u \notin$ local proof structure
>   female(θu)
> CHOOSE u = Mary
> love:$e \to (e \to t)$
> v:e   condition: $\theta v \notin$ local proof structure
>   male(θv)
> CHOOSE v = John
> love(John):$e \to t$ Modus Ponens
> love(John)(Mary):t   Modus Ponens

The information lexically provided by a pronoun can now be characterised in a unitary way. The information intrinsic to an anaphoric expression is a procedure for building structure. The expression does not itself provide a fully specified label, but it provides a constraint on how that label should be identified – whether non-locally as with pronominals, or locally as with reflexives. Reconstructed this way, anaphoric linkage is a relation established across structure – proof-theoretic structure. Locality restrictions on this process, whether to some non-local domain as with pronominals, or to some local domain as with anaphors, are naturally expressible as side conditions on the process (θ) of instantiating the initial assumed variable. We have principle A and principle B of the Binding theory stated directly as a specification given in the lexicon as definitional of anaphors/pronominals but implemented on proof structures as part of the process of arriving at some labelled conclusion, here:

love(John)(Mary):t

Notice how what on standard assumptions is a syntactic restriction has become part of the intrinsic content of the pronominal, part of the information conveyed by an expression in virtue of being a pronominal, and in this sense constituting part of its meaning.

Utterance interpretation can now be defined as a process of natural deduction from some initiating set of premises to some conclusion 'α:t', 'α' being the proposition expressed, with some of the words presented as premises to that conclusion, others determining how the conclusion is reached. A sentence is said to be well formed if and only if from some sequence of words, a conclusion of the form 'α:t' is derivable using all the information presented by the sequence of words once and once only. With this mode of explanation the concept of interpretation is essentially structural: the linguistic content of an expression is characterised in a general way as a procedure the word makes available to the inferential task of utterance interpretation. So far we have seen how words may contribute premises and other procedures. Some expressions, on the other hand, contribute solely by providing some constraint on the proof process. For this we need to turn to the other characteristic of the LDS framework – its articulation of local and non-local forms of reasoning and possible relations between them.

2.2 Wh-*expressions and linked databases*

As part of such a global logic concern, we define a concept of linked databases. Two databases are said to be linked as in figure 4.4 if and only if some free variable in each, 'x' and 'y', is replaced by some common unifier – here 'x' (for a formal definition, see Gabbay & Kempson, 1992).

Figure 4.4

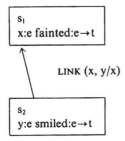

The natural-language vehicle for projecting such linked structures is the relative-clause construction: relative-clause markers are a means of creating one local piece of reasoning linked to another – through some unifying variable. Suppose, for example, we wish to link together two pieces of information, that a man fainted and that that man smiled. We can do so through the relative-clause structure:

(34) A man who smiled fainted.

Reflecting this, *wh* in English can be characterised as initiating, from the lexicon, a database to be so linked. We assign to *wh* the lexical specification that it instigate the building of a proof structure which leads to a particular form of conclusion – viz. that the conclusion of type 't' be labelled by some open formula containing a variable, that variable to be linked to the initiating database (for details of the lexical specification, see Gabbay & Kempson, 1992). The effect is that its occurrence will drive the building of such linked structures. Let us take the process stage by stage. Schematically, with *wh* as a relative, we have s_0, the point of departure to which words are projecting some internal structure. At some arbitrary point in s_0, we enter 'v:e' as induced by some name or determiner, here a variable corresponding to the indefinite. With *wh* as a following relative marker, the instruction, diagrammatically displayed in figure 4.5, is to build a new database s_1, imposing on it the more specific requirement of a formula containing a new variable 'w' linked to the variable 'v'.

Figure 4.5

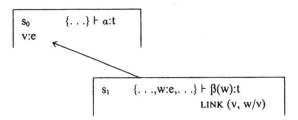

This subroutine is thus only successfully completed if at some point an assumption 'w:e', with 'w' linked (unified) with 'v' of the host database, can be constructed satisfying this goal requirement. This will only be possible if at some one point in the ensuing database, the words in sequence fail to provide all the information necessary to reach some conclusion 'a:t'. At just this point, the required assumption can be constructed and the result is success in fulfilling the imposed goal. Once the subroutine s_1 is complete, the parsing routine proceeds in s_0 and s_0 is duly completed. The lexical content of *wh* thus does not itself constitute a premise to be manipulated in any proof structure; rather, it provides a restriction on the form of conclusion that must be established. It is, that is, a goal specification on a newly initiated database.

3 The proof discipline as inducing syntactic constraints

This concept of linked databases, independent save only for the sharing of the linked variables, enables us to predict a range of syntactic phenomena in virtue of the procedural analysis of *wh* itself. Take first the restriction of 'no vacuous quantification' as in (35):

(35) The man who Bill saw Mary fainted.

The relative *wh* induces the building of a linked database, subject to the further restriction on the goal to be achieved in that database, that the outcome be a formula '$\beta(u)$:t', the conclusion 't' to be labelled by some predication on a variable, that variable to be linked on line to the point from which the *wh* initiated the building of this new database. The problem with (35) is that this required outcome is not obtainable. The database to be built for that *wh* is set out as containing a two-place predicate, 'saw:$e \rightarrow (e \rightarrow t)$', allowing for just two minor premises with which to combine to yield some labelled conclusion 'a:t'. But these two minor premises are both provided by *Bill* and *Mary* respectively. There is no room in the database to construct some assumption 'u:e' linked to the variable 'w' associated with *the*. With no position at which such an assumption could be provided, the requisite goal specification is unattainable, the imposed form of the conclusion cannot be reached, the parsing process grinds to a halt, and the string is thereby predicted to be not well formed. See figure 4.6.

Figure 4.6

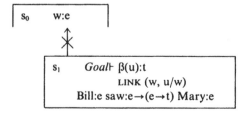

A similar problem arises with more regular 'complex NP' island constraints (modelled in figure 4.7):

(36) John has reviewed that book which Bill dislikes everyone who read.

Figure 4.7

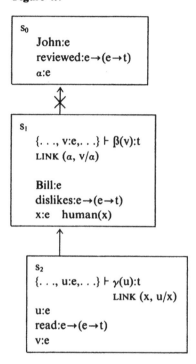

The parsing process, as induced by the relative *which*, imposes the need in s_1 to reach a conclusion of the form '$\beta(v){:}t$', 'v' linked to 'a', within the local reasoning task which constitutes the database s_1. As things turn out in (36), this goal specification cannot be fulfilled in s_1, for s_1 – as the ensuing words make plain – contains a full array of premises, 'Bill:e', 'dislike:e→(e→t)', and 'x:e, human(x)'. Fulfilling it by proxy in s_2, as is indicated by the dependency into the relative clause, will not, however, suffice to satisfy the target goal specification assigned to s_1: a local reasoning task has to be fulfilled locally to that imposed goal. Hence the lack of dependency from some *wh*-expression into a relative clause. This preclusion of satisfaction of some reasoning task for some initiating database in a database linked to it (via a relative marker) will not apply in databases nested one within another. In a case such as (37) the sub-database is contained within the initiating database, and, just as in subproofs within some overall proof structure, the fulfilment of some goal for that overall proof is carried down to all subgoals until the overall goal is fulfilled (figure 4.8).

(37) Who do you think Bill likes?

Figure 4.8

```
┌─────────────────────────────────────────────────────────┐
│  s₀                                    ⊢ β(u):t           │
│        you:e                                              │
│        think:e→(e→t)                                      │
│        s₁:e                                               │
│     ┌─────────────────────────────────────────────┐      │
│     │  s₁                             ⊢ γ(u):t     │      │
│     │      Bill:e                                  │      │
│     │      like:e→(e→t)                            │      │
│     │      u:e                                     │      │
│     │      like(u):e→t                             │      │
│     │      like(u)(Bill):t                         │      │
│     └─────────────────────────────────────────────┘      │
│        think(s₁:like(u)(Bill)):e→t                        │
│        think(s₁:like(u)(Bill))(you):t                     │
└─────────────────────────────────────────────────────────┘
```

The overall goal dictates the form of all subgoals. And satisfying that subgoal by the creation of the necessary assumption 'u:e' in the subordinate contained s_2 guarantees that the outcome in s_1 is some function on the variable 'u'.

The problem with databases linked only through a variable is precisely that they are otherwise independent. One database is not nested inside the other, so the creation of the necessary assumption 'u:e' in the database to be linked is not itself recorded in the labelling internal to the host database. Hence the inability to use a linked database to satisfy inferential actions required in the host database. Notice how a restriction normally seen as a restriction on syntactic dependency is here explained as the imposition of a certain outcome on some reasoning task, that of an imposed goal specification, by definition, having to be satisfied within the database on which the goal specification is imposed.[2]

3.1 Ellipsis and the island constraints

This pattern of explanation extends beyond the case of *wh*-dependency. Indeed many so-called syntactic phenomena emerge as consequences of the proof discipline itself. One such is the island-constraint phenomenon displayed in the interpretation of elliptical fragments. Furthermore we can now see the extent to which ellipsis interpretation and *wh*-dependencies parallel each other, and the extent to which they do not.

Recall first (23) (repeated here):

(23) Joan wants Sue to visit Bill in hospital. And Mary too.

We have in the interpretation of the first sentence some complex database leading to the conclusion:

want(visit(Bill)(Sue))(Joan)):t

With the fragment *and Mary too*, the hearer faces the goal-directed task of reaching some conclusion 'a:t' but here he has only *Mary* provided as input. In order to arrive at some conclusion, the hearer must create the one-place predicate with which to use the premise 'Mary:e' and establish the necessary propositional structure. We want to be able to use steps in the conditional logic to establish this. We have one ready made – the rule of →Introduction.

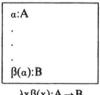

$$\lambda x \beta(x):A \to B$$

If from some assumption 'a:A' some conclusion 'β(a):B' is derived using 'a' and some further body of premises labelled 'β', the assumption 'a:A' may be withdrawn by incorporating 'A' within the body of the proof as antecedent to 'B'. The label resulting from this step records that all assumptions with respect to 'A' and its label are closed off, withdrawn. The rule is a box-exit device. From some subroutine based on the assumption 'a:A' and leading successfully to the conclusion 'β(a):B', the local subroutine is left, exiting from it by this step of →Introduction.

This rule matches exactly the step needed to create a one-place predicate out of some antecedent database for the purpose of ellipsis construal. Take (23) with the task it imposes of creating some one-place predicate for the fragment *and Mary too* to apply to, to create a database successfully yielding a conclusion 'a:t'. To achieve this end, the hearer reuses the database constructed from the entire previous clause, and retracts from it the premise 'Bill:e', in so doing creating a one-place predicate. This step of building a lambda abstract is licensed because it is a move from some premise of the form 'α:t' to a premise of the form 'λx(α):e→t', a perfectly licit step of conditional-introduction. The result is now a declarative unit 'β:e→t' in the containing database, needing to apply to some single 'γ:e' to complete the new database. The created predicate duly applies to the premise projected from the fragment 'Mary:e', and the hearer deduces a conclusion of the form 'α:t' on the basis of the words given and other information established on-line. We predict directly the diversity open to fragment interpretation. Depending upon which position is abstracted over, we can create any of the interpretations 1–3 for the fragment *and Mary too* in (23):

1 'Mary wants Sue to visit Bill in hospital.'
2 'Joan wants Mary to visit Bill in hospital.'
3 'Joan wants Sue to visit Mary in hospital.'

We are now in a position to see why fragment interpretation, like *wh*-dependency, gives rise to the island-constraint phenomena. Relative clauses, as we have already seen, are a structure initiated by the *wh*-element imposing a goal direction on the database to be linked. Like this target specification induced by *wh*, the presentation of a fragment also imposes a requirement on some local reasoning task. In these cases, the local reasoning task is to use →Introduction. As with *wh*-dependencies, the relative-clause island phenomena follow directly.

(38) Joan visited the woman who likes Bill in hospital. And Mary too.

We build for an interpretation of the first sentence of (38) the linked database in figure 4.9.

Figure 4.9

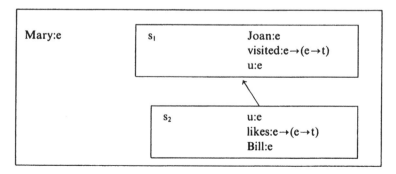

To reconstruct the fragment we need to take one step of conditional introduction; but on which local structure should we carry out this step? In order to create the complex reading substituting 'Mary' in place of 'Bill' in the relative clause, we would need to carry out conditional introduction on the first of these local structures (corresponding to the matrix clause) retracting a premise from that database, so establishing an interim conclusion of the form '$\lambda x \ \beta(x):e \to t$'. But the premise which we wish to withdraw is not there – it is only in some separate, albeit linked, structure. But conditional introduction *is* a local step of reasoning – it cannot be vacuously carried out in one structure as a record of some such step in another structure. The step of abstraction as indicated in figure 4.10 purporting to remove the assumption projected by Bill in figure 4.9 is not possible.

Figure 4.10

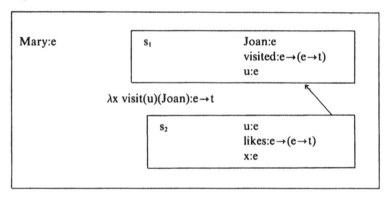

Exiting s_1 in figure 4.10 there is no operation upon the label which is the outcome of s_1 commensurate with the exit move of $\to$Introduction. And there is nothing to justify the substitution of 'x' for 'Bill' in s_2. Such steps are not licensed. The overall restriction directly parallels that precluding *wh*-dependency into relative clauses. The logical steps involved are different: one involves satisfaction of a goal specification, the other involves carrying out $\to$Introduction. But the restriction is the same: a local reasoning task for some local domain. By definition this *has* to be satisfied in that domain – no other domain will suffice. Hence the lack of dependency into relative clauses displayed by *wh*-constructions *and* by ellipsis.[3]

3.2 The asymmetry between wh-gap dependencies and 'LF movement'

A puzzle for most analyses reflecting the island-constraint sensitivity in *wh*-gap dependency and in ellipsis (reconstructed as LF movement of some abstract operator in Reinhart, 1991) is that the parallelism does not extend to all cases. There are two cases where such asymmetry arises. The difficulty of *wh*-dependency into sentential subject position, for example, does not extend to ellipsis. So here we face an asymmetry between *wh*-dependency and ellipsis. The data are as follows:

(39) *Who is that Bill will hug likely?

(40) Who is it likely that Bill will hug?

(41) That Diana admired Gilbey is well known. And Captain Hewitt too.

The explanation of (39) turns on the fact that the nesting of the secondary included database initiates the task of building a label containing the requisite variable rather than being some relatively late step in the completion of that task. The task the hearer faces in (39) is to construct in the database some assumption 'u:e' such that the outcome be 'β(u):t'. At the outset of the database there is no necessity to enter *any* subroutine to satisfy this requirement as every entry in the database remains to be made. Thus, despite the initiation of some nested database at this first entry in the database, there is no motivation for setting up any stronger target on the outcome of that database. Hence though such a parse is not precluded, it will never be constructed. To the contrary, when the structure is right-branching, the richer goal in the routine of building the subordinate database is imposed because this is, at this stage, the only way of fulfilling the initially imposed task.

In ellipsis constructions, the reconstruction of the fragment – driven by the presented premise and the need to establish some vehicle for inference of the form 'α:t' – does not depend on building a database step by step. Rather, it depends on taking some entire previous database and carrying out one step of →Introduction. Given that the database is here nested, there is no reason to preclude the application of →Introduction in the primary database while withdrawing assumptions with respect to some argument in that nested database, because, as the labelling makes plain, all such arguments are part of the complex label to the primary database as a whole. Hence the possibility of the interpretation for (41) – figure 4.11.

Figure 4.11

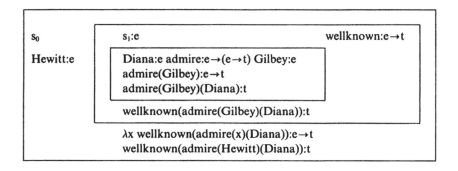

There is also an asymmetry between *wh*-binding and ellipsis reconstruction with respect to the so-called '*that*-trace effect'. Though *wh*-dependencies are not licensed if the gap immediately follows the complementiser *that*, no such restriction holds of the ellipsis analogue. Again the explanation of the contrast between the two constructions turns on the different processes by which they are assigned an interpretation. With *wh*-constructions, the hearer is building the structure step by step. With ellipsis constructions, however, she is taking some whole database and substituting one premise. To characterise the restriction itself, all we have to add is a low-level language-specific restriction on the English complementiser *that*. We specify it as inducing the building of a new database at whatever point in the proof process it occurs, requiring in addition that the first entry in this database be projected from a word. With just this addition, we get both the *that*-trace effects in *wh*-constructions:

(42) *Who do you think that likes Bill?

and the lack of them in ellipsis construction. In constructing an interpretation of *wh*, the hearer is required to use all information as presented step by step, and a requirement on some database initiated by *that* that its first entry be projected from a word will be precluded in (42). In fragment reconstruction, however, by claim, the hearer is taking the entire preceding database, carrying out one step of →Introduction and re-applying the result to the presented fragment. This process does not require reworking through that preceding database step by step from the words. So it is insensitive to any such lexical restriction to be satisfied as a step *en route* to the successful building of its antecedent database. The lack of *that*-trace effects in ellipsis reconstruction follows directly. We predict that (43)

(43) John thinks that Sue likes Bill. Mary too.

freely allows the fragment to have the interpretation 'John thinks that Mary likes Bill'.

We are thus able to predict the partial extent of the parallelism between *wh*-gap dependencies and the reconstruction of ellipsis. They are not the same process. One is a step-by-step computation of a database through successive steps of building premises and carrying out →Elimination: the other involves just one step of →Introduction, and one subsequent step of →Elimination with the new premise. Yet again, through the proof-theoretic mode of characterisation, we find that subtle differences, familiarly thought to require explication by some discrete module of syntax, have emerged solely from the pairing of lexical statement and the dynamics of the logic discipline.

4 Syntax and logic: modularity reconsidered

Where has all this led us? We started out from the argument that we needed to model the interpretation process for natural language as a structure-building process from some underdetermined input. To achieve this, I adopted a model of reasoning which systematically blurs syntax–semantics dichotomies (through the labelling discipline). We have a new construal of the nature of interpretation: lexical items contain specifications which constrain the building of a proof structure from which the more orthodox concept of truth content will be derivable. The essence of linguistic content so defined is that it is meta to any such level and hence essentially syntactic. The result is a radical blurring of the semantics–syntax dichotomy. The proof-theoretic structure we assign to a string is at one and the same time a syntactic analysis of the string, and the progressive assignment of an interpretation.

It is also a blurring of the familiar dichotomy between the language faculty seen as a grammar with a syntactic component at its heart and other central cognitive faculties such as reasoning. The model advocated here licenses strings as well formed. It assigns such strings structure; it articulates restrictions on the structures assignable to strings. The system of structures assigned to strings has, that is, well-founded syntactic properties. But these are the properties of a logic which, far from being set up specific to the natural-language enterprise (as are the feature logics of HPSG devised by e.g. Carpenter, 1989), are motivated by quite general properties of reasoning. The apparent interaction of syntactic constraints and cognitive processes of reasoning is now unproblematic. The constraints are retained as configurational constraints on the dynamic incrementation of the syntactic system – but this system is reconstrued as the reasoning system itself. We thus abandon, at last, the assumption retained earlier – the assumption that the language faculty is encapsulated, and independent of other faculties of the mind.

This reneging on traditional perspectives on linguistic knowledge is not, however, a wild jettisoning of the modularity theory of mind. To the contrary. First, despite the apparent merging of syntax and logical deduction, the knowledge of language acquired in learning a language remains isolable as a discrete construct. The input information, characterised as the lexicon, is the necessary input to the deduction process, its own internal statements encapsulated from any subsequent processes of deduction in the sense that they are irreversible, unaffected by any subsequent choices to be made. We abandon the concept of the language faculty as a body of knowledge divorced from our faculty for reasoning, but we retain the concept of encapsulation *vis-à-vis* the *a priori* nature of information drawn from the lexicon, the essential input to any cognitive processing of linguistic stimuli.

Second, however, even the view that the internal properties of natural-language grammars are dictated by our capacity for reasoning is not in conflict with a modular theory of mind. The articulation of the LDS framework is part of a new move to define mixed forms of reasoning, itself a general framework within which discrete logics can be embedded, nested one within another, one as a labelling system to another, and so on. In this new light, we can see reasoning itself as a heterogeneous activity taking different forms set within a single liberal framework which allows us to define different local forms of reasoning, even mixed modes of reasoning, each a subpart of a global reasoning framework. This study is in its infancy, but we look forward to articulating reasoning with vision-specific formats, reasoning with linked databases specific to natural-language input, reasoning with mixed modes of reasoning according as the input is mixed, and so on (see Barwise & Etchemendy, 1990; Gabbay, forthcoming). With such a framework as a promise, we can retain a modular view of the mind, while jettisoning encapsulation of the individual modules. All our separate, task-specific faculties can be seen both as having their distinctive properties and yet being founded in the overall human activity of reasoning. Finally, thus, we can retain our conception of a language faculty while nevertheless seeing it as independently motivated by our capacity for reasoning.

NOTES

1 One common argument that this cannot be a pragmatic process is that even without knowing the meaning of the noun associated with the definite article in a structure such as (20), and so not able to manipulate encyclopedic knowledge associated with any such concept, speakers can construe the structure as licensing an interpretation in which the definite NP is dependent on the quantified expression preceding it. This argument is not well founded. Even without any other provided context, such an interpretation of the definite NP is not made in a null context: it is made in the context provided by the expressions preceding the definite NP. On the supposition that definite NPs are construed as providing an argument contextually identified using the predicate provided but subject to the restriction that the value to be assigned must not be identical to some argument internal to the same clause, one possible interpretation is to construe the expression as picking out some entity functionally dependent on but not identical to that assigned to some expression already made available in the same string. If the only other available expression in the string is a variable introduced by *every*, then any such identification will result in a dependent interpretation. Nothing particular to the definite NP introducing an extra implicit second argument in the syntax need be provided. The process does not have to be seen encoded because it is made available by reasoning over the linguistic context.

2 The only possible means of licensing apparent violations of this restriction is if the head of the relative clause is itself identified as some function on the variable constituting the assumption to be created, as in (i):

    (i) The Mercedes is the car which I know someone who will rent.

In this case, *someone* is identified as a function on 'u, car(u)'. With this identification of the variable hosting the linked database as f(u), the goal specification to create some predication on 'u' is in fact locally satisfied by this variable, the 'gap' itself merely being the means of identifying that variable. The details turn on an analysis of indefinites (see Kempson, forthcoming). It is this strategy which is manipulated in the Scandinavian languages licensing *wh*-gap dependencies into relative clauses through the determiner head.

3 As with relative clauses, there is the possibility for indefinite and definite articles heading a relative clause that they can allow reconstruction through the value assigned to some dependent variable projected by the determiner, as in *I know someone who will rent the Mercedes. But not the Rolls*. In so far as this is available with other determiners, such as *every* in *Princess Di spoke to every patient who had TB. And Aids too*, this is due to the construed identification of the set variable associated with *patient* as dependent on the illness they suffered.

REFERENCES

Barwise, J. & J. Etchemendy (1990) Visual information and valid reasoning. In W. Zimmerman (ed.) *Visualization in Mathematics*, Washington, DC: Mathematical Association of America.

Barwise, J. & J. Perry (1983) *Situations and Attitudes*, Cambridge, MA: MIT Press.

Carpenter, R. (1989) Phrase meaning and categorial grammar. Ph.D dissertation, Edinburgh University.

Chierchia, G. (1992) Anaphora and dynamic binding. *Linguistics and Philosophy* 15: 111–84.

Chomsky, N. (1986) *Knowledge of Language*, New York: Praeger.

Cooper, R. (1979) The interpretation of pronouns. In F. Heny & H. Schnelle (eds.) *Syntax and Semantics, vol. X*, London: Academic Press, 61–92.

Dalrymple, M., S. Shieker & F. Pereira (1991) Ellipsis and higher-order unification. *Linguistics and Philosophy* 14: 399–42.

Evans, G. (1980) Pronouns. *Linguistic Inquiry* 11: 337–62.

Fodor, J.A. (1983) *Modularity of Mind*, Cambridge, MA: MIT Press.

Gabbay, D. (forthcoming) *Labelled Deductive Systems*, Oxford University Press.

Gabbay, D. & R. Kempson (1992) Natural-language content: a truth-theoretic perspective. In P. Dekker and M. Stokhof (eds.) *Proceedings of The Eighth Amsterdam Formal Semantics Colloquium*. Amsterdam.

Heim, I. (1990) E-type pronouns and donkey anaphora. *Linguistics and Philosophy* 13: 137–78.

Kamp, J.A.W. (1984) A theory of truth and semantic representation. In J. Groenendijk, T. Janssen & M. Stockhof (eds.), *Varieties of Formal Semantics*, Dordrecht: Foris.

Kaplan, D. (1979) On the logic of demonstratives. In P. French, T. Uehling & H. Wettstein (eds.), *Contemporary Perspectives in the Philosophy of Language*, Minneapolis: University of Minnesota Press, 401–12.

Karttunen, L. (1968) What do referential indices refer to? Santa Monica publication no. P-3554.

Katz, J. (1972) *Semantic Theory*, New York: Harper and Row.

Kempson, R. (1988) Logical form: the language and cognition interface. *Journal of Linguistics* 24: 398–432.

(forthcoming) Semantics, pragmatics, and natural-language interpretation. In S. Lappin (ed.) *Handbook of Contemporary Semantic Theory*. Oxford: Blackwell.

Klein, E. (1980) A semantics for positive and comparative adjectives. *Linguistics and Philosophy* 4: 1–45.

Lewis, D. (1972) General semantics. In D. Davidson & G. Harman (eds.) *Semantics of Natural Languages*, Dordrecht: Reidel, 169–218.

May, R. (1985) *Logical Form: its Structure and Derivation*, Cambridge, MA: MIT Press.

Montague, R. (1974) *Formal Philosophy: Selected Papers of Richard Montague*, ed. R. Thomason, New Haven, CT: Yale University Press.

Morgan, J. (1973) Sentence fragments and the notion 'sentence'. In B. Kachru, R. Lees, Y. Malkiel, A. Pietrangeli & S. Saporta (eds.) *Issues in Linguistics: Papers in Honor of Henry and Renee Kahane*, Urbana: University of Illinois Press, 719–51.

Partee, B. (1984a) Nominal and temporal anaphora. *Linguistics and Philosophy* 7: 243–86.

(1984b) Compositionality. In F. Landman & F. Veltman (eds.) *Varieties of Formal Semantics*, Dordrecht: Foris, 281–312.

(1989) Binding implicit variables in quantified contexts. *Chicago Linguistic Society* 25: 100–24.

Pereira, F. (1991) Deductive interpretation. In E. Klein & F. Veltman (eds.) *Natural Language and Speech*, Heidelberg: Springer, 117–34.

Reinhart, T. (1983a) *Anaphora and Semantic Interpretation*, London: Croom Helm.

(1983b) Coreference and bound anaphora: a restatement of the anaphora question. *Linguistics and Philosophy* 6: 47–88.

(1986) Center and periphery in the grammar of anaphora. In B. Lust (ed.) *Studies in the Acquisition of Anaphora*, Dordrecht: Reidel, 123–50.

(1991) Elliptic conjunctions: non-quantificational LF. In A. Kasher (ed.) *The Chomskyan Turn*, Oxford: Blackwell, 360–84.

Sperber, D. & D. Wilson (1986) *Relevance: Communication and Cognition*, Oxford: Blackwell.

Stump, G. (1981) The formal semantics and pragmatics of free adjuncts and absolutes in English. PhD dissertation, Ohio State University.

van Benthem, J. (1986) *Essays in Logical Semantics*, Dordrecht: Reidel.

5

Three levels of meaning

STEPHEN C. LEVINSON

1 Introduction

Many a student must have sighed when faced with what might seem the almost medieval casuistry of many of the distinctions in John Lyons' (1977) two-volume handbook, *Semantics*. Ambiguities and unclarities of every kind in our frail metalanguage for semantic analysis are there laid out for all to see; a formidable reef of difficult distinctions – types and tokens, acts and products, uses and mentions, originals and replicas, ambiguities of level, etc. – upon which we are all guaranteed sooner or later to founder. Introducing the type/token distinction in a straightforward manner, he goes on to tease us by showing how identifying different tokens of the same type can require a complex measure of similarity or identity of type, and then, having raised our anxieties, announces that it would be 'unnecessarily pedantic' to identify each such distinction (1977: 13–16).

One such distinction Lyons alludes to throughout the volumes may look particularly pedantic, the distinction between utterance-types and utterance-tokens, coming on top, as it does, of the distinctions between system-sentences and text-sentences, sentence-types and sentence-tokens, utterance-acts and -signals and so on. He himself seems to hint (1977: 570ff.) that the distinction may not be of any great utility (since utterance-tokens are rarely constrained to type, and such types could in any case be given formal definition, for example, in terms of sentence-types or forms).

In this chapter I want to suggest that this distinction between utterance-type meaning and utterance-token meaning, or something rather like it, may indeed prove to be an important division in levels of meaning. In finding utility in one of those obscure and seemingly pedantic distinctions, we can be thankful not only to John Lyons but to those generations of scholars in the western tradition, whose work Lyons has so usefully synthesised, who have laboured to hone these fundamental tools of semantic analysis.[1]

90

2 Levels of meaning

It has long been observed that we need a basic distinction between sentence-meaning and utterance-meaning, where sentence-meaning is understood as the overall meaning composed from the meanings of all the constituents together with the meaning of the constructions in which they occur, while utterance-meaning refers to the import of, say, the very same sentence when uttered in a particular context. (Utterances are thus often treated as pairings of sentences and contexts, namely the contexts in which they occur.) Thus a sentence with deictic elements like *I am sixty-three today* will clearly have different interpretations depending on who says it when, and mismatches between sentence-meaning and utterance-meaning are of course exploited in ironies and other tropes.

This observation is the foundation for the distinction between semantics and pragmatics however this is construed theoretically (see Levinson 1983: ch. 1 for a review; Lyons' *Semantics* of course encompassed both of these levels and the interactions between them).[2] That distinction established two fundamental explanatory levels in a theory of meaning, one responsible for the systematic process whereby the meaning of complex expressions can be built out of the meaning of their parts, and another responsible for explaining how the same expressions might have different meanings or interpretations in different contexts. Theoretical developments will tend to push the boundary one way or the other, but the distinction between the two levels, each with its different explanatory principles, seems certain to survive. It was partly the work of the speech act theorists (Austin and Searle in particular), but especially the work of Paul Grice, that opened up the prospect of a systematic pragmatics. Grice (1957) held that ultimately meaning could be reduced to matters of speaker's intentions, to meaning-$_{nn}$; but proximately, he held that meaning is a composite notion (see Grice 1989). He considered that the full import of an utterance could only be captured by distinguishing many different kinds of content – even the coded content (roughly, our sentence-meaning) was divided between 'the said' and 'the conventionally implicated' (and later he added 'the presupposed'), while the inferred content (our utterance-meaning) was divisible between particularised and generalised conversational implicatures and perhaps other kinds of inference altogether. (See Levinson, 1983: ch. 3, for an introductory exposition.)

It is this distinction between generalised and particularised implicatures that is the focus of this chapter. This distinction, I will argue, should force us to recognise not only the two major levels of a theory of meaning, semantics and pragmatics, but also a major distinction within pragmatics: a distinction between utterance-type meaning and utterance-token meaning. On general grounds of parsimony, this may be resisted; but I think that by recognising this further bifurcation, we will be greatly aided in understanding the relation of grammar to meaning.

Grice's (1975: 56f.; 1989: 37f.) distinction between particularised and generalised conversational implicatures needs a little exposition. A conversational implicature (henceforth 'implicature' for short), it will be recollected, is an inference that derives from what has been said in context taken together with some general background 'maxims of conversation', enjoining veracity, relevance, perspicacity and the provision of just the right amount of information. Because the inferences derive from both the linguistic expressions and these background assumptions, they are always *defeasible* (or cancellable) whenever the assumptions clearly do not hold. Now, Grice observed, some conversational implicatures seem context-bound, while others have a very general currency. Consider, for example, how a single utterance-form might suggest fundamentally different propositions (particularised conversational implicatures or PCIs) in two different contexts, while at the same time implicating something else (a generalised conversational implicature or GCI) in both these contexts and many others too:[3]

(1) Two possible contexts for B's utterance(-form):
a. Context 1:
    A: "What time is it?"
    B: "Some of the guests are already leaving."
    PCI: 'It must be late.'
    GCI: 'Not all of the guests are already leaving.'
b. Context 2:
    A: "Where's John?"
    B: "Some of the guests are already leaving."
    PCI: 'Perhaps John is already leaving.'
    GCI: 'Not all of the guests are already leaving.'

The inference labelled 'GCI' here is indeed one of very general currency: normally by stating "Some x are G", a speaker will implicate 'Not all x are G'. So general is the inference indeed that it might be mistaken for part of the meaning of *some* in English; but that it is a pragmatic inference is shown by (a) its predictability by general principle or maxim, (b) the semantic compatibility of its overt denial (as in *Some, in fact all, of the guests are already leaving*).

Some commentators (notably Sperber & Wilson, 1987: 748) have claimed that Grice attributed no real importance to this distinction,[4] but on the contrary the evidence is that he thought GCIs to be the source of many mistakes in the semantic analysis of, for example, the 'logical' connectives in English. Thus he was keen to point out that the inference from *S's saying "p or q"* to 'S doesn't know that p, or that q' is a regularity of interpretation not to be confused with the conventional or coded meaning of the disjunction. It is the regularity of association that makes the confusion so tempting.

In any case, since Grice much work has shown how useful the notion of a generalised conversational implicature is in linguistic analysis, even if it is not often so explicitly distinguished (see e.g. Gazdar & Pullum, 1976; Gazdar, 1979; Atlas & Levinson, 1981; Horn, 1989). Its utility lies precisely in the idea that certain linguistic expressions will tend to be associated with specific pragmatic inferences across a broad range of contexts, so that these associated inferences can be predicted in a systematic way, and play a systematic role in shaping patterns of lexicalisation and grammaticalisation.

The overall picture of a general theory of communication that then emerges is rather different from the standard picture. According to the standard line, there are just two levels to a theory of linguistic communication, a level of sentence-meaning (to be explicated by the theory of grammar in the broad sense) and a level of speaker-meaning (to be explicated by a theory of pragmatics, perhaps centrally employing Grice's notion of meaning-$_{nn}$). Speaker-meaning, or utterance-token-meaning, will be a matter of the actual 'nonce' or once-off inferences made in actual contexts by specific recipients with all of their rich particularities. This view, though parsimonious, is surely inadequate, indeed potentially pernicious, because it underestimates the regularity, recurrence and systematicity of many kinds of pragmatic inferences.

What it omits is a third layer, intermediate between coded meaning and nonce speaker-meaning, what we may call the level of *statement-* or *utterance-type-meaning*. This third layer is a level of systematic pragmatic inference based *not* on direct computations about speaker-intentions, but rather on *general expectations about how language is normally used*. These expectations give rise to presumptions, default inferences, about both content and force; and it is at this level (if at all) that we can sensibly talk about *speech acts, presuppositions, felicity conditions, conversational pre-sequences, preference organisation* and, of especial concern to us, *genera-lised conversational implicatures*. It is also at this level, naturally, that we can expect the systematicity of inference that might be deeply interconnected to linguistic structure and meaning, to the extent that it can become problematic to decide which phenomena should be rendered unto grammar and lexicon and which unto pragmatics (witness the long-standing disputes about the semantic or pragmatic status of illocutionary force and presupposition).

The supposition of this third, intermediate layer in a theory of communication is nothing new. Austin (1962), for example, clearly had something of this kind in mind when he proposed the three-way distinction between locutionary, illocutionary and perlocutionary acts; the locutionary level corresponds to the level of sentence-meaning, the illocutionary to our intermediate layer formed of conventions or habits of use, and the perlocutionary to the level of speaker-intentions. Other theorists have energetically tried to defend the notion of a *convention of use* to be distinguished from a *convention of language*; for example, such a distinction seems essential if we are to retain the idea that indirect speech acts are both partially conventional and inferentially motivated (Searle, 1975). Without admitting the existence of such an intermediate layer, how are we to explain the use of routine formulae (like *Good luck, Bless you, See you later*) which, although meaning what they literally mean, simultaneously perform habitual everyday rituals (Morgan, 1978)? Why is it that I can introduce myself with *My name is Steve*, but not *I was given the name Steve*; that I can express sympathy with you with *I am really sorry* but not conventionally with *That really saddens me*; that I express outrage with *Really!* but not with *In truth!*; that I can say *I am delighted to meet you* but not idiomatically *I am gratified to meet you*; that I can choose a pastry by saying *I would like that one* but not *I would desire that one* and so on? And to every specification of proper usage there tends to be a restriction on interpretation (Levinson, 1992). There is a great body of language lore here, beyond knowledge of grammar and semantics, extensively studied of course by both ethnographers of speaking and students of second-language learning. That two ways of 'saying the same thing' might be unequal in their conversational import, or that one way of saying something might pre-empt another, these are surely not radical doctrines.

The theory of GCIs is not of course a theory of conventional idioms, clichés and formulae; but it is a *generative theory of idiomaticity*, that is to say a set of principles guiding the choice of the right expression to suggest a specific interpretation, and as a corollary, a theory accounting for preferred interpretations. GCI theory offers a systematic account of why, for example, saying "See you on Tuesday" when tomorrow is Tuesday would suggest not seeing you tomorrow, why saying "If you help, I'll finish it" suggests that otherwise I will not do so, or why saying "Some of my colleagues are competent" would suggest that not all of them are, and so on, matching a 'way of putting things' with a favoured interpretation in each case. The theory thus belongs to the intermediate level of a theory of communication, the level of utterance-type-meaning.

Nevertheless, that intermediate level is constantly under attack by reductionists seeking to assimilate it either to the level of sentence-meaning or to the level of speaker-meaning; thus, for example, in the case of the inferences we are here calling GCIs, many theorists (Kamp, Peters, Barwise and others) have suggested that they should be in effect semanticised, while Sperber and Wilson and some so-called local-pragmatics theorists have presumed that on the contrary they should be assimilated to matters of nonce-inference at the level of speaker-intention.[5] But generalised implicatures are not going to reduce so easily in either direction, for they sit midway, systematically influencing grammar and semantics on the one hand and speaker-meaning on the other. I shall therefore presume that we do indeed need such a three-tiered theory of communication.

This presumption does not presuppose that the distinctions between the middle layer of utterance-type-meaning and the upper and lower levels is in any way cut and dried. Indeed, there is every reason to suppose that matters of utterance-type-meaning will shade into speaker-meaning at the one end and sentence-meaning at the other. This is in part because there is plenty of evidence that language use is the source for grammaticalised patterns, and that there is a diachronic path from speaker-meanings to utterance-type-meanings to sentence-meanings. Thus grey areas at the boundaries do not constitute evidence against the tripartite view, while evidence for it is the existence of preferred interpretations, default presumptions of the kind we shall illustrate in detail below.

3 Overcoming the bottleneck in human communication: Grice's maxims as heuristics

No student of language can fail to be awed by the intricacies and efficiency of human communication, and the underlying capacities that support it: the specialised physiology, the neurological pathways and the learning abilities that support the structural complexities of language, and above all the sheer miracle of the apparent speed and effortlessness whereby communicative intentions are encoded in articulatory gestures and acoustic signals converted into meanings. It may seem a bit like looking a gift horse in the mouth to point to one part of this miraculous process and identify it as a relatively slow and inefficient process, which acts as a bottleneck in the entire communicative procedure. Still, if we do so, the finger points inevitably to the articulation process itself: we can think faster than we can speak (e.g. we can do other complex things at the same time, including planning speech ahead), and we can easily understand pitch-corrected speech at double speed, or scan a printed page far faster than it can be read aloud. In fact the psycholinguistic evidence seems to suggest that all the other processes in the entire complex chain of production and comprehension systems could run three to four times faster than the normal pace dictated by the articulation process.[6] Those with a technical turn of mind may like to ruminate on the fact that, even making optimistic assumptions, the transmission rate for human speech is still under 100 BAUD.[7]

The articulation bottleneck in human communication raises interesting questions from, as it were, a design perspective. We can see immediately that any trade-off from coded content to inferential meaning may greatly increase the speed of communication: it will pay to say little and infer much, provided of course the inferential content can be recovered (a) reliably, and (b) speedily. Although we may admire the rich monosyllables of husband–wife communication, the process of recovery of nonce speaker-meaning generally guarantees neither speed nor reliability: the process requires computation of indefinitely nested models of the other's train of thought – what the speaker intended the recipient would think the speaker intended, and so on (see Cohen, Morgan & Pollack, 1990). Even these considerations greatly underestimate the problem of the recovery (by the recipient) of speaker-meaning: there is what might be called the *logical* problem of reconstructed reasoning – since a single conclusion can be reached from an infinite series of different sets of premises, how can the recipient reconstruct the Gricean intentions that lay behind the utterance (Levinson, 1995)?

A much simpler solution would be the provision of some general *default heuristics*, frameworks of assumption that can be taken to amplify the coded content of messages in predictable ways unless there is an indication that they do not apply.

Those default heuristics, I will argue, can be identified with Grice's maxims, or at least a version of them. The heuristics have *default* application; that is, they are applied unless there are explicit indications (in the nature of the context or the content of the message) that they should not be. They then invoke and filter further information of two kinds: information about the structure of the world (or, rather, of stereotypical properties of the relevant domain) and metalinguistic knowledge, that is, information about semantically related expressions. This information, together with the heuristics and the content of the utterance, provide a set of premises yielding inferences that greatly enrich the informational content of the utterance.[8]

Let me exemplify with three such heuristics, which interact in an interesting way. The details are complex and lie beyond the scope of this chapter, and we must therefore treat them in the most informal way. Let us introduce the cast of characters loosely as follows:

(2) *Three heuristics*

Q1: 'What is not said is not the case'
   Constrained to expression-alternates; e.g.
   If "x is G" is said, and G and F form a contrast set of expressions, then 'x is not F' is implicated.
   Characteristics:
      metalinguistic (makes reference to contrast sets e.g. {F, G});
      negative (e.g. 'x is *not* F').

Q2: 'What is simply described is stereotypically and specifically exemplified'
      (a) unmarked expressions warrant rich interpretations to the stereotype;
      (b) minimal forms warrant maximal interpretations.
   Constraint: only of unmarked, minimal expressions
   Characteristics:
      not fundamentally metalinguistic;
      invokes world-knowledge of stereotypical relations;
      positive inference to specific subcase.

M: 'Marked descriptions warn "marked situation"'
   Constraint: only of marked, unusual or periphrastic expressions
   Characteristics:
      metalinguistic (marked compared to unmarked);
      the inference is to the *complement* of the inference that would have been induced by the unmarked expression.

The idea is the following: suppose that the speaker and recipient each know that the other will use exactly these heuristics, then there are many things that will not need to be spelt out (i.e. coded in the linguistic expressions). So, for example, under the first heuristic, if I say "The flag is white", I will implicate (and you will understand) 'The flag is only white, not red, white and blue'. Under the second heuristic, if I say "He opened the door", I will suggest that he entered in the normal way, not using a crowbar or dynamite. Under the third heuristic, if I say "He turned the handle and pushed open the door" I will suggest that he opened the door in some non-stereotypical manner (e.g. with extra force or speed). In each of these cases, the inference is predictable and clear, and the speaker, knowing this, has – other things being equal – committed himself by a turn of phrase to an interpretation that he knows the recipient will make.

Of course these inferences are defeasible. There is no contradiction in saying "She was wearing a white dress. It had beautiful blue lace trim." Nor, when we are trying to decide whether we are looking at a British or a Russian warship does the observation "The flag is white" or "The flag is red" carry the suggestion 'wholly white' or 'wholly red'. And in complex sentences, the inferences in question may be cancelled by other inferences, as in "They're waving a white flag, even if it's stained red with blood". That is the nature of conversational implicature. Nevertheless, the striking fact is that *ceteris paribus* these inferences do go through by default.

These three heuristics each produce large families of defeasible inferences. By combining all three heuristics, and by presuming that both speaker and recipient will mutually expect them to be in operation, we can greatly amplify the content of what we say – thus overcoming the bottleneck provided by speech-encoding.

4 Default inferences under the three heuristics

The heuristic labels Q1, Q2 and M in (2) above are of course allusions to the corresponding Gricean maxims, the first and second maxim of Quantity and the maxim of Manner.[9] Let us take each of these in turn, and spell out how the heuristics work in a little more detail.

First, Q1, the heuristic that relies on contrast sets of expressions: what exactly is the character of these inferences and from which kinds of lexical sets do they arise? It is clear that there are different kinds of cases, and it is a matter for empirical investigation to find what different kinds of contrast set reliably yield inferences of this negative, complementary kind. Much-studied prototypes are the entailment scales, where we may set up, for example, an ordered pair $\langle S, W \rangle$ where S is the 'strong' member, and W the 'weak' member, such that when S is substituted in an arbitrary declarative sentence it will entail the same sentence with W substituted for S. In these cases, assertion of the W sentence will carry a generalised implicature that the S variant does not hold, as illustrated below.[10]

(3)　a. scale of contrastive expressions: $\langle all, some \rangle$
　　　b. S-sentence: '*All of the students were in class.*'
　　　c. W-sentence: '*Some of the students were in class.*'
　　　d. scalar GCI from the assertion of c: 'Not all of the students were in class.'

These are the prototype cases, and there are many important scalar sets in natural-language vocabularies: all the quantifiers including the cardinal numbers, the truth-functional connectives ($\langle and, or \rangle$), many gradable properties (e.g. English $\langle hot, warm \rangle$), many kinds of closed sets of morphemes with so-called 'grammatical meaning' (e.g. English $\langle the, a \rangle$), modal adjectives (e.g. $\langle necessary, possible \rangle$) and much else besides. Closely related to the scalar sets, but yielding inferences of slightly different force, are subordinating connectives of various kinds, including, for example, $\langle since, if \rangle$, as illustrated below (following Gazdar, 1979).

> (4) a. clausal subordinators: $\langle since, if \rangle$
> b. S-sentence: '*Since Ron saw my manuscript, he's a plagiarist.*'
> c. W-sentence: '*If Ron saw my manuscript, he's a plagiarist.*'
> d. clausal implicature from assertion of c:[11] 'Ron may or may not have seen my manuscript, and he may or may not be a plagiarist.'

Note that we now have Q1 default inferences attached to most of the 'logical' elements of the vocabulary: to the truth-functional connectives, conditionals, modals and quantifiers. If the systematic pragmatics of these crucial areas of the vocabulary were better appreciated by semanticists, semantic analyses might be rather different – and simpler – in character.

In addition to these cases, there are many other kinds of contrast sets capable of yielding systematic Q1 inferences. For example, as illustrated above, the colour terms {*red, white, blue, green*, etc.} denote properties that are extensionally compatible; but asserting that something is red implies that it is not also green, etc., on the grounds typical of Q1 inferences – the speaker can be relied upon to provide enough information (see Harnish, 1976). Indeed, it is possible to plunder the rich observations in structural semantics (as e.g. in Lyons, 1977, or Cruse, 1986) about many different kinds of lexical sets, and explore all the kinds of inferences that may be associated with the employment of individual lexemes from these sets. Note, for example, how the assertion of a superordinate in a taxonomy suggests that the speaker does not know (or thinks irrelevant) which subordinate term or hyponym applies:

> (5) a. "I saw an animal in the larder."
> b. Q1 implicates: 'I don't know whether it was a mouse, a rat, a squirrel or what.'

There are probably many systematic patterns here yet to be properly explored. (See Hirschberg, 1985, Levinson, forthcoming, for more ideas here.) A cursory inspection suggests a novel idea. The kinds of semantic opposition between expressions in different kinds of sets can be very different in kind, as explored, for example, in Lyons (1977): as a result the Saussurean notion of *valeur* is then decomposed to the point of loss. Yet we should rightly grieve at the premature death by dissection of a fundamental tenet of structuralist thinking. We might attempt resuscitation by suggesting that *valeur* is not at root a semantic concept at all; perhaps the force is pragmatic, and can be attributed to the Q1 inference to the inapplicability of the contrastive alternate.[12]

Let us turn now to the much less well understood heuristic sketched as Q2 in (2) above ('What is simply described is stereotypically and specifically exemplified'). That there is some such heuristic is indubitable. Consider, for example, the English spatial preposition *in*, as in *in the box*, *in the garden*, *in the cup*. Clearly *in* has a wide range of application: to closed containers (boxes), open containers (cups), bounded spaces (gardens), etc. (see Hirschberg, 1985, for illuminating complexities). Yet when I say "The coffee is in the cup", you do not mistake the relationship between the coffee and the cup for the related but distinct relation indicated in "The pencil is in the cup": we expect partial projection for pencils but not for coffee. It would be more than pedantic to spell out "The coffee is entirely within the bowl of the cup" – more than pedantic because by so saying you would implicate by the third heuristic something other than normal coffee-to-cup relations.

Semantic generality, the large range of applicability of individual expressions, is typical of most of our (non-technical) vocabulary; it is what makes our lexicon of learnable size. Hence Barwise & Perry (1983) have dubbed this property the 'efficiency' of language, neglecting to note that the property would be inefficient indeed without the complementary property of pragmatic enrichment. Semantic generality is also typical of grammatical meaning. Take, for example, the fact that the compositional principles that compute the meaning of phrases specify the composite meaning in only the most general fashion. Thus nominal compounds like *bread knife*, *steel knife*, *murder knife*, *army knife* each have presumptive interpretations along different lines: bread knives are not made of bread, but steel knives are made of steel; murder knives are not made for murder, although army knives are of a type made for armies, and so on. Similarly for the possessive in English: the construction *X's Y* merely indicates that *some* relation holds between the two noun phrases, and we resolve the relation by pragmatic inference. Thus the phrases *Jupiter's moons*, *John's ideas*, *Anne's address*, *the building's condition*, *the encyclopedia's editor*, *the year's end*, are each understood to involve different relations (gravitational capture, ideational authorship, postal access, etc.). Note that all these phrases seem to have a default interpretation: *John's pens* will naturally be taken to mean the pens belonging to John, unless the context (e.g. talk between pen-designers) warrants another less stereotypical interpretation.

What is clear then is that, hearing an utterance, we imagine a specific instantiation, a stereotypical exemplification. But why should such a tendency, perhaps psychological in origin, constitute a heuristic? Are we not confusing the private interaction between our individual knowledge of the world and our understanding of utterances with a theory of communication? The answers lie in the strange power of the reflexive reasoning that Grice introduced in his theory of meaning-$_{nn}$. The speaker, knowing the recipient's interpretation to tend in a particular direction, and knowing that the recipient knows the speaker so knows, can turn a good chance into a certainty: mutual awareness of the interpretation to the stereotype guarantees that this is what the speaker intends. The speaker *designs* his or her utterance accordingly. (The same principle holds, *mutatis mutandis*, for all the heuristics, of course.)

Closely allied to the inference to the stereotype is a class of other inferences to the more specific subcase. Many of these have to do with the maximisation of coherence, the minimisation of postulated entities and the presumptive enrichment of mentioned relations. For example, it has long been noted that conjunction, or in many languages paratactic adjunction, is presumptively enriched to suggest sequential occurrence of events and, further, intention and causality, as illustrated below, where the assertion of (a) will suggest (b), (c) and (d) even in the absence of stereotypical connections between bells and engines:

(6) *Conjunction-buttressing* (Atlas & Levinson, 1981)
    a. "Ann rang the bell and the engine started."
    b. 'Ann rang the bell and *then* the engine started.'
    c. 'Ann rang the bell and *therefore* the engine started.'
    d. 'Ann rang the bell, *thereby intending* the engine to start.'

A similar presumptive strengthening of content is typical of conditionals, as illustrated below, where the assertion of (a) will suggest (b) and thus jointly (c):[13]

(7) *Conditional perfection* (Geiss & Zwicky, 1971)
    a. "If you co-operate, there'll be no trouble."
    b. 'If you don't co-operate, there will be trouble.'
    c. 'If and only if you co-operate, will there be no trouble.'

Negative statements are of course informationally weak: from the assertion that x is not F, one is left in the dark as to whether x is G or H, etc. They are thus ripe for pragmatic enrichments of many kinds (see Horn, 1989), but a genus that comes under the rubric of the Q2 heuristic includes the many cases where contradictories are routinely 'read as' contraries:

(8) a. "I don't like the new boss."
    b. 'I positively dislike the new boss.'
(9) '*Negative-raising*'
    a. "I don't believe he will show up."
    b. 'I believe he will not show up.'

Another wide class of Q2 inferences involves interpretations that maximise cohesiveness – anaphoric linkages, for example. It is well known that anaphoric linkages are made partly on the basis of encyclopedic knowledge, but there are also clear preference patterns, for example for local (proximal) coreference which can be demonstrated in texts, as illustrated below:

(10) Then the thief$_1$ asks the butler$_2$, say, and the butler$_2$ confirms that. He$_2$ says, 'Yes the superintendent has only just left.'
                              (from Agatha Christie, *Hercule Poirot's Christmas*)

The general heuristic seems to be: do not postulate more entities than necessary, and link locally by preference.

No doubt rather specific mechanisms are involved in each of these preferences, including the inferences to the stereotype, that we currently do not fully understand; but that there are such preferences – and not just calculations of speaker-meaning – seems rather clear. Gathering them together under the rubric of the Q2 heuristic is not simply a matter of convenience, for the inferences share certain crucial properties. First, they are inferences to *more specific* interpretations, where what is implicated is a subcase, a specific instantiation, of what is said. The inferences are positive and non-metalinguistic in character, unlike Q1 or (as we shall see) M inferences. They are default inferences – not all inferences to the subcase have this character. They are tied to the use of unmarked, 'minimal' or non-prolix, semantically general expressions (or even the absence of them as in parataxis or zero anaphora). Note, for example, the following interpretative contrasts between minimal expressions (italicised in the (i) examples) and more marked expressions (italicised in the paired (ii) examples) that might be thought to paraphrase their content:

(11) a. (i) John pushed the button *and* the motor started.
            (ii) John pushed the button. *In addition*, the motor started.
     b. (i) The detective came into the room and *he* sat down.
            (ii) The detective came into the room and *the man* sat down.
     c. (i) I *don't like* garlic.
            (ii) I *have no liking* for garlic.

    d. (i) The book is *on* the desk.
       (ii) The book is *in contact with the upper surface of the desk*.
    e. (i) *John's picture* won critical acclaim.
       (ii) *The picture of John* won critical acclaim.

In addition to these shared properties, Q2 inferences share similar projection properties, to be noted below.

Any kind of inference from a general description to the special subcase clearly must be strictly constrained: we make no inference from the assertion "John drives a small car" to 'John drives a Honda Civic' even if the probabilities are so. Indeed, as discussed above, "I saw an animal in the larder" suggests that I do not know what animal I saw. How then are Q2 inferences constrained? Partly they are constrained with respect to depth; and here the notion of stereotype needs explication – as Putnam pointed out, a stereotype has nothing to do with statistical tendencies, or even with shared veracities. Fierce gorillas, gentle cows, absent-minded professors are stereotypes for which there is little evidence or even shared belief. There is no such stereotype from small cars to Honda Civics, and the speaker knows the addressee knows that the speaker will not presume so. But male surgeons are another matter, and there are many parlour puzzles of the sort "The patient went to see the surgeon. She described the problem to him and she decided at once to operate on him". Inferences to the stereotype are thus not 'generalised' in the sense that they are independent of shared beliefs (as Q1 and M inferences largely are, since they are essentially based on metalinguistic considerations), but they are 'generalised' in the sense that they follow a general principle – restrict the interpretation to what by consensus constitutes the stereotypical, central extensions.

More importantly perhaps, Q2 inferences are constrained by the other heuristics. Any Q1 inference incompatible with a Q2 inference always takes precedence. Any M inference from a marked expression likewise defeats a Q2 inference, in ways that will be explained. The result is that a Q2 inference is induced by a certain kind of expression, especially expressions that are themselves brief and colloquial. Like the following heuristic that bounds it, Q2 is thus iconic: minimal expressions invite stereotypical, rich interpretations.

Finally, we turn to the third heuristic introduced in (2) above ('Marked descriptions warn "marked situation"'), labelled M after Grice's maxim of Manner.[14] Now, we have already seen from examples in (11) that marked or more prolix expressions do not give rise to the Q2 inferences that would have arisen from their unmarked or brief counterparts. In fact, there is a systematic complementarity between unmarked expressions and their associated Q2 inferences compared to marked expressions and their M inferences.[15] The relevant sense of 'markedness' is very broad, covering formal prolixity, infrequent expressions or those of unusual formation – the M-principle is again iconic: 'non-stereotypical expressions invite interpretations to non-stereotypical extensions'. Take, for example, the following lexical doublets, and the sort of denotation they might suggest in some arbitrary utterance (the symbol + > should be read 'implicates, *ceteris paribus*'):[16]

(12) a. unmarked: *drink* Q2 + > 'alcoholic drink'
    marked: *beverage* M + > 'non-alcoholic drink'
  b. unmarked: *chair(man)* Q2 + > 'male chair person'
    marked: *chairperson* M + > 'female chair person'
  c. unmarked: *knife* Q2 + > 'kitchen-type knife'
    marked: *cutter* M + > 'not a normal knife'
  d. unmarked: *missile* Q2 + > 'rocket with warhead'
    marked: *projectile* Q2 + > 'missile other than rocket'
  e. unmarked: *letter* Q2 + > 'personal letter'
    marked: *missive, dispatch, epistle* + > 'not a personal letter'
  f. unmarked: *house* Q2 + > 'normal family house'
    marked: *residence* M + > 'grander than normal family house'
  g. unmarked: *rare* Q2 + > 'unusual and valuable'
    marked: *scarce* M + > 'in short supply'

Similarly for word formation: derivations tend to sort into two classes, the usual, colloquial with a specialised stereotypical extension, and the more unusual or prolix derivation picking up (often now by convention) the complementary interpretation (see Horn, 1989: 273ff., for discussion):

(13) a. unmarked: *informer* Q2 + > 'supplier of information against someone'
    marked: *informant* M + > 'supplier of information for someone'
  b. unmarked: *unnatural, unscientific* Q2 + > 'and bad'
    marked: *non-natural, non-scientific* M + > '(no special evaluation)'
  c. unmarked: *imprecise/immoral,* Q2 + > 'the opposite of precise/moral' (i.e. the contrary reading)
    marked: *unprecise/non-* or *amoral* M + > 'just not precise or not moral' (i.e. the contradictory reading)

There is also an opposition between simplex lexemes and derived forms which might be thought to have the same meaning and use (e.g. *sad* vs. *unhappy*, or *rude* vs. *impolite*, where the lexicalised form invariably seems to denote a more extreme property; again, see Horn 1989: 279f., also Kiparsky, 1983).

These sorts of pragmatic principles explain how specific kinds of word form may acquire specialisations of meaning: they are principles that may explain historical changes and semantic shifts. By the same token, the synchronic analysis of current lexical content is sometimes of course not so clear.

Rather clearer cases of the Q2 vs. M opposition may therefore be found in periphrastic alternatives to simple lexicalisations. Thus periphrastic modals, causatives and double negations contrast with their simpler counterparts:

(14) a. "John could solve the problem" Q2 + > 'and he did'
b. "John had the ability to solve the problem" M + > 'but he didn't'
(15) a. "James stopped the car" Q2 + > 'in the normal way, by using the foot pedal'
b. "James caused the car to stop" M + > 'in a nonstereotypical way, e.g. by using the hand-brake'
(16) a. "Sue moved the car" Q2 + > 'by driving it'
b. "Sue made the car move" M + > 'e.g. by pushing it'
(17) a. "It's possible he will recover" Q2 + > some definite probability p
b. "It's not impossible that he will recover" M + > some probability less than p
c. "The mail is reliable" Q2 + > 'to degree n'
d. "The mail is not unreliable" M + > 'to degree less than n'

Repetition and reduplication also serve to deflect interpretation from Q2-directed extensions:

(18) a. "He ate" Q2 + > 'He ate the normal meal.'
b. "He ate and ate" M + > 'He ate more than the normal meal.'

In many languages, reduplication plays an important quasi-derivational role, and it is notable how such reduplications tend to pick out, not the central or prototypical extensions of the unreduplicated form, but their complements, the peripheral or non-stereotypical extensions.[17]

These three heuristics are each responsible for large families of inferences, each of a characteristic type. In certain ways the principles are quite clearly antagonistic: they encourage inferences in opposite directions. Thus whereas Q2 invites inferences to the more specific subcase (along the lines of 'The speaker hasn't said what is obvious'), Q1 forbids the inference to the more informative interpretation (along the lines 'If the speaker didn't say it, he didn't mean it'). Similarly, M1 inferences are specified as the complement of Q2 inferences. Contradictory premises would be fatal to any deductive device, and problematic for any inferential system. They must therefore be blocked at source, or filtered by simple rule or procedure. In fact, both mechanisms seem to be involved. For example, many apparently potential Q1 inferences do not in fact arise because there are strict criteria of both form and content on the sets that give rise to them (Atlas & Levinson, 1981; Levinson, 1987a: 407). In addition, there are simple priority rules of the kind: Q1 and M inferences take precedence over inconsistent Q2 inferences; Q1 inferences take precedence over inconsistent M inferences (Levinson, 1987a: 409). Within each genus there also seem to be priorities: thus clausal Q1 inferences cancel inconsistent scalar Q1 inferences (as noted and formalised in Gazdar, 1979). In short, there is a serious projection problem for generalised implicatures, but fortunately we already have some understanding of how the problem is resolved.[18]

5 Grammar and meaning

The mechanisms reviewed here – a set of three general heuristics that induce default inferences – have completely general application across the vocabulary of a language; but they may yield inferences that are particularly precise, specific and recurrent where small closed sets of lexemes or morphemes yield contrast sets of the right kind to induce Q1 implicatures. Such sets are typical of the 'grammatical' or 'functor' words. For example, as noted above, early Gricean analyses pointed out that the English sentential connectives form a Q1 entailment set ⟨*and, or*⟩, so that an utterance of the form "p or q" will generally implicate 'not p and q', while "p and q", unbounded by a Q1 inference, will (where p and q describe events) Q2 implicate 'p and then q' and so on. Such an analysis allows us to hang on to the simple underlying invariant meaning of the connectives, while explaining all the additional variable readings.

Exactly the same kind of analysis can now be applied to any grammatically closed class of morphemes, and should yield the same kind of harvest: invariant core meanings supplemented by preferred interpretations. Take, for example, the definite/indefinite articles in English. Simple accounts of the kind 'introduce a new referent under description Y with *a Y* and a previously mentioned one under description X with *the X*' or 'Use *the X* to refer to a unique entity, *a Y* to refer to a non-unique entity' run afoul of multitudinous counter-examples, as shown by Hawkins (1978, 1991). For example, it is quite normal to introduce some entities with *the X*:

(19) a. I just met the Mayor.
    b. I'm late because I missed the train.

    c. There's something wrong with the clutch (in my car).
    d. She adores the man she met in Paris.

and indefinite articles can be used for previously introduced referents:

(20) a. All the members of the jury met for many hours because a *single member* was recalcitrant.
      b. His arms and legs were damaged in the blast, and in the end he lost *a leg*.

while some unique entities are happily referred to with an indefinite article:

(21) a. England has *a Queen* and Spain *a King*.
      b. There is *a dog* in that car.

Hawkins (1991) points out that if we adopt an account in terms of GCIs most of these puzzles evaporate. The articles form a Q1 entailment contrast set $\langle the, a \rangle$, such that *the* X entails uniqueness, while *a* Y only implicates non-uniqueness, which may thus evaporate in contexts like those immediately above. Hawkins argues that *the* X conventionally (i.e. non-defeasibly) implicates that there is a mutually salient set in which X is unique, while *a* Y Q2-implicates (i.e. defeasibly) that there is a mutually salient set to which Y belongs (hence "He lost a leg" suggests one of his own).

    There are of course many other closed sets of grammatical contrasts, often notorious for their semantic subtleties, that could benefit from a pragmatic analysis of this kind, for example, deictic adverbs or determiners, tense and aspect markers and prepositions.[19]

    Further inroads into 'grammatical meaning' may be possible. There has been much speculation about whether a pragmatic analysis might undercut the purely grammatical analysis of anaphoric dependencies typical of modern grammatical theory (Reinhart, 1983; Levinson, 1989, 1991; Huang, 1994). For example, we can think of the opposition between non-reflexive and reflexive pronouns as similar to that between indefinite and definite pronouns: wherever *him* and *himself* can contrast, for example in direct-object position, we have a Q1 scale of the kind $\langle himself, him \rangle$ such that use of *him* will implicate 'not himself' – rather than be grammatically stipulated as non-coreferential by Binding Condition B in the Government–Binding framework of Chomsky (1981). The advantage of the pragmatic account is that, since GCIs are only default inferences, it allows the possibility of coreference between subject and a non-reflexive pronominal object in unusual cases (such as *Only Felix₁ voted for him₁* – see Reinhart, 1983). Given Binding Condition A (which stipulates that reflexives must find their antecedents in certain positions), the other Binding Conditions (Binding Condition B governing the non-coreferential interpretation of non-reflexive pronouns in certain positions and Binding Condition C stipulating the non-coreferential interpretation of full lexical NPs) are regularities at least partially predicted by the system of heuristics here outlined.[20] In sketch form, consider the following patterns:

(22) a. $John_1$ likes $himself_1$.
(stipulated by Binding Condition A)
b. $John_1$ likes him_2.
(Q1 inference from the non-use of *himself* – pattern often attributed to Binding B)
c. $John_1$ told her that he_1 would come.
(Q2 inference to coreference, unblocked by Q1 inference since *himself* cannot occur in this position)
d. $John_1$ told her that the man_2 would come.
(M inference to an interpretation contrastive with that of unmarked, simpler form in (c); pattern often attributed to Binding C)

This is not the place to pursue this analysis, which can be refined – and of course countered – in various ways (see Levinson, 1987a, 1991). The point to be made here is that even if we decide that in fact these anaphoric patterns are grammaticalised in English, the very possibility of a (perhaps incomplete) pragmatic analysis undercuts Chomsky's view that the patterns in question must be specified by native 'universal grammar' because they are abstract and unpredictable from usage patterns, and thus in effect unlearnable.

The pragmatic point of view seems to be supported by the facts from languages (like many Austronesian ones, Biblical Hebrew, old Germanic languages, some Australian languages) which do not exhibit reflexives at all. In these languages a sentence glossing 'John hit him' may have a reflexive or non-reflexive reading, with the latter the default. The default reading presumably arises (as a Q2 inference) from the stereotypical agentive schema, in which an agent acts on another entity (Farmer & Harnish, 1987). To block this disjoint reading, the pronoun is normally marked by an emphatic particle or affix to indicate by M inference that the complementary interpretation is intended. Elsewhere, outside the clause, the pronoun tends to pick up coreferential readings as in English. Thus we have in schematic gloss the following pattern:

(23) a. '$John_1$ likes him_2.'
Q2 inference to stereotypical action
b. '$John_1$ likes him $EMPHATIC_1$.'
M inference to complement of (a)

    c. 'John$_1$ told her that he$_1$ would come.'
       Q2 inference to minimal domain of discourse
    d. 'John$_1$ told her that the man$_2$ would come.'
       M inference to complement of (c)

This pattern in fact suggests a general diachronic source for true reflexives in marked, emphatic forms of a normally disjoint pronoun. Certainly the history of English reflexives has normally been analysed this way (see Visser, 1963: 420–39), and in languages with continuous and ancient written traditions, like Japanese, Tamil and Chinese, there seems to be evidence in the same direction (see Faltz, 1985, and references in Levinson, 1991), while a swifter development of the same kind can perhaps be observed in creoles (Carden & Stewart, 1987, 1988).

Again, we cannot pursue these issues here (see Levinson, 1991), but the general point is that there are languages which have no reflexives, and a corresponding freedom of anaphoric interpretation (in part because they lack the strong Q1 inferences that play off the opposition between reflexive and non-reflexive pronoun). Such languages would seem to be anomalous to the Government–Binding framework, but the patterns of interpretation seem rather well predicted by our heuristics or something like them (see Huang (1991, 1994) for a developed account along similar lines of the flexible patterns of interpretation in Chinese).

In short, patterns of preferred interpretation may play an important role in the relation between grammar and meaning: grammatically or lexically stipulated meanings tend to generate a set of further default interpretations from the use of related but distinct forms. These in turn can become conventionalised or grammatically stipulated, yielding yet further default inferences. Given these diachronic tendencies, the analyst may easily mistake a default inference for a lexically or grammatically stipulated meaning, and of course vice versa (mistaking a conventionalised ex-inference for a live one).

6 Conclusion

This essay has argued for a fresh perspective on linguistic communication, where more attention is given to preferred ways of 'putting things', or the use of favoured constructions for conveying specific messages.[21] Instead of a bifurcation between grammatically and lexically specified meaning and nonce speaker-meaning, we need to develop a three-tiered theory of communication in which utterance-type meaning has a special place. The theory of utterance-type meaning should be a theory of default interpretation. This level of meaning may exhibit some relatively tight universal constraints, because (or so I have suggested) it is based on a set of heuristics that are designed to overcome an intrinsic bottleneck in the speed of communication, our slow articulation rate. Because this level of meaning sits midway between grammar and lexicon on the one hand and speaker-meaning on the other, most analysts attempt to reduce it in one or the other direction. This is a mistake, because it is a level with distinct properties – default, defeasible inferences based on the comparison of alternative linguistic expressions and on the presumption of stereotypical situations, which interact in specific ways. In addition, because these systematic mechanisms are so closely related to grammatical and lexical processes, they constrain them and, over the course of language history, feed them.[22] It is thus quite unlikely that we will have an adequate synchronic or diachronic theory of grammar and lexicon until we have a much deeper understanding of the level of utterance-type meaning.

NOTES

1 This paper is a sketch of issues treated in more depth in Levinson (forthcoming: ch. 1). A prior, spirited defence of the idea of three levels of meaning may be found in Atlas (1989: 3–4 and *passim*).

2 Lyons thus uses the term 'semantics' in a pretheoretical way to denote the full range of linguistic meaning; I will use the term in the narrower sense, opposed to pragmatics. I will, however, continue to use the term 'meaning' in the wide sense, not restricting it to coded morpheme- or sentence-meaning. For the larger field, the study of meaning in this wide sense, I will use the phrases 'the theory of meaning' or, where the wide range might not be clear, 'the theory of (linguistic) communication'.

3 Let us adopt the typographical conventions that utterances (or rather utterance-types) are indicated by double quotes, interpretations or glosses by single quotes, linguistic expressions or sentences by italics. We will also use the symbol + > for '(generally) conversationally implicates', so that "Some boys are naughty" Q2 + > 'not all boys are naughty' is read as 'The uttering of the sentence *Some boys are naughty* will by default inference under the Q2 heuristic have the additional interpretation "not all boys are naughty".'

4 Sperber & Wilson (1987: 748) wish to abolish GCIs because their proposed account of how implicatures are calculated cannot accommodate the phenomenon (see Levinson, 1987b, 1989). For other kinds of problems with the distinction, see Hirschberg (1985: 42).

5 For a representative attempt to semanticise the phenomena, see, for example, Barwise (1986); for representative attempts to reduce GCIs to nonce inferences, see, for example, Hobbs (1987), Kempson (1986) and of course Sperber & Wilson (1986).

6 For the comparative speed of pre-articulation vs. articulation processes, see Wheeldon & Levelt (forthcoming). For the ability to parse and comprehend speeded speech, see Mehler *et al.* (1993).

7 The calculation, kindly made for me by Bill Poser, assumes 7 syllables or 17.5 segments per second, and 5.5 bits per phoneme.

8 I will not here discuss the nature of the inference itself. With regard to the nature of implicature generally, there are divergent opinions: Sperber & Wilson (1986) maintain it is deductive, Grice (1973) explicitly likened it to inductive inference, while Atlas & Levinson (1981) suggested that some inferences have an abductive character. GCIs, though, are by hypothesis default inferences, both non-monotonic and presumptive. There is now a large family of formal models for such systems of inference: see, for example, the collection in Ginsberg (1987).

9 The labels Q1, Q2 and M, adopted here in deference to Grice's maxims, refer respectively to the Principles Q, I and M (or Q/M) in Levinson (1987a, 1991). Comparison with Horn's (1989) system will be aided if it is noted that his R is my Q2 (or I), while he conflates my Q1 and M under a single rubric Q. All three of my principles are conflated into one R (or Relevance principle) in Sperber & Wilson's (1986) proposal. The profusion of proposals indicates of course that this is now an active research area.

10 For much further detail see Horn (1972, 1985, 1989), Gazdar (1979), Atlas & Levinson (1981) and Hirschberg (1985). As Gazdar points out, the inferences are epistemically modified, in ways that are crucial to any formalisation, but which we ignore here.

11 That this inference is defeasible, therefore pragmatic, is shown by reasoning of the kind *He has AIDS. If he has AIDS, his wife has too.*

12 See also Clark (1993: ch. 5) for the view that *contrast* is a pragmatic strategy for language learning.

13 I have been loose about distinguishing what is implicated from what is said-and-implicated, although there is no particular problem in doing this. Incidentally, the 'conditional perfection' kind of inference is independent of the indirect illocutionary force of such utterances – promises, threats, predictions but also plain conditional assertions tend all to carry the inference.

14 The reference is particularly to Grice's first and fourth submaxims of Manner: 'avoid obscurity' and 'be brief'.

15 This observation is due to Horn (1985), who points, however, to a long tradition of essentially similar analyses in the study of morphology.

16 For reasons of space I have not spelt out the contexts of use in which the doublets might reasonably be claimed to have the same semantic content; obviously such lexical doublets are likely to have some divergence in use other than those explained by our pragmatic principles here.

17 For example, in Tamil there is a productive reduplication with rule-bound phonological alteration: thus *paittiyam* 'madness' becomes *paittiyam-giyttiyam* 'almost but not quite real insanity'. Moravcsik (1978) gives a partial account of some of these patterns. She points out that there are very different predictions where reduplication is the only signal available for some interpretation (as it is for plurality or repetition in many languages) – M implicatures after all only function by contrast to another simpler way of 'saying the same thing'.

18 Gazdar's (1979) formal system might be adapted to handle many aspects of the observable cancellation properties of the different kinds of inferences. In effect, we would set up an incremental augmentation of the contextual assumptions in a specific order: entailments > Q1-clausal > Q1-scalar > M > Q2, etc., such that inferences are added in that order only if they are consistent with what is already taken for granted. But certain problems remain: there are, for example, constraints beyond consistency.

19 Spatial prepositions in English are an interesting case: we can set up Q1 contrast sets of the kind ⟨*at, near*⟩, such that "The train is near the station" suggests 'The train is not (yet) at the station', and so on. Q2 inferences from prepositions like *in* to the relevant stereotypical relations have been illustrated above, while M contrasts like {*on, on top of*} are also easy to find.

20 Much more needs to be said of course about c-command constraints on interpretation; see Levinson (1987) and discussion there of Reinhart's (1983) proposals.

21 I borrow here the emphasis on 'favoured constructions' from John Haviland.

22 For many insights into pragmatic constraints on lexicalisation, and diachronic processes, see Gazdar & Pullum (1976), McCawley (1978) and Horn (1985, 1989).

REFERENCES

Atlas, J.D. (1989) *Philosophy without Ambiguity: a Logico-linguistic Essay*, Oxford: Clarendon Press.

Atlas, J.D. & S.C. Levinson (1981) It-clefts, informativeness and logical form. In P. Cole (ed.) *Radical Pragmatics*, New York: Academic Press, 1–61.

Austin, J.L. (1962) *How to Do Things with Words*, Oxford: Clarendon Press.

Barwise, J. (1986) Conditionals and conditional information. In E. Traugott. A. Ter Meulen, J. Reilly & C. Ferguson (eds.) *On Conditionals*, Cambridge University Press, 21–54.

Barwise, J. & J. Perry (1983) *Situations and Attitudes*, Cambridge, MA: MIT Press.

Carden, G. & W. Stewart (1987) Mauritian creole reflexives – an alternative historical scenario. MS, University of British Columbia.

(1987) Binding theory, bioprogram and creolization: evidence from Haitian creole. *Journal of Pidgin and Creole Linguistics* 3: 1–67.

Chomsky, N. (1981) *Lectures on Government and Binding*, Dordrecht: Foris.

Clark, E. (1993) *The Lexicon in Acquisition*, Cambridge University Press.

Cohen, L.J. (1971) The logical particles of natural language. In Y. Bar-Hillel (ed.), *Pragmatics of Natural Language*, Dordrecht: Reidel, 50–68.

Cohen, P., J. Morgan & M. Pollack (1990) *Intentions in Communication*, Cambridge, MA: MIT Press.

Cole, P. (1978) *Syntax and Semantics*, vol. IX: *Pragmatics*, New York: Academic Press.

Cole, P. & J. Morgan (1975) *Syntax and Semantics*, vol. III: *Speech Acts*, New York: Academic Press.

Cruse, D.A. (1986) *Lexical Semantics*, Cambridge University Press.

Faltz, L.M. (1985) *Reflexivization: a Study in Universal Grammar*, New York: Garland.

Farmer, A. & M. Harnish (1987) Communicative reference with pronouns. In M. Papi & J. Verschueren (eds.) *The Pragmatic Perspective*, Amsterdam: Benjamins, 000–00.

Gazdar, G. (1979) *Pragmatics*, New York: Academic Press.

Gazdar, G. & G. Pullum (1976) Truth-functional connectives in natural language. In *Papers from the thirteenth regional meeting of the Chicago Linguistic Society*, Chicago Linguistic Society, 137–46.

Geiss, M. & A. Zwicky (1971) On invited inferences. *Linguistic Inquiry* 2: 561–5.

Ginsberg, M.L. (ed.) (1987) *Readings in Non-monotonic Reasoning*. Los Altos: Morgan Kaufman.

Grice, H.P. (1957) Meaning. *Philosophical Review* 67: 377–88.

(1973) Probability, defeasibility and mood operators. MS, paper delivered to the Texas Conference on performatives, presuppositions and implicatures, 1973.

(1975) Logic and conversation. In P. Cole & J. Morgan (eds.) *Syntax and Semantics*, vol. III: *Speech Acts*, New York: Academic Press, 41–58.

(1989) *Studies in the Way of Words*, Cambridge, MA: Harvard University Press.

Harnish, R. (1976) Logical form and implicature. In T. Bever, J.J. Katz, & T. Langendoen (eds.) *An Integrated Theory of Linguistic Ability*, New York: Crowell, 313–92.

Hawkins, J. (1978) *Definiteness and Indefiniteness: a Study in Reference and Grammaticality Prediction*, London: Croom Helm.

(1991) On (in)definite articles: implicatures and (un)grammaticality prediction. *Journal of Linguistics* 27: 405–42.

Hirschberg, J. (1985) *A Theory of Scalar Implicature*, Moore School of Electrical Engineering, University of Pennsylvania, MS-CIS-85-56.

Hobbs, J. (1987) *Implicature and Definite Reference*, Stanford: CSLI Report 87–99.

Horn, L. (1972) *On the Semantic Properties of the Logical Operators in English*, Indiana University Linguistics Club mimeo.

(1985) Toward a new taxonomy for pragmatic inference: Q- and R-based implicature. In D. Schiffrin (ed.) *Meaning, Form and Use in Context*, Washington: Georgetown University Press, 11–42.

(1989) *A Natural History of Negation*, Chicago University Press.

Huang, Y. (1991) A neo-Gricean pragmatic theory of anaphora. *Journal of Linguistics* 27: 301–35.

(1994) *The Syntax and Pragmatics of Anaphora: a Study with Special Reference to Chinese*. Cambridge University Press.

Kempson, R. (1986) Ambiguity and the semantics-pragmatics distinction. In C. Travis (ed.) *Meaning and Interpretation*, Oxford: Blackwell, 77–104.

Kiparsky, P. (1983) Word-formation and the lexicon. In *Proceedings of the 1982 Mid-America Linguistics Conference*, Lawrence: University of Kansas, Department of Linguistics, 47–78.

Levinson, S.C. (1983) *Pragmatics*, Cambridge University Press.

(1987a) Pragmatics and the grammar of anaphora: a partial pragmatic reduction of Binding and Control phenomena. *Journal of Linguistics* 23: 379–434.

(1987b) Implicature explicated? Commentary, *Behavioural and Brain Sciences*, 10 (4): 722–3.

(1989) A review of Relevance. *Journal of Linguistics* 25: 455–72.

(1991) Pragmatic reduction of the Binding Conditions revisited. *Journal of Linguistics* 27: 107–61.

(1992) Activity types and language. In P. Drew & J. Heritage (eds.) *Talk at Work*, Cambridge University Press, 66–100.

(1995) Interactional biases in human thinking. In E. Goody (ed.) *Social Intelligence and Interaction*, Cambridge University Press, 221–60.

(forthcoming) *Generalized Conversational Implicature*, Cambridge University Press.

Lyons, J. (1977) *Semantics*, 2 vols., Cambridge University Press.

McCawley, J. (1978) Conversational implicature and the lexicon. In P. Cole (ed.), *Syntax and Semantics*, vol. IX: *Pragmatics*, New York: Academic Press, 245–59.

Mehler, J., N. Sebastian, G. Altmann, E. Dupoux, A. Christophe & C. Pallier (1993) Understanding compressed sentences: the role of rhythm and meaning. In P. Tallal, A.M. Galaburda, R. Llinas & C. von Euler (eds.) *Temporal Information Processing in the Nervous System. Annals of the New York Academy of Sciences*, 682: 272–82.

Moravcsik, E. (1978) Reduplicative constructions. In J. Greenberg (ed.) *Universals of Human Language*, vol. III: *Word Structure*, Stanford University Press, 297–335.

Morgan, J. (1978) Two types of convention in indirect speech acts. In P. Cole (ed.) *Syntax and Semantics*, vol. IX: *Pragmatics*, New York: Academic Press, 261–80.

Papi, M. & J. Verschueren (1987) *The Pragmatic Perspective*, Amsterdam: Benjamins.

Reinhart, T. (1983) *Anaphora and Semantic Interpretation*, London: Croom Helm.

Searle, J. (1975) Indirect speech acts. In P. Cole & J. Morgan (eds.) *Syntax and Semantics*, vol. III: *Speech Acts*, New York: Academic Press, 59–82.

Sperber, D. & D. Wilson (1986) *Relevance*, Oxford: Blackwell.

(1987) Response to Peer review of Sperber & Wilson: *Relevance. Brain and Behavioural Sciences*, 10 (4): 697–754.

Visser, F.T. (1963) *An Historical Syntax of the English Language*, Part I, Leiden: Brill.

Wheeldon, L. & W.J.M. Levelt (forthcoming) Monitoring the time course of phonological encoding. *Journal of Memory and Language*.

6

Does spoken language have sentences?

JIM MILLER

1 Introduction

Many linguists working on spoken language abandon the sentence as an analytic unit as a result of data like the text in (1), which is the transcription of a conversation.[1] The ' + ' signs mark brief pauses.

> (1) I used to light up a cigarette + you see because that was a very quiet way to go + now when I lit up my cigarette I used to find myself at Churchill + and the quickest way to get back from Churchill was to walk along long down Clinton Road + along + Blackford something or other it's actually an extension of Dick Place but it's called Blackford something or other it shouldn't be it's miles away from Blackford Hill + but it's called Blackford Road I think + uhm then along to Lauder Road and down Lauder Road.

As Crystal (1987: 94) observes about another, but similar, text, it is not easy to decide whether the pauses mark sentence boundaries or whether the whole text is one loosely constructed sentence. An additional problem in (1) is that one stretch uninterrupted by pauses appears to consist of what would be several sentences in writing: *It's actually an extension of Dick Place, but it's called Blackford something or other, It shouldn't be, it's miles from Blackford Hill.* Two of the clauses are conjoined by *but*, but two are simply adjacent to the preceding one. To make matters worse, the pause marking the beginning of the stretch – + *Blackford something or other* – precedes the phrase *Blackford something or other*, which is the complement of *along*, a constituent of a clause that crosses the pause boundary.

Of course the text in (1) is taken from conversation, although (1) itself is, strictly speaking, a narrative which is part of a conversation, and conversation is a special genre, with its own conventions and properties. None the less, it is spontaneous conversation and narrative that children are exposed

116

to when they learn their first language and that most adults use most of the time. These facts are good reasons for regarding spontaneous conversation and narrative as basic in the human linguistic repertoire. Since it is still controversial to suggest that sentences are foreign to spontaneous conversation and narrative, the different opinions are summarised and further arguments presented. Rhetorical structure and discourse representation are pinpointed as offering resources for an alternative analysis.

A major distinction assumed throughout this chapter is the one between language system and language behaviour. The language system consists of the syntactic, morphosyntactic, semantic, phonological and graphological principles controlling the generation of semantic and syntactic structures, the insertion of lexical items into the syntactic structures and the realisation of the structures as speech or writing.[2] The products of speaking and writing are texts, which may be spontaneous or deliberately elicited by investigators. Hypotheses about particular language systems or the general nature of language systems are based on texts and intuitions. It is essential to distinguish units that can be recognised in texts from units that belong to the hypothesised language system. Strictly speaking, the different units should be clearly kept apart by means of different terms, such as 'text-sentence', 'system-sentence', 'text-clause', 'system-clause', etc., as in Lyons (1977). In this chapter, 'sentence' and 'clause' will be used where it is clear from the context whether the unit belongs to text or to the language system.

Part of the current controversy reviewed in section 2 revolves round the question of what text units can be recognised in spoken language. In written language, sentences and clauses (and phrases, paragraphs, etc.) are obvious in any text laid out according to the conventions of the society in which it was written. The relevant conventions differ from society to society and from one period of time to another in the same society – see section 3.3. What units can be recognised in spoken language and are useful for its analysis is not so easily resolved. Some analysts maintain that sentences are not recognisable in spoken language, others that they are.[3]

The central problem is that it is far from self-evident that the language system of spoken English has sentences, for the simple reason that text-sentences are hard to locate in spoken texts. Clauses are easily recognised: even where pauses and a pitch contour with appropriate scope are missing, a given verb and its complements can be picked out. Of course, one reply to the objection is that the system-sentences employed by linguists need not correspond to text-sentences. System-sentences are postulated by linguists in order to handle distribution and dependency relations, and should be retained if this goal is achieved. Against this, it can be argued that system-sentences do not map onto text-sentences in spontaneous language because system-sentences are based on the prototype concept of a sentence as containing at least one main clause and possibly other co-ordinated main clauses and/or subordinated clauses. (That this is the prototype concept is easily verified by examining popular manuals such as Burton (1986), the literature in any generative framework or the training offered to school pupils.) It can also be argued that in fact the clause is the language-system unit that is the essential locus of both dependency relations and distributional properties (see section 4). And one can ask why, for example, the text in (1) should be thought of just as a collection of sentences or as one sentence; a third possibility is that it is a collection of clauses constituting a coherent discourse by virtue of certain rhetorical relationships.

The above remarks apply only to spontaneous spoken English. For written English (and probably all other modern written languages) it does seem self-evident that the language system has sentences and clauses, since text-sentences are easily located in written texts through the use of capital letters and full stops. The one proviso is that sentences are learned through the process of reading and writing, and are taught to the majority of language-users, whereas clauses are acquired without specific teaching. Children in the early stages of primary school typically produce single-clause sentences and have to acquire the ability (partly by instruction, partly by reading) to combine a number of clauses into a sentence.

These characteristics of clauses and sentences bear on other issues, such as whether a given language system is independent of the medium in which it is realised. If sentences are to be admitted as units of written but not spoken language, the next step is to analyse written and spoken language as having different language systems. To some extent this analysis is unavoidable anyway, since even within single clauses it is clear that written English (and other languages) permits more complex phrasal and clausal constructions, and more complex vocabulary, than occur in spoken English. In addition, written English has constructions that do not occur in spontaneous spoken English, and vice versa (see e.g. Biber, 1988, and Chafe, 1982, for English; Zemskaja, 1973, for Russian). The question is whether the differences can reasonably be hypothesised to include different units as opposed to the same units but with different degrees of complexity.

If spoken texts lack sentences, the language system must be analysed as having clauses combining into clause-complexes, as suggested by Halliday (1989). There are two major types of syntactic relationship, embedding and combining. Adverbial clauses only combine, that is, are not part of any constituent in a matrix clause. Only relative and complement clauses can be

embedded, since relative clauses are regularly part of an NP and complement clauses function as arguments to verbs. However, many occurrences
of relative clauses cannot be treated as embedded, especially if, as in (7)
below, they occur in a different turn from the head noun and come from a
different speaker. Of course, even without sentences, it would be possible to
handle examples like (7) by postulating a system-clause in which the relative
clause is embedded inside an NP and is adjacent to the head noun. The
system clause would then be mapped onto the actual arrangement of
text-clauses.

This treatment of (7) is rejected here on the ground that what must be
captured is the relationship between the relative clause and the relevant NP
in the main clause. This is just one of various relationships between clauses,
and between separate text-sentences in written language, which cannot be
handled by the usual type of syntax. The syntax is blocked by the
occurrence of sentence boundaries in writing and by the non-adjacency of
clauses in speech. Analysts can either develop rules mapping system-
structures onto text-structures or devise discourse rules handling both the
relationships among spoken clauses and the relationships among written
sentences. It is the discourse rules that are advocated here.

Of course readers are entitled to ask why they should give up a well-
developed system of sentential syntactic analysis in return for a system that
exists only in the form of a promissory note. The answer is in several parts.
Firstly, the analysis of written language still needs sentential syntactic
analysis. There is no demand that such analysis be given up altogether,
merely that limitations on its scope be recognised. Secondly, written
language cannot be completely analysed without discourse rules that
specify the relationships between separate sentences – relationships that
also hold between the clauses of speech. The relationships range from
coreference to rhetorical structure ones such as condition, elaboration and
concession (see Matthiessen & Thompson, 1988). Thirdly, the alternative
to discourse rules is a set of rules mapping tightly integrated arrangements
of system sentences onto loose arrangements of sentences (in writing) and
clauses (in speech). Such a system of rules has not even been foreshadowed,
far less explicitly proposed. Fourthly, the absence of any sentence marking
in speech compared with an abundance of clear sentence marking in writing
raises questions as to the validity of the sentence in the analysis of spoken
language. Finally, the sort of discourse rules called for already exist in
prototype form in the work of Mann, Thompson and others (see Mann &
Thompson, 1987; Matthiessen & Thompson, 1988; Hovy, 1990). Matthiessen & Thompson (1988: 300) demonstrate two essential points: the same

general relationships hold among clauses in clause combinations as among higher-level units of text, and clauses have the same combinatory structure as higher-level text units, namely as members of a list or as nucleus with satellite.

2 Sentences in spoken texts

This section briefly surveys the arguments for and against the sentence as a unit in spoken texts and as an analytical unit in accounts of spoken language. The case against has been stated most clearly by Halliday (1989: 66), who argues that the basic unit of syntax is the clause. Clauses occur singly or in complexes, and clause and clause-complex are indispensable concepts for the study of both spoken and written syntax. Sentences in written language developed from the desire to mark clause-complexes; the initial capital letter of the first word in a clause-complex and the full stop following the final word signal which clauses the writer wants the reader to construe as interconnected. Of course, clauses are also interconnected in spoken language; the difference is that interconnectedness is not signalled by adjacency nor even by the relevant clauses occurring in the same turn (in conversation) or under the same intonation contour (in narrative).

A number of researchers recognise the problematic nature of the sentence in spoken language. Quirk et al. (1985: 47) state that the sentence boundaries can be difficult to locate 'particularly in spoken language'[4] and point out that the question 'What counts as a grammatical English sentence?' does not always permit a decisive answer. They deal with the difficulty by avoiding any definition of sentence while continuing to use the term for a unit greater than the clause. Linell (1988: 54) reaffirms the lack of clearcut sentences in spoken language and adds that talk consists of phrases and clauses loosely related to each other and combining into structures less clear and hierarchical than the structures dealt with in grammar books. Similar points had been made earlier by Brown et al. (1984: 16–18).

Brown et al. and Linell are apparently satisfied to work with phrases and clauses; indeed, that is the position adopted here. Some analysts propose a thorough clearing-out of concepts: for instance, Crookes (1990) surveys a range of work whose goal is to develop an alternative basic unit for work on oral texts. His survey includes the *idea unit* of Kroll (1977), the *turn unit* of conversational analysis, the *tone unit* of Quirk et al. (1985) *inter alios*, the *t-unit* of Hunt (1966) and the *utterance* as defined by Crookes & Rulon (1985: 9). The details of these various alternative units need not concern us here, as none of them relates directly to syntactic structure. *Pace* Crookes, the analysis of dialogue requires turns and phrases and clauses, since it is quite unclear how syntactic structure could be analysed without the latter. Crookes is, however, quite correct in describing tone groups as controversial. Indeed, Brown & Yule (1983) and their phonetician colleagues found it so difficult to apply the concept of tone groups to spontaneous conversation and narrative that they abandoned tone groups and worked instead with units delimited from each other by pauses, which could be short, medium or long.

Sentences in spoken language are defended by Chafe and Danielewicz (1987: 94–6), who appeal to both clause and sentence in their analysis of spoken language. For spoken language they emphasise the central place of what they call 'prototypical intonation units', consisting of a single coherent intonation contour, possibly followed by a pause and stretching over a maximum of six words, which often constitute a clause but which may also constitute a phrase or simply a fragment of syntax. Chafe & Danielewicz (1987: 103) further say that, although the sentence is a controversial unit in the analysis of spoken language, speakers appear to produce sentence-final intonation when they judge that they have come to the end of some coherent content sequence.

3 Text-sentences in spoken language

3.1 Intonational criteria

One difficulty with Chafe & Danielewicz's account is that their sentences correspond more to short paragraphs than to the prototypical written sentence. The intonation contours they describe may encompass one or more main clauses, not conjoined but simply adjacent to each other. Conversely, the same type of intonation contour may encompass a mere phrase. Interestingly, similar difficulties occur in Russian. The transcripts of spoken Russian in Kapanadze & Zemskaja (1979) are coded for what they call completed and uncompleted intonation. The latter occurs when speakers signal that they have not completed their utterance but are merely pausing, while the former signals completion of the utterance. What Kapanadze & Zemskaja call signalling completion of an utterance appears to be equivalent to speakers signalling that they have come to the end of a coherent content sequence, as Chafe & Danielewicz put it. Consider the example in (2), where single obliques mark uncompleted utterance intonation, and double obliques mark completed utterance intonation. Sequences of three full stops indicate a pause. The capital letters and punctuation are taken from the original. The lines are assigned letters for ease of reference.

(2) a. // Potom iz   drugoj gruppy kievljan   tože/nu kak re . . .
          then   from   other   group   of Kievans   also [interpretation
                  (the)   unclear]
    b.   žalko   vse-taki . . . rebjat/   oni   ne   znajut   dorogu
         sorry   however   (for) them/ they not   know   (the) road
    c.   i   pojdut/   i   eti   tože   vstajut
         and   will-set-off/ and   these-ones   too   get-up //

'Then people from the other group of Kievans also [broken syntax] – anyway I was sorry for them [lit. the children] – they didn't know the route and were about to set off – these ones too were getting up.'

                                              (Kapanadze & Zemskaja, 1979: 95)

As the double obliques show, the speaker treats the whole sequence in (2) as a complete utterance. The sequence contains a prepositional phrase and a fragment in line (a), two main clauses in line (b) and two more main clauses in line (c). Of course, speakers can use co-ordinating and subordinating devices to combine a number of clauses into a single written sentence, but there is no justification for postulating one or more sentences here apart from the reader's/listener's intuition – and different readers or listeners have different intuitions, as will be demonstrated shortly.

3.2 Intuitions about sentences in spoken language

Wackernagel-Jolles (1971: 148–69) demonstrated that speakers do not share intuitions about what counts as a sentence in spoken language. She got groups of thirty to fifty final-year undergraduate students at a German university to listen to recordings of narratives by native speakers of German. The narratives were prompted by questions from an interviewer. Each text was played through once to allow the students to accustom themselves to the speaker's voice. They were then issued with a transcription of the recording, without punctuation. The text skipped to a new line only where there was a change of speaker. The recording was then played through a second time and the students were asked to draw a line in the text wherever they thought a sentence ended. Agreement as to sentence-endings ranged from 13 out of 20 in one text to 6 out of 29 in another. The former text was the telling of a fairy-tale, the latter a panel-beater recounting his early life and his war experiences.

Wackernagel-Jolles comments (1971: 149) that uninterrupted story-telling was especially conducive to clear intonation signals. But the factors governing the recognition of sentence boundaries are far from obvious. The students were agreed on 20.6 per cent of the sentence boundaries in a text produced by a slow-speaking man but agreed on 42.8 per cent of the boundaries in a text produced by a fast and 'lazy' male student. They agreed on 41 per cent of the boundaries in a text produced by a non-academic female student who failed to complete many syntactic constructions but only on 30 per cent in a text from a clergyman with very expressive intonation. Ignoring the differences between the various text types, we see that the essential point is that naive speakers/writers, who as university students can doubtless organise their own written texts into acceptable sentences, were unanimous about the final boundary for less than half of the sentences in the texts.[5] For these subjects the sentence is a relatively fluid unit.

3.3 The sentence – a changing concept

It was remarked in section 1 that young children in general appear not to have a clear notion of sentence but learn to write complex sentences at school. In this connection it is interesting that in written English text-sentence boundaries vary from one historical period to another, from one genre to another, from one individual to another and from one culture to another. This variation can be interpreted as evidence that the text-sentence is not a stable unit of syntax but a discourse unit whose composition and complexity is subject to cultural variation and rhetorical fashion. Clauses (and phrases) are not subject to such variation and fashion. Unstable text-sentences indicate that even for written language system-sentences do not map onto text-sentences in any straightforward fashion, and they throw doubt on the text-sentence as a unit in spoken language and on the system-sentence as a useful unit in the analysis of spoken language.

Changing rhetorical fashion can be seen from (3), from Pepys' Diary. The editor (see Latham, 1978) explains that Pepys used full stops to mark the final boundary of both sentences and phrases and dashes to mark some boundaries inside sentences. Latham has replaced Pepys' dashes with semi-colons. Example (3), which is typical of Pepys' writing, shows an awareness of phrases and clauses and of larger discourse units, but not of the prototype sentence as described in section 1 above, with a main finite clause and possibly co-ordinated or subordinated final clauses.

(3) to Whitehall to the Duke, who met us in his closett; and there he did desire of us to know what hath been the common practice about making of forrayne ships to strike sail to us: which they did all do as much as they could, but I could say nothing to it, which I was sorry for; so endeed, I was forced to study a lie; and so after we were gone from the Duke, I told Mr Coventry that I had heard Mr Selden often say that he could prove that in Henry the 7ths time he did give commission to his captains to make the King of Denmark's ships to strike to him in the Baltique.

(Latham, 1978: 34)

The arrangement of clauses in (3) is not peculiar to Pepys or to diary-writing but is found in other authors and other genres, such as Jane Austen's novels. Even modern authors can produce paragraph-like sentences, though rather shorter than (3). Compare (4):

(4) When Homer got close to the carton, he saw it was not empty; David Copperfield, Junior, was in the bottom of the carton – Curly Day was giving him a ride.

(John Irving, *Cider House Rules* (Black Swan, 1991), p. 217)

The concept of text-sentence is not stable across cultural boundaries. The French weekly *L'Express* has a house style that encourages phrases and subordinate clauses of all types to be presented as single text-sentences. Farther afield, the Qur'an is said to have no unit between the clause and a unit corresponding roughly to the paragraph in the European literary tradition. In Turkey sentence-writing conventions have been consciously changed in recent times. Lewis (1953) talks of traditional Turkish prose writers rambling happily on adding participial phrase after participial phrase but observes that modern writers try to keep their sentences short, a practice now being taught in Turkish schools.

The elaboration of clause sequences into complex sentences has been traced for various languages: for example, Palmer (1954: 119), discussing the development of prose style in Latin, comments on how progression from the earliest to later Latin texts shows how 'the naive juxtaposition of simple sentences is gradually built up into the complex period with careful subordination of its constituent parts'. That is, the earliest written texts had text-sentences consisting of few clauses, and over time more complex written text-sentences were elaborated by Latin writers. This development resulted from conscious effort, unlike changes in spontaneous spoken language; the development did not take place in the spoken language, and the resulting written text-units had to be taught.

4 The sentence as a unit of analysis

We turn now to sentence and clause in linguistic analysis. The burden of the preceding discussion is that the sentence is not a unit that can be recognised in spoken texts or applied in their analysis. In contrast, the sentence is a prominent unit in written texts and requires a corresponding analytical unit. Interestingly, there is evidence that the clause should be taken as the major locus of distributional and dependency relations and not the (system) sentence.

We can usefully begin by returning to the problems discussed in section 1 in connection with the text in (1). Consider the examples in (5)–(8):

(5) B: right if you go from the front giraffe's foot about
       hold on let me see –
       if you go down about straight down about 6 cms.
       you find the waterhole
       and it's a big hole . . . with reeds round the side of it . . . and animals
          drinking
       out of it
       and it's about
       it's an oval hole
       it's about 2 cms. wide north to south
       and from the side to side it's about – 3 cms. wide . . .

(6) A: you go down to the bridge
    B: uhuh to the left of the swamp?
    A: to the left of the swamp – taking a gentle curve south west

(7) A: . . . the first day we went canoeing
    L: where I capsized

(8) A1: eh you've got an East Lake haven't you
    B1: aye away at the top?
    A2: uhuh
    B2: of the page?

Example (5) illustrates the way in which in spontaneous spoken language information is carefully staged, in the sense of being spread out over different clauses. Most of the clauses are simple clauses and are simple in structure, though one clause has two prepositional phrases with a participial phrase inside one of the latter – *with reeds round the side of it* and (*with*) *animals drinking out of it.* It would be possible to gather the clauses into sentences, but various possibilities are open. For example, we might decide to have *You find the waterhole and it's a big hole . . . [and it's about]. It's an oval hole. It's about 2 cms. wide north to south. And from . . .* Another possible version is *You find the waterhole. And it's a big hole . . . It's about 2 cms. wide north to south and from . . .*

The basic difficulty is that in collecting the clauses into sentences we rely on recognising clauses and on our knowledge of the stylistic conventions for written dialogue. As in (1), the intonation and pause boundaries do not coincide with the possible sentence boundaries, and to add to the difficulties the prepositional phrases *with reeds round the side of it* and (*with*) *animals drinking out of it* were separated from the initial part of the clause and from each other by a long pause. It is in fact unclear whether these chunks should be analysed as combining into a single clause. The analyst can combine the clauses into sentences, but the combining process is arbitrary and the sentences would not contribute to the analysis of the data as a coherent text. Coherence relations (say, as part of a discourse representation theory) must apply to clauses and indeed phrases, and sentences are not necessary.

The same problem arises in (8), where B2 modifies B1, but B1 has a completed intonation contour, and is separated from B2 by A2. A2, part of the conversation management, does not overlap with B1 or B2. While the speaker could have uttered B1 and B2 as part of the same pause and intonation unit, he did not, and there are no criteria that justify treating them in any way except as two separate but discourse-related phrases. The fact that the speaker might well have written the two phrases as part of a single sentence, given planning time, is irrelevant. Similarly, (5) could have been *written* as the compact, dense, syntactically integrated piece of prose in (9), but the characteristics of (9) cannot be invoked as criteria in the analysis of (5). It would be rather like taking a piece of written language, rewriting it, analysing the rewritten piece, and presenting the analysis as pertaining to the original passage!

> (9) It's a big oval waterhole about 2 cms. wide north to south and about 3 cms. wide from side to side, surrounded by reeds and with animals drinking out of it.

Examples (6) and (7) exemplify other relationships that cannot reasonably be analysed by invoking a single sentence. Example (6) presents a free participial phrase *taking a gentle curve south west*, modifying the clause produced in a previous turn by the same speaker, and (7) presents a relative clause *where I capsized*, modifying a constituent in the clause produced by the previous speaker. Participial phrases are discourse-dependent in the sense that the listener cannot interpret them without reference to a previous piece of text; at the very least, a subject has to be found for the participle itself. The nearest candidate for the subject is in the first line of (6), but this is not a reason for analysing the participial phrase as belonging to one and the same sentence as *you go down to the bridge*. Note that speaker A was not interrupted in the process of producing a single sentence. *You go down to the bridge* is a completed utterance, with appropriate intonation. B signals acceptance of the instruction with *uhuh*, looks at the map and realises that he needs more information: *to the left of the swamp?* A produces the participial phrase in response to B's question.

It will be useful to consider the role of the sentence in syntactic analysis. Bloomfield (1935: 170), having discussed an invented text *How are you? It's a fine day. Are you going to play tennis this afternoon?*, makes the declaration in (10):

> (10) It is evident that the sentences in any utterance are marked off by the mere fact that each sentence is an independent linguistic form, not included by virtue of any grammatical construction in any larger linguistic form.

Crystal (1987: 94) puts it more concisely: a sentence is the largest unit to which syntactic rules apply. While representing an enormous advance over statements about sentences expressing complete thoughts, this sort of definition is itself open to objection. One self-evident fact about (10) is that Bloomfield's sentences each consist of a single finite clause. Bloomfield does treat the problem of parataxis – two or more main clauses juxtaposed with no pauses or intonation breaks to mark the putative sentence boundaries, as in (1) above – by invoking a set of pitch phonemes. This treatment is decisively countered by Matthews (1981: 30–4), on the grounds that intonation is continuous, the phonemic principle of sameness/distinctness does not apply and there are no rules governing parataxis. Matthews (1981: 35–8, 46), on the basis of tag questions and the distribution of *please*, further points out that not all phenomena in a given language lend themselves to a rigorous rule-based account, for the simple reason that any natural language has areas of indeterminacy.

Matthews' objection can be restated thus: what units of syntax (in spoken or written language) are affected by the rules of distribution and dependency relations? The answer is that the clause is the locus of the densest dependency and distributional properties, that a few dependency relations cross clause boundaries, and that, even in written language, a few dependency relations cross sentence boundaries. The first part of the answer will be used to support the view that the sentence is not required as an analytical unit in spoken language (and may be less central in written language than previously thought). The second part of the answer, dependency relations crossing clause boundaries, could be interpreted as supporting the sentence as an analytical unit even in spoken language, but this potential argument is counteracted by the third part, dependency relations crossing text-sentence boundaries in written language. Because dependency relations cross text-sentence boundaries, a complete grammatical theory must have a mechanism for specifying such dependencies, and whatever the mechanism is, it will undoubtedly be able to specify dependencies from clause to clause when the clauses are gathered, not into a sentence but into a text.

Let us consider first the dependency relations in the Russian examples in (11):

(11) a. Molodaja   devuška   verila   ee   materi.
         (the) young girl   believed   her   mother
      b. Molodaja   devuška   verila,   čto   mat'   pomogaet   ej.
         (the) young girl   believed   that   (her) mother   was-helping her

Example (11a) consists of a single main clause which can stand on its own (and constitute a sentence in written Russian). Within that clause there is a dense network of dependencies. *Verila* has the two NPs as complements – it requires both a subject and an object NP. Being singular number and feminine gender, *verila* requires its subject noun to be singular and feminine, and also in the nominative case. *Devuška* has all these properties. *Verila* requires its direct object to be in the dative case – most transitive Russian verbs govern their direct object in the accusative case.[6] *Materi* is a dative case form. The adjective *molodaja* agrees in number, gender and case with its head noun. In copula clauses with BYT' (BE), the subject noun agrees with adjective complements of BYT' in gender and number: *Vrač byl simpatičnyj* ((the) doctor – was – nice), where *vrač* and *simpatičnyj* are both nominative case, singular number and masculine gender.

Example (11b) demonstrates another property of VERIT' (BELIEVE). Verbs control how many constituents co-occur with them in clauses, and what type. VERIT' allows direct object NPs as its complement, but it also allows clauses. This is an important property, since many verbs exclude clauses and some verbs allow only clauses.

Only one property of rection crosses the clause boundary, the mood of the clause. In Russian this is signalled by the complementiser – *čto* with *verila*, but some verbs require *čtoby* and a past-tense verb – as in *Devuška xotela, čtoby mat' pomagala ej* ((the) girl – wanted – that – (her) mother – help – her), where *pomagala* is a past-tense form. All the other dependencies in the complement clause are controlled by the verb in that clause.

Another example of cross-clause dependency is found in Russian relative clauses, exemplified in (12).

(12) Nekotorye   bojalis'   politiki,   kotoruju   vvel   Stalin.
     certain (ones) fear   (the) policy which   introduced Stalin
     'Certain people fear the policy which Stalin introduced.'

The relative clause in (12) is *kotoruju vvel Stalin*. *Kotoruju* is a relative pronoun with feminine gender, singular number and accusative case. The accusative case is assigned by *vvel* ('introduced'), which also assigns nominative case to the subject noun *Stalin* and agrees with it in number. In the main clause *bojalis'* ('fear') is third-person plural, as is the subject noun *nekotorye*. *Politiki*, the object of *bojalis'*, is in the genitive case, which is required by that verb. In addition, *politiki* is feminine gender and singular number, the very properties that turn up in the relative pronoun. That is, the case of the relative pronoun is determined by the verb in the relative clause and whether the pronoun is the subject or object of the verb, but the gender and number of the relative pronoun are determined by the noun modified by the relative clause.

Dependencies do not cross clause boundaries into adverbial clauses. Certain combinations of adverbial clause and main clause appear to involve cross-clause dependencies, such as the rules in Classical Greek governing clause combinations expressing fulfilled or unfulfilled conditions as in (13):

(13) a. ei touto epoioun,   ēdikoun.
        if this   they-were-doing they-were-wrong
     b. ei touto epraksen,   ēdikēsan   an.
        if this   they-had-done they-would-have-been-wrong PARTICLE

The English copula + adjective structure corresponds to a single verb in Greek. Example (13a) expresses a fulfilled condition; the conditional clause contains an imperfective past-tense verb, *ēdikoun*. Example (13b) expresses a remote, unfulfilled condition. The conditional clause contains a perfective past-tense form, *epraksen*, and the main clause contains a perfective past-tense form and the particle *an*. Such examples, however (both the Classical Greek ones and their English equivalents), are not instances of dependencies crossing from one clause to another. The syntactic constraints affect both the main and adverbial clauses, and the dependencies appear to be associated with the entire combination, rather than flowing from the main clause to the adverbial clause.

Relative clauses and complement clauses differ from adverbial clauses in being embedded, relative clauses occurring inside NPs and complement clauses functioning as arguments of verbs. Given these close relationships, the cross-clause dependencies are not surprising, but note that for relative clauses it is only agreement in number and gender (which applies to full NPs and succeeding pronoun anaphors in different sentences), while for complement clauses it is only mood – but see the comments below on the type of constructions that are common in spoken language.

Relative clauses are interesting in another respect. Non-restrictive relative clauses are often separated from their antecedent NP by a long pause, or a break in intonation or a change of conversational turn. Compare the change of turn in (7) and the break in intonation in (14):

(14) on   zastavil [ego] nam   čitat'   kurs   tureckogo jazyka//
      he   made   him   to-us to-read course of-Turkish language
      'He made him give us a course of lectures on Turkish.'
      Očen' interesnyj//   iz   kotorogo ja massu vynes//
      very interesting (one) from   which   I   mass   took-out
      'A very interesting course, from which I learned a lot.'

(Kapanadze & Zemskaja 1979)

Kapanadze & Zemskaja use double obliques to mark the end of a completed-utterance intonation contour and the beginning of a new contour. In (14) the relative clause *iz kotorogo ja massu vynes* is separated from the previous phrase by a double oblique.

The close relationship between the complement clause and the matrix clause in which it is embedded is undeniable, but one phenomenon must be mentioned here: constructions that are quite regular and frequent in written language simply do not occur, or are very rare, in spontaneous speech. For instance, what would be a complement clause in writing is typically expressed in speech as though a speaker's exact words were being reported direct, as in *So I asked what are you doing* versus *I asked what he was doing*; *I said we'll help* versus *I said that we would help*; and *Then she explained – the baby was ill and she had to stay at home* versus *Then she explained that the baby was ill and she had to stay at home*. Admittedly, the frequency of the different constructions in a large body of spontaneous speech has yet to be rigorously calculated, but an examination of a sample of the conversation mentioned in [1] showed no occurrences of verbs of saying followed by a complement clause as opposed to ten occurrences of verbs of saying followed by the purported words of the person being talked about.

To close this discussion of dependencies, let us consider (15) and (16), which exemplify dependencies crossing text-sentence boundaries:

(15) *Etot portnoj* byl ...   krasivo   starejuščij   mužčina ...
      this tailor   was   handsomely growing-old   man

Šest' večerov v nedelju stojal *on* za stolom . . .
six evenings in week stood he at table
rezal, šil, proglažival švy utjugom.
(he) cut (cloth) (he) sewed (cloth) (he) smoothed seams with-iron
Zarabatyval den'gi. Voskresen'je provodil na ippodrome.
(he) earned money Sunday (he) spent at (the) racecourse
'This tailor was growing old but keeping his good looks. He spent six
evenings in the week at the table cutting, sewing, ironing seams and
earning good money. Sunday he spent at the racecourse.

(Anatolij Rybakov, *Deti Arbata* (Tashkent: Gafura Guljama Press,
1988), p. 25)

(16) A ona molčit. Idet, ladoški v rukava svitera/
but she is-silent (she) walks hands into sleeves of sweater
sprjatala, i molčit
has-hidden and is-silent.
'But she says nothing. She walks along with her hands hidden in the sleeves
of her jersey.'

(Al'bert Ivanov & Evgenij Karelov, Rebjata ja ziv. In *Mir Priključenij*,
(Moscow: Detskaja Literatura, 1986), p. 11)

In (15) the first sentence has the full masculine singular NP *etot portnoj;* the
second sentence has the masculine singular pronoun *on*; and the third and
fourth sentences have the subjectless masculine singular verbs *zarabatyval*
and *provodil*. The properties 'masculine' and 'singular' are projected by *etot
portnoj* into the pronoun in the second sentence and then into the verb
forms in the third and fourth sentences. In (16) the Agent is referred to by
the feminine singular pronoun *ona*, which itself refers back to a full NP
omitted here. In the second sentence the verb *idet* has the properties
'singular' and 'third person' (but not 'feminine') and the verb *sprjatala* has
the properties 'feminine', 'singular' and 'third person'.

With respect to distribution it is equally obvious that the classic
distributional criteria apply within clauses rather than sentences. For
example, in a recent introduction to transformational grammar (Radford,
1988: 69–75), the vast bulk of the distributional evidence relates to single
main clauses. Where there is more than one clause, one reason is that the
additional material is needed to provide a convincing linguistic context; for
example, in *Down the hill John ran, as fast as he could* the adverbial clause of
manner, *as fast as he could,* lends naturalness to the fronted prepositional
phrase, *down the hill.* A second reason is that the extra clause is a relative
clause or a complement clause; that is, clauses that are embedded inside
arguments of the verb in the main clause. One example is *He explained to*

her all the terrible problems that he had encountered, where the relative clause gives the necessary weight to the final noun phrase. In any case, distributional analysis runs into the same problem as verbs and complement clauses, complex sentences of the sort appealed to in the literature on syntax are missing from spontaneous spoken language.

The only clauses that have distribution inside a unit bigger than the clauses: complex sentences of the sort appealed to in the literature on syntax are missing from spontaneous spoken language.

precede or follow the main clause with which they combine, but in formal spoken English they tend to follow the main clause. That is, since their distribution even in written English is limited, they are no more than mild exceptions to the rule that the clause is the main focus of distributional properties. In informal spoken English, in any case, the analysis advocated here is that adverbial clauses combine with main clauses to form a clause-complex, and that the relationships between the clause-complexes should be handled by discourse rules.[7]

5 Conclusion

There is very little evidence to support either text-sentences or system-sentences in spontaneous spoken language. Planned or semi-planned spoken language is different, but is typically heavily influenced by the units and organisation of written language. Much of the language system of a given language is medium-independent, but some is dependent, most obviously the complex syntactic constructions and the vocabulary that are typical of written language but not spoken language. Equally, there are constructions and vocabulary that occur in spontaneous spoken language but not in written language. The system differences can be kept to a minimum by appealing to the notion of discourse rules specific to a given medium. The discourse rules for written language map one or more clauses into sentences where appropriate; the discourse rules for spontaneous spoken language do not.

The final words in this chapter come from Heath (1985: 108). He was writing about another phenomenon, but his sentiments are appropriate to the study of spoken language in general:

> There has been a recurrent tendency in much syntactic research to distinguish between an underlying, rather crystalline 'grammar', which then interacts in real speech with a distinct outer 'psycholinguistic' component, the latter being especially concerned with short-term memory limitations, linear ordering of major clause constituents, resolution of

surface ambiguities, etc. My view is that these two aspects of language are far more tightly welded to each other than it seems at first sight.

It is clear to the writer, in the spirit of Heath's view, that a major challenge for linguistic theory lies in the combination of process and structure residing in spoken language.

NOTES

1 John Anderson, Ellen Bard and Bob Ladd kindly read and commented on the first draft of this chapter, thereby excising unclarity and error. The example in (1), part of a tutorial exercise with postgraduate students in Applied Linguistics in 1980 at the University of Edinburgh, was supplied by Gill Brown and George Yule. The analysis is based on a corpus of spontaneous conversation and a corpus of task-oriented dialogues.

2 The term 'semantic' is intended to apply to the set of principles that are divided by many linguists into 'semantic' and 'pragmatic'.

3 The distinction between spoken and written language *tout court* is clearly wrong. Many types of written and spoken text can and must be recognised. Prepared spoken material such as lectures and sermons is quite different from spontaneous conversation and unscripted narrative. For the purpose of this chapter, it is convenient to talk simply of spoken language, but what is meant by this term is spontaneous conversation and impromptu narrative. These are particularly important types of text, as they constitute the vast bulk of speakers' experience of language.

4 It is not clear why it should be difficult to recognise sentences in written English, provided a given writer has used capital letters and full stops according to convention. Whether readers find that writer's usage stylistically acceptable is quite another question.

5 The data from Wackernagel-Jolles not having been subjected to statistical analysis, it is impossible to state whether the students were in greater agreement on the sentence boundaries than chance would permit. For present purposes that question is not directly relevant, since the point being made is that even with a transcript there was a conspicuous lack of agreement about the location of the sentence boundaries. It would be surprising if listeners were to disagree about the boundaries and the constituents of individual clauses, though admittedly the relevant results must come from an experiment that is yet to be conducted.

6 Whether dative complement NPs are direct objects is open to question. Since nothing in this chapter depends on a decision one way or the other, the term 'direct object' is used for convenience.

7 Note that the recent major works based on fieldwork on 'exotic' languages focus exclusively on the clause (Nichols & Woodbury, 1985; Foley & Van Valin, 1984).

REFERENCES

Biber, D. (1988) *Variation across Speech and Writing*. Cambridge University Press.

Bloomfield, L. (1935) *Language*, London: Allen and Unwin.

Brown, G., A. Anderson, R. Shillcock & G. Yule (1984) *Teaching Talk: Strategies for Production and Assessment*, Cambridge University Press.

Brown, G. and G. Yule (1983) *Discourse Analysis*, Cambridge University Press.

Burton, S.H. (1986) *ABC of Common Errors* (Longman English Guides). Harlow: Longman.

Chafe, W. (1982) Integration and involvement in speaking, writing and oral literature. In D. Tannen (ed.) *Spoken and Written Language: Exploring Orality and Literacy*, Norwood, NJ: Ablex, 35–53.

Chafe, W. & J. Danielewicz (1987) Properties of written and spoken language. In R. Horowitz & S.J. Samuels (eds.) *Comprehending Oral and Written Language*, New York: Academic Press, 83–113.

Crookes, G. (1990) The utterance and other basic units for second language discourse analysis. *Applied Linguistics* 11 (2): 183–99.

Crookes, G.V. & K. Rulon (1985) *Incorporation of Corrective Feedback in Native Speaker/Non-native Speaker Conversation* (Technical Report no. 3, Center for Second Language Classroom Research, Social Science Research Institute), Honolulu: University of Hawaii.

Crystal, D. (1987) *The Cambridge Encyclopaedia of Language*, Cambridge University Press.

Foley, W.D. & R.D. Van Valin Jnr (1984) *Functional Syntax and Universal Grammar*, Cambridge University Press.

Halliday, M.A.K. (1989) *Spoken and Writen Language*, Oxford University Press.

Heath, J. (1985) Clause structure in Ngandi. In Nichols & Woodbury (eds.): 89–110.

Hovy, E. (1990) Unresolved issues in paragraph planning. In R. Dale, C. Mellish and M. Zock (eds.) *Current Research in Natural Language Generation*, New York: Academic Press, 17–45.

Hunt, K.W. (1966) Recent measures in syntactic development. *Elementary English* 43: 732–9.

Kapanadze, M. & E.O. Zemskaja (1979) *Teksty*, Moscow: Nauka.

Kroll, B. (1977) Combining ideas in written and spoken English: a look at subordination and coordination. In E. Ochs Keenan & T.L. Bennett (eds.) *Discourse across Time and Space* (Southern California Occasional Papers in Linguistics, 5), Los Angeles: University of Southern California, 69–108.

Lapteva, O.A. (1976) *Russkij razgovornyj sintaksis*, Moscow: Nauka.

Latham, R. (1978) *The Illustrated Pepys*, London: Bell and Hyman.

Lewis, G.L. (1953) *Teach Yourself Turkish*, London: Hodder and Stoughton.

Linell, P. (1988) The impact of literacy on the conception of language: the case of linguistics. In R. Saljö (ed.) *The Written World*, Berlin: Springer, 41–58.

Lyons, J. (1977) *Semantics*, vol. I, Cambridge University Press.

Mann, W.C. & S.A. Thompson (1987) Rhetorical structure theory: a theory of text organization. ISI/RS-87-190. Marina del Rey, California: Information Sciences Institute.

Matthews, P. (1981) *Syntax*, Cambridge University Press.

Matthiessen, C. & S.A. Thompson (1988) The structure of discourse and subordination. In J. Haiman & S.A. Thompson (eds.) *Clause Combining in Grammar and Discourse*, Amsterdam: Benjamins, 275–329.

Nichols, J. & A.C. Woodbury (1985) *Grammar Inside and Outside the Clause*, Cambridge University Press.

Palmer, L.R. (1954) *The Latin Language*, London: Faber and Faber.

Quirk, R., S. Greenbaum, G. Leech & J. Svartvik (1985) *A Comprehensive Grammar of the English Language*, London: Longman.

Radford, A. (1988) *Transformational Grammar: a First Course*, Cambridge University Press.

Wackernagel-Jolles, B. (1971) *Untersuchungen zur gesprochenen Sprache: Beobachtungen zur Verknüpfung spontanen Sprechens*, Göttingen: Alfred Kümmerle.

Zemskaja E.A. (1973) *Russkaja razgovornaja reč'*. Moscow: Nauka.

7

Grammaticalisation and social structure: non-standard conjunction-formation in East Anglian English

PETER TRUDGILL

In this chapter I focus on a particular form of grammaticalisation process, the development of non-standard conjunctions in the rural traditional dialects (see Trudgill, 1990) of East Anglia. The factual grammatical information provided here is derived from my own personal knowledge of the dialects in question. The examples I supply for illustrative purposes are taken from dialect texts (presented here in normalised orthography) written by East Anglian writers who have made self-conscious attempts to write in the local dialect. The advantages of using this sort of material are obvious. There are now relatively few speakers of the traditional dialects left, and obtaining texts from native speakers that are of sufficient length to permit the study of grammatical features would be an extremely time-consuming process. There are also, of course, very obvious dangers with using this type of material as data. Dialect writing may be unreliable as a representation of actual dialect speech, employing inaccurate stereotypes and hyperdialectisms (Trudgill, 1986). In this particular case, however, I have selected only texts which I am confident are accurate representations of the dialect and have been written by genuine native speakers of the dialects in question. My confidence comes from a lifetime of living in East Anglia, from having had many older relatives and acquaintances who spoke the traditional dialect and from twenty-five years of academic study of these dialects. The examples, that is, should not be regarded as data as such, but simply as illustrations which support and confirm my own understanding of how these dialects work.

Grammatical features typical of East Anglian dialects which should be noted are:

1 lack of present-tense third-person singular -s: e.g. *he know;*
2 third-person non-personal subject pronoun *that* vs. oblique *it*: e.g. *That's raining; Feed the cat – that's hungry;*
3 second-person imperatives with inverted verb: e.g. *Shut you up!*

1 Non-standard conjunctions in East Anglian dialects

The grammaticalisation process that we are interested in here involves the regrammaticalisation in the dialects in question of nouns, verbs, adverbs and adjuncts as conjunctions, with corresponding reduction in lexical-semantic content. The extent to which grammaticalisation is the result of pragmatic and cognitive (Heine, Claudi & Hünnemeyer, 1991), discourse (Givón, 1979), semantic (see Traugott, 1980), syntactic (see Li, 1975) or phonological (e.g. Comrie, 1980) processes is, of course, an open question. In this particular case, however, I would suggest that grammaticalisation has occurred because of phonological reduction and eventual omission of lexical material initially associated with the original nouns etc., and their consequent re-interpretation and recategorisation.

The way in which phonological reduction can have grammatical consequences can be illustrated by the following examples of grammaticalisation. The first case we consider involves the form *yet*, which can be seen to have a (non-standard) phrasal conjoining function equivalent to *nor* in East Anglian constructions such as:

(1) There weren't no laburnum, yet no lilac.
    'There wasn't any laburnum, or any lilac.'
(2) There wouldn't be nothing yet nobody to start things off again.
    'There wouldn't be anything or anybody to start things off again.'

The form *yet* has acquired or is at least acquiring conjunction status as a result, I would suggest, of the omission of material previously associated with it. That this recategorisation is indeed the result of reduction and omission can be confirmed by the occurrence in the dialect of alternative, synonymous and presumably less advanced examples of phrasal and clausal conjunction where *yet* is actually preceded by *nor*:

(3) That snew that there hard you couldn't see no hedges nor yet anything else.
    'It snowed so hard that you couldn't see any hedges or anything else.'
(4) Education is all very well but that won't keep a house clean, nor yet cook a dinner.
    'Education is all very well but it won't keep a house clean, or cook a dinner.'
(5) You can't curry-comb a tractor, nor yet you can't coax it.
    'You can't curry-comb a tractor, and you can't coax it either.'

We can assume that *yet* has begun to be used as a conjunction as a result of phonological reduction and elision processes which have led to the loss of *nor*; thus:

[nɔː jɪʔ > nəjɪʔ > njɪʔ > jɪʔ],

all of which forms can, crucially, still be heard in the dialect.

This argument is strengthened by other, apparently similar, cases of conjunction development: for example, a similar phenomenon can be observed in the use of *more* as a conjunction, or perhaps conjunct, equivalent to *nor* or *neither*. This is illustrated by examples such as:

(6) Aunt Agatha she say 'You don't know the difference.' Granfar say 'More don't you.'
    'Aunt Agatha says "You don't know the difference." Grandfather says "Neither do you."'

(7) The fruit and vegetables weren't as big as last year, more weren't the taters and onions.
    'The fruit and vegetables weren't as big as last year, and neither were the potatoes and onions.'

The amount of phonological material that we have to suppose has been diachronically deleted in this case is rather extensive. We have to look for an origin for forms such as *He don't like it, more don't I* in (non-standard) grammatical structures such as *He don't like it, and no more don't I*, which are still also current in the dialects. Here *no more* is equivalent to Standard English *neither* (with non-standard multiple negation, of course). It would be quite normal for *and no more* to be realised in lento speech in traditional East Anglian dialect as [ən nə mɔː] (see below), and so we can suppose a phonological development of the type:

[> ņnə mɔː > ņņ mɔː > ņn mɔː > nmɔː > mɔː].

Once again, each of these forms can still be heard in the dialect. The phonological reduction does, however, ultimately have a drastic effect on the grammatical categorisation of *more* itself.

A further interesting example is provided by the form *case*:

(8) We mustn't carry any, case they stop us,

which has clearly resulted from the deletion of *in*. We can suppose a phonological development of the type:

[ɪn > ɪŋ > əŋ > ŋ̩ > ŋ > ∅],

and indeed fuller forms with *in case* do still appear in the dialect, so that the regrammaticalisation of *case* is by no means complete.

In each of the above instances, grammaticalisation can be seen in our dialect texts as well as in the dialects themselves to be ongoing or incipient, since in addition to *yet, more, case* we also find instances of *nor yet, and no more, in case*. The form *time*, however, has progressed beyond this stage. *Time* is an East Anglian conjunction which demonstrates complete grammaticalisation with concomitant loss of lexical content. It is very well known to older East Anglians that in the traditional dialects of the county of Norfolk (at least), *time* operates in a way which is equivalent to the Standard English subordinating conjunction *while*, as the following examples show:

(9) Go you and have a good wash and a change, time I get tea ready.

(10) You remember what old Martha used to say, time she were alive.

Here we have had a change in grammatical status from noun to conjunction, with corresponding loss of semantic content. Our discussions of *yet*, *more* and *case* suggest that the origins of this development must lie in the phonological reduction and, ultimately, omission of preceding elements such as *during the* or *for the*, but this is no longer recoverable, since alternative uncontracted forms no longer occur. (We can observe in passing that Standard English *while* can also be a noun.)

2 The conjunction *do*

In order to support this phonological hypothesis concerning the nature of conjunction formation in rather more detail, we now turn to a discussion of perhaps the most interesting grammaticalised conjunction in the older East Anglian dialects, namely the use of the obviously originally verbal form *do* as a conjunction approximately equivalent to *otherwise*. (The *English Dialect Dictionary* shows that this was once found in the rural dialects of Norfolk, Suffolk, Cambridgeshire and northern Essex.) The most advanced East Anglian traditional dialect function of this form can be seen in the following example:

(11) You lot must have moved it, do I wouldn't have fell in.
'You lot must have moved it, or I wouldn't have fallen in.'

It is clear here that *do* is functioning as a non-verbal form with no semantic content connected to 'doing' anything, and with a function entirely equivalent to Standard English *otherwise*.

The interesting question is: how exactly did this change from verb to conjunction status come about? Our discussion above leads us to suppose that it is probably ultimately due to phonological developments involving the loss of phonetic material. Happily, this supposition is in part confirmed by (I would suggest) somewhat less advanced, less completely grammaticalised forms which can still be found in some parts of the dialect area. That is, many of the putative different stages of the diachronic development of *do* as a conjunction can be revealed by a synchronic examination of different texts. Consider, for example the following:

(12) Don't you take yours off, do you'll get rheumatism.
     'Don't take yours off, or you'll get rheumatism.'
(13) Don't you tell your Aunt Agatha about the coupons, do she'll mob me.
     'Don't tell your Aunt Agatha about the coupons, or she'll tell me off.'
(14) Don't you walk upstairs yet, do you'll whitewash the whole stair carpet.
(15) Don't sleep there, do you'll be a-laughing on the wrong side of your face.
(16) Don't you put her proper name in, do she'll pull both of us for libel.

And compare with the following examples where *don't* appears rather than *do*:

(17) Put that there antimacassar over her face, don't she'll give me nightmares.
     'Put that antimacassar over her face, or she'll give me nightmares.'
(18) You'd better turn that broom the other way up, don't you'll be breaking someone's neck.
     'You'd better turn that broom the other way up, otherwise you'll be breaking someone's neck.'
(19) Put your hand in front of your mouth when you cough, don't you'll have them germs all over the house.

I take it that these forms represent the earliest stage in the grammaticalisation process, that is, simple omission of lexical material. In examples (12)–(19), it is apparent that we can, as it were, supply for ourselves the missing lexical material: in each case, the insertion of *and/because if you* will supply forms transparent to speakers of all English dialects, such as:

Don't you take yours off, [because if you] do you'll get rheumatism.

(Forms with pronouns other than *you* also occur in the dialect. Note, however, that verbal or quasi-verbal *do/don't* occur with all persons, because of the lack of third-person singular -*s*.)

We can therefore assume that the initial impetus for this grammaticalisation was indeed the omission of phrases such as *because if Pronoun*. We can point to very considerable phonological reduction and eventual increasingly institutionalised omission of rather large amounts of lexical material as a causal mechanism. But we also have to note that a verbal-type negative/positive distinction between *do* and *don't* is still maintained in (12)–(19), together with the grammatical (tense) link between the verb in the first clause and the quasi-auxiliary verb form in the second.

The second stage in the grammaticalisation process shows a weakening of this link and is illustrated by the following:

> (20) Have the fox left? – No that ain't, do Bailey would've let them went.
> 'Has the fox left?' – 'No, it hasn't or Bailey would've let them [the hounds] go.'

which can be compared to forms with *don't* such as:

> (21) He pinned ahold of her other leg, don't she'd have been in.
> 'He pinned hold of her other leg, otherwise she'd have been in.'

Here a distinction between positive and negative quasi-verbal forms is still maintained, since we have a positive form *do* in the second clause corresponding to a negative form in the first clause in (20), and vice versa in (21). But some regrammaticalisation has clearly taken place, since the grammatical link with the tense of the verb in the first clause has been broken, that is, the originally present-tense forms *do* and *don't* are now being applied in past-tense contexts, as is illustrated by the fact that expansion to sentences with fully verbal *do* and *don't* is no longer possible – we would rather expect *had* and *hadn't*. Thus, the correct paraphrase for (20) is not *because if it does* but *because if it had*. The verbal history of the form is thus still apparent in the *do/don't* distinction, but the grammatical link in terms of tense to the verb of the preceding clause has been lost; and the semantic content is now almost entirely equivalent to Standard English *or, otherwise*.

The final stage in the grammaticalisation process is demonstrated in examples (22)–(24).

> (22) Sing out, do we shall be drownded!
> 'Call out, or we shall be drowned!'
> (23) Where's the ladder? – That stand in the stackyard, do that did do.
> 'Where's the ladder?' – 'It's standing in the stackyard, or at least it was.'
> (24) Keep you them elephants still, do we shan't half be in a mess.
> 'Keep those elephants still, or we won't half be in a mess.'

In these examples, as it happens, there still appears to be grammatical agreement between present tense forms in both clauses, but we see that the originally verbal negative/positive distinction has now been entirely lost, with *do* appearing where in earlier stages *don't* would have been expected, that is the *do/don't* distinction has been neutralised in favour of *do*.

Examples (11) and (25)–(29) show more clearly that the process has now gone to completion, in that there is no quasi-verbal grammatical link at all either to the tense or to the negative/positive polarity of the preceding clause:

> (25) That's a good job we came out of that there field, do he'd've had us!
> 'It's a good job we came out of that field, or he would have had us!'
> (26) She say that wouldn't have done to have done nothing to the boy, do I might have gone round for nothing, not knowing.
> 'She said that it wouldn't have done to do anything to the boy, or I might have gone round for nothing, not knowing.'
> (27) That was up to him to do his job proper, do there wouldn't be nothing yet nobody to start things off again.
> (28) We stabled them elephants right in the middle, do we should've capsized.
> (29) Things must be wonderful bad, do master would never have broke.
> 'Things must be extremely bad, or master would never have gone bust.'

The complete life-history of East Anglian conjunction *do* is thus:

> 1 phonological reduction and loss of lexical material of the type *because if Pronoun*;
> 2 loss of tense marking of *do* and *don't*;
> 3 loss of negative/positive polarity and neutralisation in favour of *do*.

3 The role of social networks

We have thus seen that, compared to Standard English, the traditional dialects of this rural area of eastern England demonstrate ongoing or completed grammaticalisation of no fewer than five different forms as conjunctions. This kind of process is, of course, not unique to this dialect, but the developments do appear to have been very extensive. This raises the question of whether the degree to which this process has taken place in this dialect is in some way unusual, and, if so, whether we can explain why it has happened to the extent that it has.

In an attempt to answer this question, we can first of all point to the now widely accepted fact that social-network structure can have a powerful effect on linguistic change. In particular, the work of James Milroy (1982) and Lesley Milroy (1987) in Belfast has shown that dense, multiplex social networks with strong ties have the effect of reducing inter-individual linguistic variation, and of accelerating ongoing linguistic changes. In subsequent work (Milroy & Milroy, 1985), they have also argued that *weak* ties play an important role in the diffusion of innovations.

Considering the work of Milroy and Milroy, as well as of others who have produced insights through a consideration of the importance of social networks (e.g. Bortoni-Ricardo, 1985), I have suggested elsewhere (Trudgill, 1992) that social-network structure may have an effect not only on *rate* of linguistic change, but also on *type* of linguistic change. For example, I have proposed that morphological simplification may be more typical of fluid, high-contact, more open societal types, while retention or even increase in morphological complexity may be more associated with (usually small) more tightly knit communities. This is what is suggested by a comparison of, for example, the morphological structures of Danish and Faroese. I have also cited evidence that phonological systems may vary as between high- and low-contact dialects. The indications are that imperfect dialect- and language-learning by post-adolescents leads to simplification, while tight social-network structure helps the maintenance of complex norms from generation to generation. As far as linguistic change is concerned, I have also suggested (Trudgill, forthcoming) that small, dense network-type communities may similarly be relatively more able to sustain and enforce 'unusual' sound changes.

In this chapter, however, I have concentrated on a type of change that appears to have to do with the amounts of linguistic *information* that are variously required in different types of community. We can note, for example, the work of Bernstein (1971), who argued that speakers from tightly knit working-class communities who were not accustomed to communicating with outsiders were more likely to use 'restricted code', that is, a form of discourse which was less explicit and took a higher degree of shared information for granted. The explanation is obviously that, in the experience of these speakers, taking large amounts of shared information for granted has been the norm which they have become used to.

4 Fast-speech phenomena

Similarly, it may well be the case that certain sorts of phonological change are more typical of some sorts of communities than others for the same kind of reason. For example, if we consider fast-speech phenomena such as assimilation and elision, we can suggest the following. Efficient communication is sometimes said to result from achieving an equilibrium between the needs of the speaker and the needs of the listener (see Martinet, 1962). The speaker wants to communicate quickly or at least with little effort, while the listener needs enough information to process the message accurately. In phonological terms, we can say, with Dressler (1984), that phonological processes 'serve the communicative function of language by serving their proper functions: pronounceability and perceptibility' but that 'the goals of better perception and better articulation often conflict with each other'. In more open societies, I would like to suggest, this equilibrium is disturbed, and this conflict is complicated by the needs of the outsider as listener. Fast-speech phenomena make things easier for the native speaker: the same message can be got across more quickly and with less articulatory effort. However, crucially, they also make life much more difficult for outsiders, who do not share information with insiders, as well as for non-native speakers, who lack close familiarity with the particular linguistic system, by reducing the amount of phonetic information available for processing.

One of the developments which often occurs in linguistic change is that fast-speech phenomena become institutionalised, that is, they become slow-speech phenomena as well (*pace* Hock (1986: 49), who claims that 'by and large, fast speech phenomena do not seem to have any lasting effect on linguistic change'). As Dressler (1984: 35) says: 'A typical scenario of diachronic change consists in the generalisation of assimilatory processes which are first limited to casual speech into more and more formal speech situations until they become obligatory processes.' If it is true that outsiders have problems with such processes, then we would expect this institutionalisation to occur less often in more fluid, open societies in which many social outsiders are participating in verbal interactions and where languages and dialects may be being employed by speakers for whom they are not the mother-tongue.

Fast-speech phenomena are thus more likely to occur, and to become institutionalised, in small, tightly knit, perhaps isolated communities which have large amounts of shared information in common and where individual personalities are known to all, than in larger communities or communities with looser network ties where more phonetic information may be required. How tightly knit a community is in network terms may therefore have an influence on the phonetics of its language or dialect. There are clear similarities between the ultimately semantic point made by Bernstein and the phonological point being made here. In both cases we are dealing with the same principle, namely that listeners who are operating in a familiar environment in interaction with speakers whose language or dialect they are familiar with, with whom they are well acquainted, with whom they interact frequently and with whom they share a large fund of common knowledge, can make do with less phonetic and semantic information than listeners who are less familiar with the situation, the topic and the other interlocutors.

I now want to suggest that this principle may be operative not only in influencing phonological change, but also in influencing certain types of grammatical change. It may be that the type of grammaticalisation process that we have noted in the traditional dialects of rural East Anglia may be more typical of smaller, relatively isolated communities with tight social-network structures than of other sorts of communities. It is presumably not a coincidence that the main mechanism behind this grammaticalisation process seems to be phonological in origin, and that it has to do with phonological reduction of a type which is typically associated with fast speech. There is a connection, that is, with the extent to which fast speech processes become institutionalised, as discussed above.

5 East Anglian phonology

It is also important that the phonology of the traditional East Anglian dialects is characterised by a number of features which can generally be labelled reduction and which would seem to be highly relevant:

1 There is a very marked tendency to reduction and deletion of unstressed vowels (see Trudgill, 1974): for example, the only vowel permitted in word-final unstressed position is /ə/. Thus, not only are *hammer, sooner,* etc. /hæmə, sʉːnə/ as expected in non-rhotic varieties, and *window, barrow,* etc. /wɪndə, bærə/, as in many other varieties, but also *money, city, very,* etc. are /mʌnə, sɪtə, wɛrə/, etc.

2 In other phonological contexts reduction to /ə/ occurs where many other varieties of English have unstressed /ɪ/: *David* [dɛːvəʔ]; *village* [wɪləj]; *motorist* [mʊʔəɹəst].

3 Unstressed /ə/ is also highly susceptible to deletion, as in *forty-three* [fɔːʔːθrii]; *very good* [wɛɹgʊd]; *at home* [tʊm].

4 And even stressed vowels may be deleted if they do not bear primary sentence stress: *Have you got any money?* [hæ jə gɑʔ nə mʌnə]?

It is quite possible that this tendency to reduction and loss of unstressed material may well be a characteristic more typical of non-standard than of standard varieties.

6 Conclusion

I do not of course want to claim that the processes which have led to the widespread development of new conjunctions in traditional East Anglian dialects are confined to such village dialects; clearly they are not. Rather, I want simply to argue that they are very probably much more *common* in small, rural communities than they are in the more koinéised non-standard varieties of urban areas, or in standardised varieties. The suggestion is that the fact that this sort of development appears to be so productive in these particular dialects is due to the greater tendency to phonological reduction that is characteristic of the dialects of those communities which have dense, multiplex social networks and which also have relatively few contacts with other, outside communities. It is significant that the new conjunctions under discussion in this chapter are much more typical of the older East Anglian dialects exemplified here, and that many of them are no longer to be found in the speech of younger, urban, more mobile speakers in the geographical area in question.

NOTES

I would like to thank Andrew Radford for comments on an earlier draft of this chapter; and John Lyons, without whom I would never have had the opportunity to study East Anglian or any other dialects.

SOURCES

Benham, C.E. *Essex Ballads*, Colchester: Benham Newspapers, 1895; reissued 1960.
Claxton, A.O.D. *The Suffolk Dialect of the Twentieth Century*, Woodbridge: Boydell Press, 1954; 3rd edn 1968.
Cooper, E.R. *Mardles from Suffolk*, Newbury: Countryside Books, 1932; reissued 1984.
Grapes, S. *The Boy John Letters*, Norwich: Wensum Books, 1958; reissued 1974.
Mardle, J. (E. Fowler) *Broad Norfolk*, Norwich: Wensum Books, 1973.
Riches, C. *Orl Bewtiful and New*, Norwich: F. Crowe, 1978.
West, H.M. *East Anglian Tales*, Newbury: Countryside Books, 1983.
The East Anglian and His Humour, Ipswich: Anglian, 1966.

REFERENCES

Bernstein, B. (1971) *Class, Codes and Control*, vol. I, London: Routledge.
Bortoni-Ricardo, S. (1985) *The Urbanisation of Rural Dialect Speakers*, Cambridge University Press.
Comrie, B. (1980) Morphology and word order reconstruction: problems and prospects. In J. Fisiak (ed.), *Historical Morphology*, The Hague: Mouton, 83–96.
Dressler, W. (1984) Explaining natural phonology. *Phonology Yearbook* 1: 29–51.
Givón, T. (1979) *On Understanding Grammar*, New York: Academic Press.

Heine, B., U. Claudi & F. Hünnemeyer (1991) *Grammaticalization: a Conceptual Framework*, University of Chicago Press.

Hock, H.H. (1986) *Principles of Historical Linguistics*, Berlin: Mouton de Gruyter.

Li, C.N. (ed.) (1975) *Word Order and Word Order Change*, Austin: University of Texas Press.

Martinet, A. (1962) *A Functional View of Language*, Oxford University Press.

Milroy, J. (1982) Probing under the tip of the iceberg: phonological normalisation and the shape of speech communities. In S. Romaine (ed.) *Sociolinguistic Variation in Speech Communities*, London: Arnold, 32–48.

Milroy, J. & L. Milroy (1985) Linguistic change, social network and speaker innovation. *Journal of Linguistics* 21: 339–84.

Milroy, L. (1987) *Language and Social Networks*, 2nd edn, Oxford: Blackwell.

Traugott, E. (1980) Meaning-change in the development of grammatical markers. *Language Science* 2: 44–61.

Trudgill, P. (1974) *The Social Differentiation of English in Norwich*, Cambridge University Press.

(1986) *Dialects in Contact*, Oxford: Blackwell.

(1990) *The Dialects of England*, Oxford: Blackwell.

(1992) Dialect typology and social structure. In E.H. Jahr (ed.) *Language Contact: Theoretical and Empirical Studies*, Berlin: Mouton de Gruyter.

(forthcoming) Dialect typology: isolation, social network and phonological structure. In G. Guy (ed.) *Language Variation and Language Change: Papers in Honour of William Labov*. Amsterdam: Benjamins.

8

German Perfekt and Präteritum: speculations on meaning and interpretation

BERNARD COMRIE

1 Introduction

In comparison with English, German appears at first sight to have a very simple tense–aspect system, certainly if we restrict the terms tense and aspect to grammatical categories of the languages, whether expressed by synthetic or periphrastic means. German has two simple forms, the Present (as in *ich liebe* 'I love') and a simple past form, which I will henceforth, following German usage, call the Präteritum (as in *ich liebte* 'I loved'). In addition, there is a compound past form, as in *ich habe geliebt* 'I have loved', which I will henceforth, following German usage, refer to as the Perfekt. Other periphrastic forms include the Pluperfect (as in *ich hatte geliebt* 'I had loved'), the Future (as in *ich werde lieben* 'I shall love') and the Future Perfect (in German conventionally called the Futur II, as in *ich werde geliebt haben* 'I will have loved'), although, as in many other languages, the question arises whether the Future and Future Perfect are more properly to be classified as tenses or moods. Some varieties of German also have Double Perfect and Double Pluperfect periphrastic forms, as in *ich habe geliebt gehabt* and *ich hatte geliebt gehabt*; English has no corresponding forms. The focus of interest in this article will be the distinction between the Perfekt and the Präteritum, the two major verb forms used with past time reference.

In some varieties of German, the system is even simpler, through loss of the Präteritum, leaving the Perfekt as the only form with past time reference as part of its basic meaning. This loss of the Präteritum is particularly characteristic of the Upper German dialects and local varieties close to the standard language based on these dialects. In some such varieties the Präteritum has been lost completely. In others it may survive in a handful of verbs, for instance in the modal verbs 'to be'. However, in other varieties of German, including the current northern-based standard of Germany itself, both the Perfekt and the Präteritum are used, and the question arises of the distinction between them. This article is intended as a partial answer to this question. It is also, let me be the first to admit, very speculative; I believe that it points towards a possible approach for resolving the problem of the Perfekt/Präteritum opposition, although much more empirical and analytical work would be needed in order to justify the approach.

One major characteristic of the approach is careful delimitation of the contribution of semantics and of pragmatics to the overall interpretation of a linguistic form. In most previous approaches to the Perfekt/Präteritum opposition (Bamberg (1990) is a notable exception), the general line of analysis has been to isolate the interpretations that the two forms can have, in different contexts (for instance, with verbs of different aktionsarten), to present these interpretations as the informal analysis, perhaps proceeding to a further stage of formalising these interpretations. This line of analysis, first initiated in breadth for the German tense–aspect system by Wunderlich (1970), is continued, for instance, in Ehrich (1992), an impressive work that combines extensive empirical material with sophisticated semantic analysis. This line of analysis, moreover, tends to lead to analyses where the same verbal form is given different analyses depending on particular contexts. While I do not deny that in certain circumstances it may be necessary to recognise that a single morphological category has more than one meaning, general considerations of economy suggest that such analyses should be dispreferred to those that provide a single semantic characterisation, other things being equal. In this paper, therefore, I try to find a single characterisation that covers all, or at least as wide a range as possible, of the differences between the Perfekt and the Präteritum.

An analogy from my suggestions concerning future time in German (Comrie, 1989: 57) may clarify my position. Previous analyses had suggested a generalisation along the lines that the German Present, as in *ich bin in Berlin*, literally 'I am in Berlin', can have future time reference if there is a future time adverbial, but that otherwise the Present receives present time reference, and future time reference must be indicated explicitly, for instance by the auxiliary verb *werden*. This means that the German Present has different meanings dependent on context: present time reference in the absence of a future time adverbial, future time reference in the presence of a time adverbial. In Comrie (1989) I suggested that by distinguishing between the semantic and the pragmatic contributions to the overall interpretation of the German Present, a single meaning can be posited, with different contexts having different effects on the final interpretation. The overall meaning posited for the German Present is non-past time reference. In combination with a future time adverbial, this clearly gives future time reference, as the only interpretation that is compatible both with the tense of the verb and with the meaning of the time adverbial. The problem is why the Present receives present time reference, to the virtual exclusion of future time reference, in the absence of such a time adverbial. General considerations of relevance play a role here: the addressee needs to interpret an utterance in such a way that it makes sense relevant to the given context. If no future time context is given, then only the ever-present 'here and now', in particular the present moment, is available and relevant, and considerations of relevance force the addressee to tie the time reference to the present. Thus, strictly speaking, *ich bin in Berlin* does not have only present time reference; rather, it has the potential for both present and future time reference, but in the absence of a contextual indicator licensing future time reference it will be interpreted by default as having present time reference.

This approach means that great care must be taken in distinguishing semantic and pragmatic contributions to overall interpretation. In particular, native-speaker judgments (and this is likely to apply as much to the judgments of native-speaker linguists) are initially directed towards the interpretation, and it requires subtle analysis to disentangle the different contributions. However, once this is done, further advantages accrue. In the example of the German Present with future time reference, for instance, we can readily account for the following facts. First, it is not absolutely necessary for a future time adverbial to be present, so long as the broader context (for instance, preceding utterances) makes the context of future time reference available. Secondly, with certain aspectual interpretations, for instance of a single action, strict present-time interpretation is unlikely, and here one gets future time reference even in the absence of a future time adverbial, as in example (1):

(1) Also gut, ich gehe hin und schmeiße es ins Feuer.
    'All right, I will go and throw it in the fire.'

If we exclude the implausible possibility that the speaker is giving a running commentary on his actions, and likewise that the reference is to a habitual action, then any kind of present time reference is excluded, leaving future time reference as the only possibility, as indicated in the English translation. Thus, by combining relatively general semantic representations and pragmatic principles in this way we arrive at a simple analysis that accounts for the apparently bewildering effects of different time adverbials, aktionsarten, etc. More generally: the effect of context is to select among interpretations allowed by the semantics, not to change the semantic representation.

2 Perfekt and Präteritum: a distinction

The difference between the Perfekt and the Präteritum in German is clearly different from that between the Perfect and Simple Past in English, despite the etymological identity or near-identity of the two pairs. One characteristic of the English distinction is that the Perfect requires continuing relevance of the past situation to the present moment, while the Simple Past does not have any such requirement. In German, the Perfekt can be used in examples that have no continuing present relevance, as in examples (2) (Drosdowski, 1984: 150) and (3) (Ehrich, 1992):

> (2) Kolumbus hat Amerika entdeckt.
> 'Columbus discovered (literally: has discovered) America.'
> (3) Mozart hat Klavier gespielt.
> 'Mozart played (literally: has played) the piano.'

Since it is not my aim here to give a full characterisation of the difference between the Perfect and the Simple Past in English, I will discuss English at a relatively informal level, in particular bearing in mind that the generalisations given here may ultimately turn out to represent an intermediate stage of analysis, subsumable under some more general principle. One further caveat is relevant: in speaking of 'continuing relevance', I am throughout referring to the speaker's indication that there is or is not continuing relevance. Even assuming that objective continuing relevance can be defined, what is important for linguistic purposes is not this objective relevance, but rather the speaker's assessment of whether an earlier situation has continuing relevance at a later time point.

In English in general, the Perfect expresses continuous relevance, while the Simple Past expresses absence of continuing relevance.[1] It follows from this that the Perfect and Simple Past are not in general substitutable for one another, without clearly changing the speaker's communicative intent. However, there are some instances where, even in the presence of the factor continuing relevance, English grammar requires the Simple Past, most noticeably with explicit time adverbials referring to a point of time in the past, as in (4):

> (4) Have you seen Marty? – I saw him an hour ago.

Overall then, in English the Perfect requires present relevance, while the Simple Past usually disallows present relevance, but under certain circumstances is neutral with respect to present relevance.

In German, on the other hand, the Perfekt neither requires nor disallows present relevance. This suggests that we might at least try to characterise the German Präteritum by completing the square: the German Präteritum denotes a past situation and explicitly instructs the addressee not to seek to relate it through continuing relevance to the present moment. The Perfekt, by contrast, is neutral with respect to continuing relevance, and is thus the only form appropriate where the speaker does not wish to exclude continuing relevance. The body of this paper will be devoted to exploring some consequences of this simple characterisation of the semantics of the Präteritum versus Perfekt opposition, especially the interaction of this quite general semantics with pragmatic factors.

Before proceeding to detailed consideration of examples, some preliminary caveats are in order. Strictly speaking, all that the following will indicate is that lack of continuing relevance is one factor distinguishing Präteritum from Perfekt. It is conceivable that there may be other additional factors. Indeed, I will argue below that the two are also distinguished by the nature of the reference point, which is freer in the case of the Perfekt than in the case of the Präteritum. In addition, there are some sets of examples where the analysis advocated in this article either does not make correct predictions or seems to require a certain amount of legerdemain to fit in with the observed facts. There thus remains plenty of scope for future work, hopefully in elaborating the approach put forward here, though possibly in elaborating alternatives.

Let us examine, in the light of this hypothesis, some of the characteristic examples of distinctions in use between the Perfekt and the Präteritum as they appear in some of the earlier literature. In most instances, what is of significance is the impossibility of substituting the Präteritum for the Perfekt.

The most obvious case where the Perfekt cannot be replaced by the Präteritum is where the speaker's communicative intention is to indicate continuing relevance. Since German, on the analysis advanced here, has no specific form that explicitly indicates continuing relevance, the best the speaker can do, in terms of verb forms, is to use that form that does not exclude present relevance, namely the Perfekt. In an example like (5), for instance, spoken as a reason for not going skiing, only the Perfekt is appropriate:

(5) Ich habe mein Bein gebrochen.
    'I have broken my leg.'

To replace the Perfekt *habe ... gebrochen* with the Präteritum *brach* would make the sentence quite inappropriate for its intended communicative function.

Part of the meaning of the Präteritum is reference to a time preceding the present moment: it is, in the strict sense, an (absolute) past tense. By contrast, part of the meaning of the Perfekt is reference to a time preceding a non-past reference point, which need not necessarily be the present moment but may also be a point of time in the future. From this it follows that the Perfekt, but not the Präteritum, may be used for situations anterior to a reference point in the future, as in (6) (Drosdowski, 1984: 150, 151):

(6) Wirklich gesiegt haben wir nur, wenn die Eingeborenen den Sinn der Schutzgebiete einsehen.
'We will only really have won when the indigenous people understand the purpose of the [nature] reserves.'

Substitution of Präteritum *siegten* for Perfekt *gesiegt haben* (with the past participle preceding the auxiliary because the past participle is fronted for pragmatic prominence) produces nonsense. Thus, this slight difference in reference points needs to be added to the overall characterisation of the Perfekt/Präteritum distinction.

Example (5) referred to a specific occasion in the present. As noted by Drosdowski (1984: 151), the same generalisation applies when the Present tense is used with generic time reference, as in (7), where the Perfekt *verlassen hat* cannot be replaced by the Präteritum *verließ*:

(7) Wenn der Pfeil die Sehne des Bogens verlassen hat, so fliegt er seine Bahn.
'When/if the arrow has left the string of the bow, it flies its path.'

If one were to reformulate this sentence referring to a single event, as in (8), then still only the Perfekt would be possible, to the exclusion of the Präteritum:

(8) Da der Pfeil die Sehne des Bogens verlassen hat, fliegt er seine Bahn.
'Since the arrow has left the string of the bow, it is flying its path.'

In this single-event sentence, it is clear that the arrow's having left the bow has continuing relevance to the arrow's flying along its path. The same is true for each individual occurrence of the generic, so that if one takes the generic as being an operator with, in this interpretation of the sentence, scope over the whole sentence, then the Perfekt is required in order not to exclude continuing relevance in (8) just as much as in (7).[2]

One of the examples used by Ehrich (1992) to illustrate the distinction between Perfekt and Präteritum can also be used as an illustration here, especially as the other member of the pair will be cited below. In (9), the Perfekt *ist . . . geworden* cannot be replaced by the Präteritum *wurde* without changing the interpretation:

(9) Nach dem zweiten Weltkrieg ist Kleve immer mehr zu einer Klinkerstadt
geworden.
'Since the Second World War Kleve has become more and more a city of
clinker brick.'

The context of this sentence is a discussion of the change of Kleve from
being a city of white buildings to being a city of buildings constructed out of
clinker brick, a change that took hold increasingly after the Second World
War and whose result – the fact that Kleve is now essentially a city of clinker
brick – still holds. Clearly, it is crucial that the transformation undergone
by Kleve has led to the results currently visible, so that the Präteritum,
telling the addressee not to link the transformation to the present, would be
incoherent.

While the account advocated here provides an explanation of a range of
cases where the Perfekt cannot be replaced by the Präteritum, it can also go
at least some way towards accounting for preferences in the distribution of
Perfekt and Präteritum in cases where, in principle, both are possible. In his
study of the use of Perfekt and Präteritum in German news broadcasts,
Bamberg (1990) notes a tendency not to use the Präteritum in the first
sentence of a report, but rather to use the Perfekt if reference is to a past
event, as in example (10) (Bamberg, 1990: 274):

(10) Der ehemalige Bürgermeister von Florenz, Lando Conti, ist heute abend
ermordet worden. Nach Angaben der Polizei wurde er in den Bergen
außerhalb der Stadt aus einem Auto heraus von zwei Männern
erschossen.
'The former mayor of Florence, Lando Conti, was (literally: has been)
murdered this evening. According to the police, he was shot from a car by
two men in the mountains outside the city.'

In (10), the first sentence has a Perfekt verb form *ist . . . ermordet worden*,
literally 'has been murdered', while the second, *wurde erschossen* 'was shot',
is in the Präteritum. My impression is that in English, the Simple Past is
most natural in both clauses, as in the free translation given above. Since the
Präteritum specifically instructs the addressee not to relate the situation to
the present moment, it is at least somewhat inappropriate for an 'out-of-
the-blue' announcement in a news broadcast, which, by definition, is
providing its audience with recent world, national or local events of current
relevance. But once the story is introduced by the first Perfekt, subsequent
events can be linked to that first event, and do not need to be linked to the
present moment. Actually, the recentness of the events described, though
clearly true of example (10), is probably not a necessary feature of this

sequence of Perfekt followed by Präteritum. In fact, the most natural temporal reference point to take in interpreting the second sentence in (10) is the event described by the first sentence in (10), making the dissociative function of the Imperfekt (i.e. the instruction not to attempt to forge a link of continuing relevance with the present moment) particularly appropriate.

One finds something similar even with the narration of events from the more distant past, as in example (11) (Drosdowski, 1984: 151); Charles V reigned as Emperor from 1519 to 1556:

> (11) Die Sorge um das Schicksal seiner Völker hat Kaiser Karl V. in mancher Nacht des Schlafes geraubt. Er pflegte dann, in seine Pelze gehüllt, am Kamin zu sitzen. Die Sorge, in ihren sekulären Lumpen, saß ihm gegenüber, bis die Nacht vorüber war – zwei Majestäten, die miteinander Geschäfte hatten.
> 'Worry about the fate of his peoples robbed Emperor Charles V of sleep on many a night. He was accustomed then, wrapped in his furs, to sit by the fireside. Care, in its secular rags, sat opposite him till the night was over – two majesties who had business with one another.'

In this example, the behaviour of Charles V is first presented in the Perfekt (*hat ... geraubt*), a possibility allowed by the essentially unmarked nature of the Perfekt relative to the Präteritum in German; note that English would here require the Simple Past. Thereafter, however, it is more plausible for the addressee to be led to link later events to the preceding event, and the use of the Präteritum (*pflegte, saß*) indeed leads the addressee in this direction, with its explicit dissociation from the present moment. This, of course, leads to the oft-noted more general conclusion that the Präteritum is the basic tense in standard written German for narration (Drosdowski 1984: 150).

More testing for accounts of the difference between the Perfekt and the Präteritum are those instances where only the Präteritum is possible, or where it is at least strongly preferred. If the Präteritum specifically instructs the addressee not to look for a link to the present, while the Perfekt is neutral in this respect, then one might predict that the Präteritum would always be replaceable by the Perfekt. It is here, however, that pragmatics really comes to the fore. In particular, the relevance factor becomes crucial, that is the requirement on the part of the addressee that what is heard must be relatable to the context, which in the absence of any independently given context means must be relatable to the here-and-now. Thus, while the Perfekt in its meaning does not require a link to be established to the present moment, if the situation to which it refers cannot otherwise be made relevant to some other time frame, then pragmatics will require relevance to be established to the present moment. The example used by Ehrich (1992) to parallel (9), namely (12), provides a good illustration:

> (12) Am 30. September 1956 übernahm Ehepaar Klören das Hotel. Sie brachten das Gebäude auf den neuesten Stand und gaben ihm eine elegante Note.
> 'On 30 September 1956 Mr and Mrs Klören took over the hotel. They completely modernized the building and gave it an elegant tone.'

Why the Präteritum (*übernahm, brachten, gaben*) in this example? It emerges from the subsequent discussion that, despite all the efforts of the Klören family, the hotel in question ceased to exist in 1971. The Perfekt, in a variety of German where the Präteritum is still a vital category, would tend to suggest that the hotel still exists, not because this is part of the meaning of the Perfekt, but because in the absence of any indication to the contrary this interpretation is suggested pragmatically by the relevance factor ('make things relevant to the here-and-now'). Note that in English the only possibility is the Simple Past, so that there is no comparable possibility of expressing the contrast expressed by the German Präteritum versus Perfekt; and indeed the English translation given above reads very much as if it were the introduction to a continuing success story, rather than one leading up to the disappearance of the hotel.

We may now return to one of the apparently simplest examples treated above, namely (3), repeated here as (13):

> (13) Mozart hat Klavier gespielt.
> 'Mozart played (literally: has played) the piano.'

In this example, there is surely no continuing relevance – while Mozart's compositions may be of continuing relevance, the fact that he played the piano hardly is. And as we would expect, given this, the Präteritum is also possible in German, as in (14):

> (14) Mozart spielte Klavier.

But if the Perfekt is used in (13), and if we assume that there is no indication that the speaker is not to derive an interpretation of continuing relevance, then surely the analysis advocated here would suggest that the speaker will derive such an interpretation. Here it is necessary to bear in mind that while pragmatic principles are of great generality, the empirical facts that the addressee may bring to bear (and that the speaker may expect the addressee to bring to bear) can be quite multifarious. Given that Mozart is a well-known composer, and that it is widely known that he died a long time ago (actually, in 1791), the addressee is unlikely even to attempt to draw any interpretation of continuing relevance, because factual information excludes the plausibility of such an interpretation. Note that, by contrast, if someone were to overhear (15), with no indication of who Hans is, then the most likely reaction would be something like 'but I haven't heard anyone playing the piano':

(15) Hans hat Klavier gespielt.

3 Further problems

I believe that the distinction outlined in section 2 provides an explanatory basis for a wide range of differences that have been observed in the behaviour of the Perfekt and the Präteritum in German. However, there are some further uses that do not fall so obviously under this distinction, and in this section I will make some attempt to show how they might be brought under the general account.

One use of the Präteritum, to the exclusion of the Perfekt, that has been noted in many accounts as pragmatically conditioned is the following. Imagine that a waiter has taken orders from a table, including an order for goulash soup. On returning to the table with the dishes, he wishes to ascertain which customer ordered the goulash soup. One possible way of asking this in German is as in (16):

(16) Wer bekam die Gulaschsuppe?
      'Who ordered (literally: received) the goulash soup?'

The lexical meaning of the verb *bekommen*, Präteritum *bekam*, is clearly 'receive', so that the sentence literally says, 'Who received the goulash soup?', although this is not, of course, a possible translation into English, where it would imply that the goulash soup has already been received. If one replaces the Präteritum *bekam* by the Perfekt *hat . . . bekommen* in German, this suggests that the soup has already been received, so the sentence is no longer appropriate to its context. This is thus one of the few instances where the Präteritum absolutely cannot be replaced by the Perfekt. Actually, this is part of a broader phenomenon, since we find the same lack of substitutability in an example like (17), with the interpretation 'Who was going to travel to Leipzig?'

(17) Wer fuhr nach Leipzig?
      'Who was travelling to Leipzig?'

Note that English here also uses the Past rather than the Perfect, though in the Progressive aspect – the non-Progressive would suggest that this was a question of who actually did travel to Leipzig, as would replacement of the Präteritum *fuhr* by the Perfekt *ist . . . gefahren* in German.

To some extent, this use of a past tense is idiomatic in both languages: while reference is to the past, namely to a past propensity (as is made clear in the English version with *was going to travel*), the action of travelling itself is clearly not located in the past, certainly not at the past moment to which the sentence refers.[3] This idiomaticity – namely, interpretation of a verb form to indicate propensity to carry out the action denoted by that verb, rather than the action itself – must, I assume, be stated explicitly, and does not follow from general properties of the verb form. But taking the idiomaticity for granted, why is it the Präteritum rather than the Perfekt that is judged appropriate to carry this idiomatic meaning? The crucial point seems to be that this idiom necessarily dissociates the reference time of the sentence (which, let it be emphasised once again, is the time of the propensity, not of the possibly resulting action), that is, reference is exclusively to a past propensity irrespective of its subsequent results. The Präteritum is compatible with this because it explicitly instructs the addressee not to establish continuing relevance; the Perfekt, by not excluding the possibility of continuing relevance, would tend to suggest this interpretation pragmatically because of the general propensity to interpret utterances as being relevant to the here-and-now.

In some cases, the difference between the Perfekt and the Präteritum is apparently aspectual, with the Präteritum receiving a completive interpretation, the Perfekt a non-progressive interpretation, as in the contrast between (18) and (19):

    (18) Hans aß schon.
           'Hans was already eating (literally: already ate).'
    (19) Hans hat schon gegessen.
           'Hans has already eaten.'

These are not, however, the only interpretations that can be assigned, especially in richer contexts. Both the Präteritum and the Perfekt with *schon* 'already' can, for instance, be assigned a habitual interpretation. However, the difference between types (18) and (19) is none the less striking. Can the analysis advocated in this article account for the distinction? To some extent, the answer is in the affirmative. Let us take (19) with the Perfekt first. This sentence gives no contextual indication of a reference point other than the present moment, therefore pragmatically, from the relevance constraint, the present moment is selected as the reference point. The meaning of *schon* 'already' is, roughly, 'by a specified time', and in the absence of any other indication of time the only time point available to be the specified time is the present moment. The Perfekt denotes a situation holding before the reference point, that is, in this case, the present moment, so the only interpretation consistent with all this is that Hans' eating has taken place by the present moment. With respect to (18), note first of all that the sentence is odd out of context, requiring some contextual indication of when Hans was doing the eating, and of the 'specified time' required by the meaning of *schon*. Given the meaning component of the Präteritum that instructs the speaker not to relate the situation to the present moment, the present moment is explicitly made unavailable as a reference point. Let us suppose that (18) occurred immediately after the sentence *Es war fünf Uhr* 'It was five o'clock'. Then 'at five o'clock' provides both the reference point necessary for the interpretation of *schon* (that is, 'by five o'clock'), and the reference point necessary for anchoring the Präteritum (that is, his eating took place at, or at least encompassed, five o'clock). Given that the same reference point anchors both *schon* and the Präteritum, the only possible interpretation is that the two are simultaneous, that is, that his eating took place at five o'clock, or, given that his eating was probably not a momentary affair, that his eating was taking place at five o'clock.

Whether this account can be expanded to all instances of aspect-like values of the Perfekt/Präteritum distinction remains to be seen. At the moment, for instance, I am not sure how to account for the apparently similar distinction between sentences like (20) and (21), where (21), but not (20), seems to allow a progressive interpretation:

(20) Als Hans zurückkam, haben wir gegessen.
'When Hans came back, we ate.'
(21) Als Hans zurückkam, aßen wir.
'When Hans came back, we ate/were eating.'

One problem in investigating examples of this kind is unravelling judgments strictly within a system that distinguishes Perfekt from Präteritum from those within systems that allow greater incursion of the Perfekt into the realm of the Präteritum. With just a slight change in lexical content, we find (22), where the Perfekt seems not to exclude a progressive interpretation, so clearly a number of factors are potentially involved, and it is not the case that the Perfekt invariably excludes a progressive interpretation:

(22) Als Hans zurückkam, haben wir geschlafen.
'When Hans came back, we slept/were sleeping.'

4 Conclusions

At first sight, the use of the Perfekt and Präteritum in those varieties of German that maintain the distinction involves a number of disparate distinguishing features. I have tried to show that at least some order can be brought to this apparent ebullience by adopting an analysis that makes a clear distinction between semantics and pragmatics. The meaning of the Präteritum, as given by the semantics, is past time reference with an instruction to the addressee not to relate the situation as relevant to a non-past reference point. The meaning of the Perfekt is time reference before a non-past reference point, with no indication to the addressee whether or not the situation is relevant to the reference point. All the rest follows, or at least should follow, from pragmatics. In particular, while the Perfekt does not require establishment of a relation between the situation and the reference point, pragmatic considerations of relevance give the Perfekt a default interpretation whereby the situation it denotes is relevant to the present moment. This default interpretation can, however, be suspended by the broader context. While a number of problems remain that are not directly addressed by this analysis, I feel that it is at least deserving of further consideration, especially in relation to other approaches that retreat ever further into the particularities of specific contexts.

NOTES

I am grateful to Veronika Ehrich for discussions on the German past tenses and for making her work available to me before its publication.

1 This does not, of course, refer to those varieties, like some varieties of colloquial American English, which use the Simple Past in sentences like *Did you eat already?*, where other varieties would require *Have you eaten already?*

2 The Präteritum is probably also excluded by the requirement that its reference point be the present moment, whereas in example (7) the reference point is each relevant occasion on which the arrow flies its path. However, one could also interpret the use of the Present in (7) as taking a single present situation and using it to stand for a class of situations, in which case the Präteritum might not be excluded on this particular ground.

3 This idiomatic interpretation does not, of course, exclude the possibility of the travel having been completed in the past, but only if subsequent to the time to which sentence (17) refers – just as in (16) it is possible, and indeed in such a context highly likely, that the person who was going to receive the goulash soup

will indeed receive it. Thus possible continuations of (17) might specify that someone did indeed travel to Leipzig, or that someone will indeed still travel to Leipzig, but might equally continue by specifying that someone planned to travel to Leipzig but this plan has now changed.

REFERENCES

Bamberg, Michael (1990) The German Perfekt: form and function of tense alternations. *Studies in Language* 14: 253–90.

Comrie, Bernard (1989) On identifying future tenses. In Werner Abraham & Theo Janssen (eds.) *Tempus–Aspekt–Modus: die lexikalischen und grammatischen Formen in den germanischen Sprachen*, Tübingen: Max Niemeyer, 51–63.

Drosdowski, Günter (ed.) (1984) *Duden Grammatik der deutschen Gegenwartssprache*, 4th edn, Mannheim: Dudenverlag.

Ehrich, Veronika (1992) *Hier und jetzt: Studien zur lokalen und temporalen Deixis im Deutschen*, Tübingen: Niemeyer.

Wunderlich, Dieter (1970) *Tempus und Zeitreferenz im Deutschen*, Munich: Huebner.

9

The possessed

JOHN ANDERSON

1 Concord, rection and dependency

Concord and rection both involve the assignment of a value (term) for a morphological category or categories to a victim word by a trigger or controller. Traditionally, they are differentiated, roughly, in terms of the substantive role of the trigger (see e.g. Matthews, 1981: 246). Thus, the Latin sentence in (1):

(1) Hostis habet muros.
'The enemy holds the walls.'

can be said to show concord between subject (*hostis*, the trigger) and verb (*habet*, the victim), which latter is said to agree with the subject – that is, is assigned (some of) the same category values, singular number and third person; while assignment of the value for the case category (accusative) to the post-verbal argument (*muros*) is simply determined by presence of the verb (in Latin, of a particular class) – it is not a copy of a category also manifested in the structure of the verb and thus is rectional.[1]

This brief formulation of the traditional characterisation of concord and rection is in need of some refinement. It is not obvious that all concord, for instance, involves simply the copying of a particular member of a category. For example, a controller involving co-ordinate items of discrepant gender may trigger yet another gender selection in the victim (see e.g. Corbett, 1983, 1989, on this and other complications). But it is at least appropriate to attribute the same particular morphological category to both trigger and victim, whatever the mechanisms of matching the members (apart from simple copying). This is not the case with rection, where only the victim shows the relevant morphological differentiation.

Concord is thus more general than 'copying' might imply. Rection, on the other hand, perhaps needs to be distinguished more narrowly from

162

other phenomena apparently showing morphological reflection of the presence of another element. For example, some languages (e.g. the Algonquian) have an affix marking transitive verbs as such (S.R. Anderson, 1985; section 2.2.2); but this is arguably a manifestation of derivational morphology rather than involving an inflectional category determined by the presence or absence of an object. I shall not include such morphological manifestations as instances of rection, which I assume to be strictly inflectional.

I thus take the traditional distinction and domain as my starting point, while recognising that there may arise doubtful cases which will have to be evaluated individually. J.M. Anderson (1979) distinguishes between concord and rection also in terms of the (independently established) dependency relation which holds between victim and trigger: rection proceeds from governor (head) to dependent (modifier), as with verb and (object) argument in (1); the concord victim in (1), on the other hand, governs the trigger – both nouns are dependents of the verb. While concord is triggered by a dependent, rection is determined by the governor. 'Rection' is also traditionally labelled 'government'; it seems to me that this is not fortuitous, given the basis for dependency assignment discussed below: see, for example, 'some "transitive" verbs govern a "direct object" in the genitive or dative' (Mitchell, 1985: 534).

This distinction in the status of the triggers of concord and rection is rather compactly illustrated by the morphosyntax of Old English noun phrases such as that represented in (2):

(2)
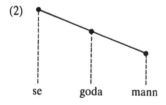

se   goda   mann

(see J.M. Anderson 1986a), where concord in gender spreads from the dependent *mann* (masculine, 'man') to its head *goda* ('good') and to the head of the latter, *se* ('that/the'); whereas the weak form of the adjective (*goda* rather than the strong *god* – cf. *Se mann bið god* 'That man is good', *god mann* '(a) good man') is required by the presence of a demonstrative as head of the phrase, it is determined rectionally. Such headhood assignments are not uncontroversial, and require some comment, despite recent advocacy of Determiners as heads (see e.g. Hudson, 1984).

Anderson (1986a) regards these phenomena of Old English as evidence of the mutual support given by the hypothesis concerning the relationship between concord and rection and dependency (as suggested in J.M. Anderson, 1979) and the analysis of noun phrases assumed in (2) (proposed in J.M. Anderson, 1976, 1989, etc.), which views them as centrifugal. This is in accordance with the subcategorisation requirements, which determine dependency: heads are subcategorised for their dependents (see e.g. J.M. Anderson, 1986b, 1990, 1991, 1992). As noted, a similar analysis, with Determiners as the head of their constructions, has been suggested by Hudson (1984) and within some recent developments in the Government–Binding framework. I do not assume here (and elsewhere), however, that (2), for example, constitutes a 'Determiner Phrase', in that I interpret determiners as transitive (pro)nouns; nor are simple adjectives modifiers of the noun with which they are in construction.[2]

J.M. Anderson (1986a) formulates, in an informal way, as (3):

(3) *The Principle of Concord and Rection Determination*
    a. Determination of concord is counter-dependency.
    b. Determination of rection is the reverse.

the dependency relationship between trigger and victim in a rectional or concordial relation. However makeshift, this formulation is at least vulnerable to questioning with respect to putative counter-examples. For instance, as S.R. Anderson again observes (1985: section 2.2.2), there are languages (such as the Circassian) where a transitive verb assumes a particular morphological shape when the object is absent: that is, the shape reflects the absence of an expected modifier, apparent 'detransitivisation'. If this is an instance of rection, then it runs counter to (3). However such phenomena again differ rather sharply from central cases of rection, which (as illustrated further in section 2 immediately below) involve morphological form responding to the presence of a particular element which the victim is in construction with; and it is perhaps unsurprising that morphology should reflect on the one hand presence of a particular governor but on the other absence of a modifier for which the governing element is subcategorised. I therefore take it that such phenomena do not conflict with the spirit of (3). However, we shall encounter some further problematical instances in section 6 below.

2 Concord, rection and Old English verbs

Other manifestations of (the applicability of) the Principle in Old English are associated with prepositional and verbal constructions:

(4) Þa gewearþ þam hlaforde and þam hyrigmannum wið anum peninge.
   'Then there was agreement between the lord and the hired men on one penny.'

(with the datives *hlaforde* and *hyrigmannum* determined by the verb *gewearþ* and the dative *peninge* determined by the preposition *wið*), including verb and participle (see e.g. J.M. Anderson, 1976: ch. 2, 1990, 1993: section 3), as illustrated in (5):

(5) Eastengle   hæfdon Ælfrede cyninge aþas   geseald.
    the East-Angles had   to King Alfred   oaths   given

with dependency relations as in (6):

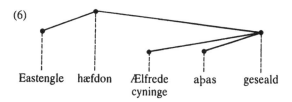

such that all of *Ælfrede cyninge*, *aþas* and *geseald* are inflected, as dative, accusative and 'second participle' (Mitchell, 1985), respectively, in accordance with the demands of their (respective) governors, and *hæfdon* shows (plural) concord with its dependent *Eastengle*. And we can associate similar phenomena with Present-day English, despite the paucity of case-marking. We return to the present-day situation below; at this point, further observations concerning the Old English weak/strong adjective distinction demand our attention.

Before proceeding to this, let us note further in relation to such 'participles' with 'transitive perfects' that they can also exhibit concord, appropriately anti-dependency, with their objects. In Old English, such concord is not always present, and many instances are ambivalent (between presence vs. absence of concord). In Italian such concord is usual only with pronoun objects, as in (7) (see e.g. Matthews, 1981: 250):

(7) Li/Le   ha   visti/viste.
    (he/she) them-MASC/FEM-PL has   seen-MASC/FEM-PL

(MASC = masculine, FEM = feminine gender; PL = plural number). Other 'uses' of 'participles' show subject-determined concord, again in accord with (or, rather, in accordance with (3), counter to) the dependency relations, as seen in (8):

(8)

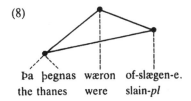

Þa þegnas wæron of-slægen-e.
the thanes were slain-*pl*

with *þa þegnas* determining (plural) concord on both of *wæron* and *of-slægene*. (On such representations, see e.g. J.M. Anderson, 1990, 1991, 1993: section 3.) All of these phenomena are compatible with the Principle suggested in (3).

3 Rection and possessives

As we have noted, the weak declension of the Old English adjective in (2) is determined by the presence of the demonstrative, again in accordance with (3), given the structural representation in (2). The weak declension is also determined by possessives, as in (9):

(9) min ealda freond 'my old friend'

In terms of Principle (3), this suggests that the possessive *min* also governs the adjective *ealda*. And the same conclusion concerning possessives emerges from a consideration of the construction in Makonde, and indeed from similar *status constructus* ('construct state') phenomena elsewhere. In a number of languages (particularly some Semitic and Nilotic) a possessed noun is inflected to mark its possessedness: it is 'put in the so-called "construct state", or "appertentive" form' (S.R. Anderson, 1985: 185). That this is an instance of rection is indicated by Anderson's (*ibid.*) observation that: 'This situation can be distinguished from that of possessive inflection on nouns . . . since a "construct state" form does not indicate the person, number, gender or other features of the subordinate noun, but only that there is one.' Again, given Principle (3), the possessive is not a dependent of the possessed noun but the governing element in the phrase, which determines rection. The phenomenon of concord with possessives alluded to by S.R. Anderson will, however, require our attention below, for obvious reasons.

In Makonde a possessive has the effect of removing all high tones on preceding words in the possessive phrase and assigns a high tone to the last vowel of the word therein immediately preceding it. I take this to be a manifestation of rection, realised not by affixation but by tonal modification. So the forms in (10) (with high tone symbolised with an acute accent):

(10) a. nyaáma 'meat'
     b. méléméénde 'cockroach'
     c. kaanya 'mouth'

emerge as shown in (11) when possessed:

(11) a. nyamá yaangu 'my meat'
     b. melemendé waangu 'my cockroach'
     c. kanyá yaangu 'my mouth'

(Odden, 1990: 164); and if another 'modifier' intervenes between the noun and the possessive it is the (final) modifier which bears the rectional high tone, as in (12d):

(12) a. chínduuli 'cassava'
     b. chindulí chaangu 'my cassava'
     c. chínduli chibaáya 'bad cassava'
     d. chinduli chibayá chaangu 'my bad cassava'

which also shows removal of all high tones (except that assigned by the possessive) on the pre-possessive elements in the phrase.

Odden shows further that possessed 'infinitives' exhibit the effects of rection in an analogous fashion; all elements headed by the 'infinitive' have their high tones removed and a high tone is assigned to the final vowel of the element adjacent to the possessive. Compare (13), wherein the 'infinitive' is not possessed:

(13) kutéléká nyámá yaake 'to cook his meat'

and retains its high tones (and indeed, as elsewhere, assigns one to its object), with (14):

(14) kuteleka nyama yoé kwaangu 'my cooking all the meat'

with only the final high on *yoé* assigned by the following possessive.

Of further interest here is the fact that while the phrase which is deprived of high tones is that headed by the dependent (the 'infinitive') of the possessive, the locus of the rectional high tone in (14) is a subordinate (here a dependent of a dependent) of the possessive merely, not a dependent, as represented in (15).

(15)

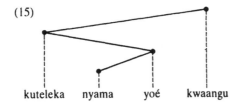

kuteleka   nyama   yoé   kwaangu

But the locus is the subordinate which is adjacent to the trigger of rection, the possessive.

An adjacency requirement has also been attributed to rection of case in Present-day English, for instance. I do not pursue here, however, the articulation of the adjacency and subordination parameters that it seems ought to be recognised in relation to the operability of rection, and thus incorporated into a more comprehensive version of (3). Perhaps something based on (3'):

(3') *The Principle of Concord and Rection Determination*
    a. Determination of concord is counter-dependency.
    b. Determination of rection is the reverse.
        Preferred options: dependency (rather than subordination)
                    adjacency (rather than non-)

might be appropriate, at least as far as rection parameters are concerned. Here, though, I want to continue to focus on the interaction between possessives and concord/rection, particularly in relation to the core of the proposed Principle.

We should note at this point, however, that the status of the adjective in constructions like (2) or (9) as governor of the noun (as assumed here) or dependent is indeterminate with respect to rection, provided the demonstrative can assign weak declension to a subordinate, not merely a dependent. But the concord direction (noun to adjective) supports the position I have adopted, that pre-nominal attributives are organised centrifugally (see J.M. Anderson, 1976: ch. 3, 1989). However, questions of concord lead us back to a problem in the analysis of possessives; indeed, to an apparent contradiction in terms of Principle (3).

4 Concord and possessives

The rectional phenomena we have briefly surveyed are consonant with Principle (3), provided that possessives govern (as in (15)) the phrases which also contain the possessed element. But there is, of course, much evidence that possessives can be determined by the possessed element, and that the possessed element can show concord with the possessive. The latter phenomenon is noted by S.R. Anderson (1985: section 2.1.3) as characteristic of 'Turkish, Finnish, Athabaskan, Muskogean, Mayan, Algonquian, and a great many others' (see too Moravcsik, 1971). Such concord suggests, in terms of Principle (3), that in these cases, at least, the possessed element governs the possessive. The former phenomenon, the attribution of a (genitive) inflection to the possessive by virtue of its being in construction with a possessed element, is very familiar, and (again, given (3)) leads apparently, as an instance of rection, to the same conclusion concerning the dependency relations involved, that is, the reverse of that suggested by the phenomena surveyed earlier.

This discrepancy cannot be taken as an indication of two different linguistic types (even if the recognition of this were in such a case desirable), in that the discrepancy arises within individual languages. So, for instance, Old English possessives, as well as determining weak declension on dependent adjectives, are themselves inflected rectionally. The possessive in (9) is arguably a derived adjective, and it indeed inflects according to the strong (non-rectionally determined) declension. But third-person possessives (apart from the archaic *sin* – Mitchell, 1985: sections 290–3) are clearly genitives whose case-marking as such is required by their being part of a possessive construction:

> (16) his goda freond 'his good friend'

as in Present-day English. (On occasional first- and second-person examples parallel to this, see Mitchell, 1985: section 296.) In terms of (3), the possessive in (16) must be dependent on the possessed noun and govern the adjective, but the adjective, in turn, must govern the noun, in order to receive (gender, etc.) concord from it – recall the discussion of (2) above.

In the light of Principle (3), the evidence is apparently contradictory: the existence of bilateral rection suggests that the possessive both governs (or has subordinate to it) and is governed by the possessed element. Perhaps, then, at least the part of (3) concerned with rection should be abandoned as such. But the apparent contradiction is manifested in other phenomena, phenomena which are central to the determination of dependency.

5 Possessives as biconstructional

Dependency reflects direction of subcategorisation (see again J.M. Anderson, 1986b, 1990, 1991, 1992): heads are subcategorised for their dependents. Also, in terms of (3), rection follows dependency. Thus, for example, 'perfect *have*' in (6) determines rection on its dependent verb and is also subcategorised therefor. More generally, verbs are subcategorised for their arguments, and assign them case.

Similarly, the possessive in (17):

(17) John's destruction of the ghetto-blaster

is both determined rectionally by the possessed element and an argument for which it is subcategorised. Rection and subcategorisation coincide in selecting the possessive as a modifier of *destruction*. But a reversed dependency relation is suggested not merely by the rection of weak declension in Old English and the Makonde tone phenomena but also by the fact that possessives, like other 'attributives', must be subcategorised for a dependent noun phrase (J.M. Anderson, 1989, 1991, 1992): Modern English *my* is a 'transitive' noun (specifically, pronoun); this is what differentiates it syntactically from the other members of the paradigm. (So too are demonstratives, quantifiers, numerals, attributive adjectives, etc.)

Say we accept the apparent contradiction: the possessive both governs and is governed by the possessed element. That is, a configuration like that in (18) is appropriate for possessive phrases:

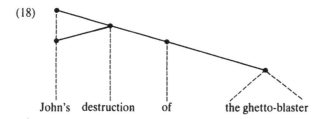

(18)

John's   destruction   of   the ghetto-blaster

wherein the possessive functions simultaneously as an argument in the lower construction headed by *destruction* and as head of the phrase as a whole, subcategorised for a noun phrase. The two functions are expressed distinctively in (19):

(19) the destruction by John of the ghetto-blaster

wherein (the transitive pronoun) *the* heads the entire phrase and is subcategorised for a noun phrase (see again J.M. Anderson, 1989) and *John* and *the ghetto-blaster* are marked by adposition as arguments of *destruction*. The apparent contradictions in morphosyntax associated with possessives can thus be related to the bifunctionality attributed by representations such as (18).

There obviously needs to be explored whether there are motivations for other cases of bifunctionality of this type. J.M. Anderson (1991) argues for a related type, whereby a single element depends on two distinct heads (see (8) above), and proposes constraints on the distribution of such, as well as indicating a formal system (wherein dependency and linearity are derivative) within which such configurations can be erected in the context of a restrictive (monotonic) theory of syntax (see too on this J.M. Anderson, 1986b, 1989, 1990, 1992, 1993); indeed, within which the achievement of monotonicity depends on the restricted availability of such violations of tree-propriety.[3]

6 Afterthoughts on the construct state

A similar approach to that advocated in section 5 above seems to be appropriate to cases where certain forms of the verb appear in the construct state. Hausa, for instance, shows a construct-state construction with possessed nouns:

(20) a. dōkī 'horse'
    b. sarkī 'chief'
    c. dōkin sarkī '(the) chief's horse'

(Taylor, 1959: section 21; cf. the Makonde examples of (11) above). Similarly, post-nominal demonstratives are associated with a noun in the construct state (Smirnova, 1982: 44). Once more, if the construct state is a manifestation of rection, its occurrence is in accord with Principle (3). However, in the (so-called) 'present tense' an overtly transitive verb is put in the construct state; that is, it is marked as a verbal noun in a rectional relation with the object:

(21) a. Sunā harbī. 'They are shooting.'
    b. Sunā harbin nāman-jējī. 'They are shooting game.'

(Taylor, 1959: sections 37, 98). This suggests, in accordance with Principle (3), that the verb in (21b) depends on its object. But we also want to say, on the basis of subcategorisation, that the verb governs its object. This is in accord with the determination of rection from verb to object in (1) above. Moreover, as we would expect, there are languages where the verb shows concord with its object, as illustrated by (22), from Lebanese Arabic:

(22) a. Samiir šaaf-u la l walad. 'Samir saw-him *object marker* the boy.'
   b. Samiir šaaf-ha la l bint. 'Samir saw-her *object marker* the girl.'
   c. Samiir šaaf-ni ili. 'Samir saw-me me.'

(Moravcsik, 1974: 27), concord here being, appropriately, anti-dependency. In this context, one might propose that the representation in (23) is appropriate for (the relevant part of) (21b):

(23)

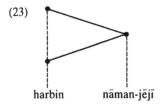

   harbin   nāman-jējī

The verb, *harbin*, is simultaneously the governor, *qua* verb, of the object and its dependent, *qua* possessed nominal.

It may be too, however, that construct state in Hausa, for instance, is not a reflection of rection, but merely an indication that the (nominal) element so marked takes a complement to its right. Pre-nominal (but not postnominal) adjectives in Hausa take the construct-state suffix (Smirnova, 1982: 29); pre-nominal demonstratives can be similarly interpreted. In each instance, the construct-state form is in construction with a complement to its right. Perhaps we have here a morphological variation that is neither concordial nor rectional, but rather an indication of 'transitivity'-orientation with nominals (including common nouns, demonstratives, adjectives and nominalised verbs): construct-state constructions are left-headed. Compare here the rejection in section 1 above of 'detransitivisation' as a manifestation of rection proper. The framework offered here at least offers a context in which this might be fruitfully explored.

NOTES

Thanks go to Fran Colman for her comments on an earlier quasi-printed version; she is never to blame, however. An intermediate version appeared, under the title 'Concord, rection and possessives in English, Makonde and elsewhere', in *Working Papers in General and Applied Linguistics* 2 (Department of English, University of Thessaloniki, 1991), ed. A. Kakouriotis, pp. 1–20.
1 I leave aside here the perhaps more controversial question of the assignment of the nominative case to *hostis*, though it does not seem to be inconsistent with the

description of rection given here, whether or not one acknowledges the legitimacy as a syntactic constituent of INFL and the like. If one does, one would, however, have to modify the description given above of the concord manifested in (1). I assume that no such modification is required; but recognition or otherwise of INFL is not crucial to the present discussion.

2 It is perhaps worth also pointing out, since (*pace* Pullum, 1984) it is Tuesday for someone somewhere, and all our yesterdays are maybe tomorrow, that such an analysis is not incompatible with the conclusions reached by Hjelmslev (1959 [1939]), who proposes that 'le terme régi est celui des deux qui est appelé nécessairement par l'autre' and that therefore prepositions govern their associated nouns, and attributive adjectives ('termes sécondaires') their nouns ('termes primaires'), while 'c'est évidemment le genre, le nombre et le cas du terme primaire qui régissent le genre, le nombre et le cas du terme sécondaire', concord thus going against the categorial dependency relation, while rection reflects the direction of that relation.

3 As with the phenomena briefly discussed by J.M. Anderson (1990, 1991), such multifunctional representations – that is, structures allowing a single category to participate in more than one dependency relation – obviate recourse to 'movement' (mutation of structure). In the present case, we allow for the apparently contradictory demands of subcategorisation and rection without positing different levels of representation mediated by mutations. Compare here one of the results of the careful discussion of possessives and related phenomena provided by Giorgi & Longobardi: 'Possessive forms, which are genitive NPs at D-structure, surface with the distribution either of Adjectives (e.g. in Italian) or of Determiners (e.g. in English); in both cases they must occur at S-structure outside N', binding a trace therein if interpreted as internal arguments' (1991: 170). Of course, it remains to be established (despite the proliferation of avowedly non-mutational programmes) that/if the (other) explanatory results offered by such mutational frameworks can at least be replicated in the absence of 'movement' and empty categories.

REFERENCES

Anderson, J.M. (1976) *On Serialisation in English Syntax* (Ludwigsburg Studies in Language and Linguistics, 1), Ludwigsburg: R.O.U. Strauch.

(1979) Serialisation, dependency and the syntax of possessives in Moru. *Studia Linguistica* 33: 1–25.

(1986a) Old English morphology and the structure of noun phrases. *Folia Linguistica Historica* 7: 219–24.

(1986b) Structural analogy and case grammar. *Lingua* 70: 79–129.

(1989) Reflections on notional grammar, with some remarks on its relevance to issues in the analysis of English and its history. In Arnold *et al.* (eds.): 13–36.

(1990) On the status of auxiliaries in notional grammar. *Journal of Linguistics* 26: 341–62.

(1991) Notional grammar and the redundancy of syntax. *Studies in Language* 15: 307–33.

(1992) *Linguistic Representation: Structural Analogy and Stratification*, Berlin: Mouton de Gruyter.

(1993) Parameters of syntactic change: a notional view. In C. Jones (ed.) *Historical Linguistics: Problems and Perspectives*, London: Longman, 1–41.

Anderson, S.R. (1985) Inflectional morphology. In T. Shopen (ed.) *Language Typology and Syntactic Description*, vol. III: *Grammatical Categories and the Lexicon*, Cambridge University Press, 150–201.

Arnold, D.J., R.M. Atkinson, J. Durand, C. Grover & L. Sadler (eds.) (1989) *Essays on Grammatical Theory and Universal Grammar*, Oxford University Press.

Corbett, G.G. (1983) *Hierarchies, Targets and Controllers*, London: Croom Helm.

(1989) An approach to the description of gender systems. In Arnold *et al.* (eds.): 53–89.

Giorgi, A. & G. Longobardi (1991) *The Syntax of Noun Phrases: Configuration, Parameters and Empty Categories*, Cambridge University Press.

Hjelmslev, L. (1959) La notion de rection. In *Essais linguistiques* (Travaux du Cercle Linguistique de Copenhague, XII), Copenhagen: Nordisk Sprog- og Kultur-forlag, 139–51. (Reprinted from *Acta Linguistica* 1 (1939): 10–23.)

Hudson, R.A. (1984) *Word Grammar*, Oxford: Blackwell.

Matthews, P.H. (1981) *Syntax*, Cambridge University Press.

Mitchell, B. (1985) *Old English Syntax*, Oxford University Press.

Moravcsik, E.A. (1971) Agreement. In *Working Papers on Language Universals* 5, Stanford University, California: A1–A69.

(1974) Object–verb agreement. In *Working Papers on Language Universals* 15, Stanford University, California: 25–140.

Odden, D. (1990) C-command or edges in Makonde. *Phonology* 7: 163–9.

Pullum, G.K. (1984) Topic . . . comment: if it's Tuesday, this must be glossematics. *Natural Language and Linguistic Theory* 2: 151–6.

Smirnova, M.A. (1982) *The Hausa Language*, London: Routledge and Kegan Paul.

Taylor, F.W. (1959) *A Practical Hausa Grammar*, 2nd edn, Oxford University Press.

10

Complement clauses and complementation strategies

R.M.W. DIXON

Grammar exists to code meaning. Every language has a similar set of semantic tasks to fulfil. There is a universal pool of grammatical construction types, and each language draws its own selection from the pool. According to the selection that is made, a similar type of meaning may be expressed by different grammatical means in different languages.

But the variation is not random. Each construction type in a language has a semantic effect, and although a given meaning may be expressed in different languages by constructions that are grammatically diverse, they will have similar semantics. This will be illustrated for complementation strategies in the Australian language Dyirbal, which are compared with the familiar complement clause constructions in English, and in Fijian.

Section 1 discusses the appropriate part of the semantic task which all languages have to perform; section 2 sketches the varied grammatical means for achieving it, paying attention to the different kinds of interclausal relation found in human languages; section 3 deals with complement clauses in English and Fijian; section 4 then discusses complementation strategies (which do not involve complement clauses *per se*) in Dyirbal; section 5 summarises the results and shows that verbs with similar meaning take complement clauses or complementation strategies, with similar meanings, across widely diverse languages.

1 The semantic task

The words of any language can be grouped into a number of lexical classes called SEMANTIC TYPES, which have a common meaning component and some shared grammatical properties. Each semantic type will, in a given language, be associated with a particular word class. Thus the DIMENSION (e.g. 'big', 'little', 'long'), COLOUR ('black', 'white'), AGE ('new', 'old') and

VALUE ('good', 'bad') types are in most languages related to the Adjective class. Words with CONCRETE reference ('woman', 'hand', 'water', 'axe', 'hill', etc.) always belong to the Noun class. The semantic types expressing MOTION (e.g. 'go', 'throw'), AFFECT ('cut', 'burn'), ATTENTION ('see', 'hear') and SPEAKING ('say', 'ask', 'tell', etc.) are always associated with the Verb class.

Every language has a large open class of Primary verbs,[1] which can make up a complete sentence by choosing appropriate NPs (with noun or pronoun as head) to fill subject, object, etc. slots. In English, and in many other languages, there are two subclasses of Primary verbs:

> PRIMARY-A verbs describe actions or states that relate only to things; their subject and object slots must be filled by NPs. Primary-A covers semantic types such as MOTION, REST (e.g. 'stand', 'put'), AFFECT, GIVING ('lend', 'pay') and CORPOREAL ('eat', 'laugh', 'die').
>
> PRIMARY-B verbs describe actions and states that can relate to things or to other actions or states. One can say *I watched the storm* or *I watched John building a wall*; and *He described the prize bull* or *He described how John tamed the bull*. Primary-B types include ATTENTION, SPEAKING and, in many languages, THINKING ('think', 'know', 'believe') and/or LIKING ('love', 'hate').

Each language must have some grammatical means for linking a PRIMARY-B verb and the verb describing the action or state that the Primary-B verb refers to. In English, as in many other languages, Primary-B verbs may have NPs filling subject and object slots (*I heard John, Mary annoys me*) or, as an alternative, they may allow a complement clause to fill one of these slots – the object slot in the case of *describe*, *watch* and *hear* (e.g. *I heard that John had died*) and the subject slot in the case of *annoy* (*John's drinking gin annoys me*).

Each language also has a set of what we can call Secondary concepts, which modify the meanings of verbs; these typically include all or most of 'not', 'can', 'must', 'begin', 'finish', 'try', 'want', 'make (do)' and 'seem'. There are varied grammatical means for realising these ideas but it appears that every language expresses some (although not all) of them through verbs, which can appropriately be called Secondary verbs. Whereas all Primary verbs can just relate to objects, and make up a complete sentence with NPs filling their argument slots, all Secondary verbs relate to some action or state and demand a grammatical link to another verb.

In English, *not*, *can* and *must* are constituents within the verbal auxiliary (effectively, modifiers to a main verb in a verb phrase), while *begin*, *finish*, *try, want, make, prevent* and *seem* are Secondary verbs, which take complement clauses, for example *John finished building the wall, I want to get a new car, John made Mary sell her bicycle.* In these sentences *finish, want* and *make* are syntactically the main verbs, with *build, get* and *sell* functioning as verbs of embedded clauses; but semantically *build, get* and *sell* are the core concepts of the sentences, with *finish, want* and *make* providing semantic modification. I have presented arguments (Dixon, 1991: 90–3, 172–85) that Secondary verbs in English always take an underlying complement clause, although the verb of this clause may sometimes be omitted (in circumstances where it could be supplied by the addressee), for instance *John finished the wall, I want a new car.*

The semantic tasks which all languages must face, and which they have different ways of fulfilling, are:

(a) there must be some grammatical or lexical means for expressing the Secondary concepts;
(b) there must be some grammatical means for linking Primary-B and Secondary verbs with verbs to which they relate, such as 'watch' and 'build' in 'I watched John building the wall'; or 'force' and 'build' in 'I forced John to build the wall'.

2 Grammatical means

2.1 For expressing secondary concepts

Dealing first with (a) above, there are four main ways in which languages express Secondary concepts:

1 as Secondary verbs, which have essentially the same array of derivational and inflectional possibilities as Primary verbs;
2 as verbal affixes;
3 as modifiers to a verb (including both adverbs and modal verbs, as in English and other European languages);
4 as non-inflecting particles within a clause.

As is well known, languages distribute descriptive tasks among their components in varying ways. What is done by morphology in one language can be the domain of syntax in another – in Latin, for instance, syntactic function is shown by case endings, with word order being relatively free, whereas in English syntactic function of core arguments is realised through word order.

In a similar fashion, what one language handles through morphological systems may be expressed by independent lexemes in another. Macushi, a Carib language spoken on the borders of Brazil, Venezuela and Guyana, has verbal affixes which include *-yənpa* 'try', *-pia'tî* 'begin' and *-aretî'ka* 'finish' (Abbot, 1991). In Bolivian Quechua verbal suffixes include *-na* 'have to, be able to' (Crapo & Aitken, 1986, II: 4). Halkomelem Salish, spoken in British Columbia, has a causative suffix *-st(əxʷ)* 'make' and a desiderative suffix *-əlmən* 'want' (Gerdts, 1991). The Tibeto-Burman language Limbu, from Eastern Nepal, has verbal affixes that mark negation *mɛ-* ~ *-nɛn* ~ *-n* 'not' (van Driem, 1987: 103–4). Many similar examples could be given, from other languages, of verbal derivational affixes which would be translated into English by Secondary verbs (*try, begin, finish, make, want*) or by modals (*can, must*) or by the auxiliary element *not*. There are also instances – as will be described in section 4, on Dyirbal – of a verbal inflection in one language corresponding semantically to a separate lexeme in another.

This exemplifies a critical difference between Primary and Secondary verbs. Secondary verbs encode meanings that relate to some other verb, and which can be expressed as verbal lexemes or as affixes or verbal modifiers or clausal particles. Primary verbs (which do not need to relate to any other verb) are always expressed as verbal lexemes.[2]

Some secondary concepts – such as 'can' and 'must' – are more likely than others to be realised as verbal affixes, although English (a language with relatively simple morphology) has *can* and *must* as modals, functioning as modifiers to a main verb, and in Irish 'modals' are main verbs, taking one of the two varieties of complement clause (Stenson, 1981: 86). 'Not' is generally realised either as a verb affix (as in Limbu, mentioned above, and in Bantu languages) or else as an element within the verb phrase (as in English) or as a non-inflecting clause particle (as in Dyirbal). But in Fijian the only way of achieving negation is through the lexical verb *sega* 'it is not the case', which then takes a subject complement clause, for example *e sega niu la'o*, literally 'It is not the case [that I am going]' translates the English sentence *I am not going* (Dixon, 1988: 279–81).

It is likely that every language has some Secondary concepts expressed as lexical verbs. And all languages have Primary-B verbs, which may relate to some other verb. Typically, languages use the same grammatical means to code the relation between a Secondary verb and the verb which it semantically modifies, and the relation between a Primary-B verb and the verb whose state or action it refers to. For instance, in English we get *They began building the wall* and *They discussed building the wall*. These two sentences have the same surface syntax but different semantic interpretations: *They began building the wall* describes an activity of building, with *begin* providing semantic modification to *build* (in languages such as Macushi or Dyirbal this would be expressed by a suffix onto 'build'); *They discussed building the wall* describes a discussion, whose topic is the building of the wall. Here, as at other places in the grammar, we find one syntactic mechanism being used for tasks which are semantically rather different.

2.2 For linking verbs

There are a number of ways in which a language can grammatically code the link between a Secondary or Primary-B verb and a second verb. The main ones are:

1 The second verb can be nominalised, and then function as head of an NP in subject or object function to the Secondary or Primary-B verb.
2 Both verbs can appear, in apposition, in the same verb phrase.
3 The verbs can occur in separate clauses, which are linked together by one of a number of grammatical strategies.

Method 1 is little used for linking a Secondary or Primary-B verb with another verb in the familiar languages of Europe, but it is a major mechanism for achieving this in many languages from Africa and South America, for example. (See, among many other sources, Derbyshire, 1979, 1985; Ameka, 1991.)

The phenomenon of 'serial verbs' is an example of method 2. In the languages in which it occurs, this can be used to link many types of verb, including the Secondary and Primary-B instances that are the concern of this paper. (See Foley & Van Valin, 1984: 189ff.; Noonan, 1985: 76ff.; Jensen, 1990: 124ff., and further references therein.)

Dyirbal has a syntactic technique of this kind whereby a verb phrase can include more than one verb with the condition that the verbs must agree in transitivity value and in tense or other inflection, and that they must of course be semantically compatible. A verb phrase may include *warrinyu* 'fly' and *waynyjin* 'go up', the whole then meaning 'fly up'. This technique of verb apposition can be used in Dyirbal for linking a Secondary verb with a verb that it semantically modifies, for instance *jaybin* 'finish' and *jangganyu* 'eat' can be combined in a verb phrase *jaybin jangganyu* 'eat (it) all up' (and see section 4.1 below).

Probably the most popular way of linking two verbs is through method 3, where each fills the predicate slot of a clause, and the clauses are then linked together in a complex sentence construction. There are basically three ways

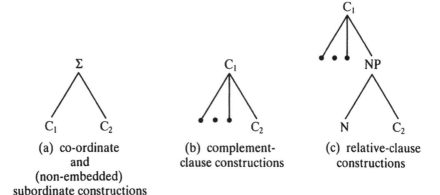

(a) co-ordinate
and
(non-embedded)
subordinate constructions

(b) complement-
clause constructions

(c) relative-clause
constructions

Figure 10.1 Types of clause linking

in which two clauses can be linked (although not all languages utilise all three). These are illustrated in figure 10.1, using Σ for sentence, C for clause, NP for noun phrase and N for noun. In (a) both clauses are immediate constituents of a sentence; in (b) one clause fills a syntactic slot (subject, object, etc) in the other clause; and in (c) one clause functions as modifier within an NP which itself fills a syntactic slot in the main clause. These three methods of clause linking can be briefly exemplified from English:

(a) *Co-ordinate and non-embedded subordinate constructions.* Clauses can be linked without embedding by (i) co-ordinate linkers such as *and, but, or*; (ii) temporal subordinate linkers such as *after, before, while*; (iii) logical subordinate linkers such as *since, because, if*; (iv) purposive linkers such as *so that, in order (that/(for . . .)to)*. There are grammatical conventions for omitting an NP which appears in both clauses and these are slightly different for each of (i)–(iv).

Linking of type (iv) is of particular interest in the context of this paper. The relator *in order* is followed by *that* or by *for X to*; if the two clauses have the same subject then *for X* (where X is the subject) is omitted. Thus, *John borrowed my car in order that he might give Mary a driving lesson, John borrowed my car (in order) for Mary to practise driving* and *John borrowed my car (in order) to give Mary a driving lesson.* The *in order* is generally omitted before *for* or *to*, although it can be retained; it is normally retained before *that*, although here it can also be omitted.

There is no grammatical restriction on either of the two clauses in a co-ordinate or non-embedded subordinate construction – either can be transitive or intransitive; there can be, but need not be, an NP common to the two clauses; and if there is, it can be in any function in each clause. (There is of course the semantic condition that the meanings of the two clauses must be compatible with that of the construction type employed.)

(b) *Complement-clause constructions.* English has a number of types of complement clause (see section 3.1), each of which has the internal structure of a clause but fills an object, subject or post-object slot in a main clause. For instance, the complement clause in *They expected* [*that Mary would win*] behaves like an object in that it can become subject of a passive, for example [*That Mary would win*] *was expected* (*by them*), or – with extraposition of the 'heavy constituent' to the end of the sentence – *It was expected* (*by them*) [*that Mary would win*].

(c) *Relative-clause constructions.* There are various kinds of modifier within an NP which can help to focus the reference of the head noun: these include demonstratives, adjectives and relative clauses, for instance *Which man were you calling to? I was calling to* [*that tall fellow* [*who lives in the old cottage*]].

Quite different types of clause linking can appear similar on the surface but have distinct underlying structures. Consider (1) and (2):

(1) [The man went] to [bathe]
(2) [The man wanted [to bathe]]

Sentence (1) is a construction of type (a), in which the intransitive clause *The man went* is linked by subordinator *to* with another clause that has an identical subject (and this is then omitted); it could be expanded to *The man went in order to bathe. Want* is a transitive verb that can have as object either an NP (e.g. *The man wanted some fish*) or a complement clause, as in (2) (the complement-clause subject is omitted under identity with the main-clause subject); *to* is here a complementiser and we could not expand this sentence to **The man wanted in order to bathe.*

Note that although (1) and (2) have similar surface structures, a speaker of English will never have any doubt concerning which construction is being used: in (1) *went* is an intransitive verb and so this must be non-embedded subordination, type (a), while in (2) *wanted* is a transitive verb which has to be followed by an object, so this must be a complement-clause construction, type (b).[3]

Another pair of sentences with different underlying structures which can, with appropriate omissions, have the same surface form, are (3) and (4):

(3) I don't like [that man('s) painting his front door blue]
(4) I don't like [that man (who is) painting his front door blue]

Sentence (3) is a complement-clause construction, with the O slot for *like* filled by the clause *that man('s) painting his front door blue*; it indicates that I do not approve of what he is doing. In (4) *like* has an NP in object slot; this has as its head the noun *man*, which is modified by demonstrative *that* and relative clause *who is painting his front door blue*. Here the relative clause simply serves to identify which man it is that I dislike – there is no implication that I do not like him because of what he is doing to his front door (it is, in fact, likely that I hate him for some quite different reason). In their full forms, with *'s* in (3) and *who is* in (4), these sentences are clearly distinct; but these elements may be omitted and then *I don't like that man painting his front door* is ambiguous between a complement-clause and a relative-clause reading.

It is also important to distinguish between complement clauses and NPs involving deverbal nouns, since *-ing* can (among other functions) mark one kind of nominalisation, and it can also mark the verb in one variety of complement clause. The sentence *I didn't like Mary's singing* is ambiguous: it could mean I disliked the way that she sang or I did not approve of the fact that she sang. Under the first reading the sentence would be a shortened form of a construction like (5), where the object of *like* is an NP whose head is the derived noun *singing*; for the second reading it could be a shortened form of a construction like (6), where the object of *like* is a complement clause.

(5) I didn't like [Mary's singing (of 'The Lord is my shepherd' in that bar)]
(6) I didn't like [Mary('s) singing ('The Lord is my shepherd' in that bar)]

That is, (5) says that I did not think she performed the psalm very well on that occasion (I have heard her sing it better in other places); but (6) implies that I did not think it proper for her to perform a sacred song in such a setting (irrespective of how well or badly she sang). The bracketed constituent in (5) has the status of an NP with *singing* as the head noun –*Mary's* could be replaced by *the*, an adjective could be included, such as *loud singing*, and there must be the preposition *of* before *'The Lord is my shepherd'*, which is the object of the underlying verb. In contrast, the bracketed constituent in (6) has the structure of a clause, with *Mary* as subject, *'The Lord is my shepherd'* as object, and *sing* as the verb phrase head (this variety of complement clause is marked by *-ing* on the verb and an optional *'s* on the subject). In (6), *Mary's* could not be replaced by *the*, the verb could not be modified by an adjective such as *loud* (only by an adverb, *loudly*) and *of* could not be included before the object.[4]

I mentioned in the first paragraph of this paper that there appears to be a universal 'pool' of grammatical construction types with each language making its own selection from the pool. Not all languages are like English in having in their grammars all three methods of clause linking illustrated in figure 10.1.

It seems that if a language does have constructions of type (b) – in which a clause can function as subject, object, etc. for another clause – then it will use this syntactic mechanism to code the link between a Secondary or Primary-B verb and another verb. Section 3 briefly surveys the varieties of complement-clause constructions in English and Fijian, and their meanings. For languages which lack complement-clause constructions, other means must be employed to code inter-verb links. Dyirbal, as described in section 4, has no constructions of type (b) but it does have what I call 'strategies of complementation', one of which involves a link of type (a) and the other a link of type (c).

I suggest the following universal: for languages which have complement-clause constructions there are always at least two possibilities: a 'potential (irrealis)' type, typically referring to something that has not happened but which people want or intend should happen (as in 'I want to go', 'I ordered him to run'); and an 'actual (realis)' type, typically referring to some existing or certain event or state (e.g. 'I remembered that he had gone', 'I decided that I would apply'). For a language that lacks complement-clause constructions there will be at least two strategies of complementation, with similar meanings.

3 Complement clauses

Little systematic study has as yet been attempted of the genetic and areal distribution of the various kinds of clause linking. From general reading, and from talking to descriptive linguists, I have the impression that complement-clause constructions are common among the languages of Europe, Oceania and Africa but rare in those of Australia and South America.[5] This section briefly surveys the grammar and meaning of complementation in a sample language from each of the first two areas, English and Fijian.

The semantic task of complement-clause constructions is to code the relation between a matrix verb (whether of Primary-B or Secondary type) and the complement-clause verb. Thus, the meanings of *describe* and of *decide* and of *ing*, *that* and 'modal' *to* complement clauses in English are reflected in the fact that *describe* only takes an *ing* clause in object slot (e.g. *He described John's painting the wall*) while *decide* can take a *that* clause (*He decided that the wall didn't need to be painted*) or a *to* clause (*He decided to paint the wall*) with a meaning difference. This will be further illustrated in the sections that follow.

Varieties of complement clause are generally marked by special words or affixes, called complementisers. Noonan (1985: 47, and see references quoted there) mentions that 'complementisers typically derive historically from pronouns, conjunctions or case markers, and, rarely, verbs'; however, Charles E. Grimes points out (personal communication) that in many languages of Indonesia and Oceania complementisers are grammaticalised from verbs (and see Schachter, 1985: 50). The great majority of complementisers are homonymous with some other grammatical form in that language. Exceptions are noteworthy: *että* which in Finnish functions only as a complementiser 'that' (Kristina Sands, personal communication; Karlsson, 1983: 170); and Latin *ut*, Arabic *ʔan* (I am grateful to Ulrike Mosel for pointing these out).

3.1 English

A great deal has been written about the syntax – and a little about the semantics – of complement clauses in English (including Dixon, 1991, which pays attention to the relation between syntax and semantics). Only a very brief summary is included here.

There are a number of forms which serve to mark complement clauses in English: *that*, *for*, *to*, *-ing*, *'s*, *from*, *if*, *whether* and *wh-* words such as *who*, *what*, *where*, *how*, *why*. With the exception of *whether*, all of these have some other function in the grammar. Of the three main kinds of complement, a *that* clause has the same structure as a main clause, with *that* preposed – it must have a stated subject, and has the full range of modal and tense–aspect possibilities; *to* and *-ing* complements can have the subject omitted when it is coreferential with an appropriate NP in the main clause, and they have limited tense–aspect possibilities in the auxiliary and cannot include a modal.

All of the types of complement clause have the internal structure of a clause – a transitive verb can be followed by an object (with no preposition intervening), the verb can be modified by an adverb, etc. – but they function in a syntactic slot within the main clause. A complement clause in object function can become passive subject, in the appropriate semantic circumstances, for example [*That Mary is cleverer than John*] *was admitted* (*by everyone*), [*John's having punched the managing director on his birthday*] *is still remembered* (*by all our staff*), [*For John to lead the parade*] *was agreed* (*on*) (*by the organisers*). *That* and *to* (but not *-ing*) complements in subject function are typically extraposed to the end of the clause, with *it* filling the subject position: *It was admitted* [*that Mary is cleverer than John*], *It was agreed* [*for John to lead the parade*].

Some verbs take just one variety of complement clause (in object or post-object or subject slot) while others may accept two or more. This is a function of the meaning of the verb, and the meanings of the complement-clause constructions. We will first briefly comment on the meanings of the complement varieties, and then survey the main semantic types of verb that take complement clauses.

A *that* complement refers to an activity or event or state as a simple unit, without any reference to its internal constitution or time duration (and a *wh*-complement has similar meaning). It often refers to a single fact, as in *John reported* [*that the horses had been fed*]. In contrast, an *-ing* complement refers to an activity as extended in time, noting the way in which it unfolds. Compare (7a) and (7b):

(7) a. I heard [that America had beaten France]
    b. I heard [America beating France]

Sentence (7a) is used when I have just heard the result, whereas (7b) would be the appropriate thing to say when I had listened to a radio commentary on the game (the first goal, the equaliser, the penalty in the closing minutes, and then the winning shot that clinched the match).

There are two main subvarieties of *to* complement: the 'modal' type and the 'judgment' type. Many verbs that take a *to* complement may also select a *that* clause; the modal subvariety corresponds to a *that* clause which includes a modal (recall that *to* clauses cannot themselves involve a modal), for example:

(8) a. I wish that John would go.
    b. I wish John to go.
(9) a. I decided that I would apply.
    b. I decided to apply.

'Modal' *to* complements relate to the subject of the complement clause becoming involved in the activity or state referred to by that clause, or to the possibility of such involvement, as in (8b) and (9b). 'Judgment' *to* complements have a rather different meaning; here the subject of the main clause ventures a judgment or opinion about the subject of the complement-clause predicate (which often commences with *be*). A 'judgment' *to* clause corresponds to a *that* complement without a modal, for instance:

> (10) a. I noticed that John was wounded.
>   b. I noticed John to be wounded.
> (11) a. I knew that Mary was cleverer than John.
>   b. I knew Mary to be cleverer than John.

Note that verbs which take 'modal' *to* may take a *that* clause without a modal, such as *I decided that I was sick*, but in this case there is no corresponding *to* construction (we can say *I decided to be sick*, but this corresponds to *I decided that I would be sick*, which does have a modal). Also, verbs that take a 'judgment' *to* clause may have a *that* clause with a modal (*I knew that Mary might be cleverer than John*) and there is then no corresponding *to* construction.

Although a 'modal' *to* construction can have a similar meaning to a *that* clause with a modal, they are never exactly synonymous. Compare (12a) and (12b):

> (12) a. I remembered that I should lock the door (but then decided not to, as a way of asserting my distaste for the rules).
>   b. I remembered to lock the door (but then Mary snatched the key and pushed it down a grating, so I couldn't).

The *that* clause in (12a) simply records a fact, what my obligation was; it says nothing about my attitude to that obligation. A 'modal' *to* complement, as in (12b), refers to the potentiality of the subject's doing something and implies that if at all possible he will do that thing (he will only not do it if something outside his control intervenes), for instance *I hope to go, John promised to call tomorrow*.

Three of the main varieties of complement clause may be compared in (13):

> (13) a. The doctor remembered that he had examined Mary Brown.
>   b. The doctor remembered examining Mary Brown.
>   c. The doctor remembered to examine Mary Brown.

Sentence (13a) might be used when he remembered that the consultation had taken place, but could not recall any of the details. Example (13b) implies that he had a clear vision of what happened – Mary's giggle when he asked her to put out her tongue, the high blood pressure, and so on. Both (13a) and (13b) refer to some actual event. Sentence (13c) is quite different, in stating that he remembered to involve himself in some activity. Unless anything is said to the contrary we would infer from (13c) that he did examine her; however, the sentence could be continued 'but when he looked in the waiting room he found she'd grown tired of waiting and gone off home'.

We can now embark on a brief survey of the various semantic types involving verbs (or other realisations of Secondary concepts) which relate to other verbs, beginning with Secondary items.

NEGATION, MODALS, ASPECTUALS – these concepts simply provide modification for a (or for another) verb, sharing its subject, object etc., for example *John didn't/must/can/began to/tried to read the book*. The negator *not* and modals (*will, should, can, might*, etc.) are in English simply grammatical modifiers to a verb. However, aspectuals such as *begin, start, finish, continue, try* and *attempt* function as full verbs. In *John started to build the wall* the verb *build* is the semantic core, with *start* providing semantic modification, although syntactically *start* is the main verb with *build* as verb of an embedded predicate clause. Most aspectual verbs take both *to* and *-ing* complements, with a difference in meaning. Compare (14a) and (14b):

(14) a. John tried to drive the car (but Mary wouldn't let him).
     b. John tried driving the car (but didn't rate its performance very highly).

The *-ing* complement indicates that he did it for a period of time, the *to* clause that he attempted to get involved in the activity (but something may have prevented him from doing so). Compare also (15a) and (15b):

(15) a. Mary began to hit John.
     b. Mary began hitting John.

Sentence (15b) implies that she did rain a few blows on him, that is, did the activity for a period, while (15a) might be used when she had just hit him once, or perhaps if she just had the stick raised (but then it was snatched off her before she could bring it down on his head) – she attempted to get involved in the activity.

Finish is unusual among aspectual verbs in that it is confined to an *-ing* complement – *John finished painting the house* but not *John finished to paint the house*; it contrasts with *cease*, which takes both complement types. The reason appears to be that *cease* has 'subject orientation' (the subject stops at his whim, even though the task may not be complete) whereas *finish* shows 'object orientation' (the activity stops because it is completed – here, the house is fully painted). A *to* complement, which refers to the subject's predisposition to do something, is semantically incompatible with the 'object orientation' of *finish*.

The WANTING type – including verbs like *want, wish (for), desire, hope (for), need, require* and *expect* – introduces one semantic role in addition to those of the complement clause verb, for example *John wanted [Mary to ride the horse]*. However, the subjects of the two clauses may coincide, and then the complement-clause occurrence may be omitted: *John wanted [to ride the horse]*. Verbs in this type may take a *to* complement referring to something attainable which the speaker can do something to achieve, such as *I hope to attend the concert this evening*; or a *that* complement relating to something over which he has less control, *I hope that I do live to draw my pension*.

Want and *need* have strong pragmatic meanings (see Dixon, 1991: 246), being generally used for something that is attainable through the efforts of the subject; they are naturally restricted to *to* complements. Compare *I want to study with Ken Hale* and *I wish that I could have studied under Sapir*.

Verbs of the MAKING type also require a semantic role additional to those of the verb to which they relate, for instance *I forced [Mary to ride the horse]*. For this type, subjects of the two verbs are unlikely to coincide and, even if they do, no omission is possible: *I forced [myself to ride the horse]*, not **I forced to ride the horse*. There are three subclasses: (i) *make, force, cause, let, allow, permit* typically imply some positive effort on the part of the main-clause subject to bring something about and are restricted to *to* complements;[6] (ii) *stop, prevent, spare, save* typically imply a definite effort to avoid something happening, and are only used with a variety of *-ing* clauses introduced by *from*, such as *I stopped Mary [(from) riding the horse]*;[7] (iii) *ensure*, alone from this type, takes a *that* complement – it refers to some general fact as in *He ensured [that the doors were locked]* (there is no information about who locked them, just that it had been done).

We can now survey the main Primary-B verb types, all of which allow a complement clause, as an alternative to an NP, in one syntactic slot.

For ATTENTION (e.g. *see, hear, feel, observe, watch*) and THINKING (*think (about), imagine, remember, believe, know*) there is some variation according to the meanings of individual items (see Dixon, 1991: 124–38), but verbs from these types typically take *-ing, that*, and 'judgment' *to* complements in object slot. A few verbs – including *remember, forget, know, learn, teach* – may relate to potentiality, and then take a 'modal' *to* complement. Examples illustrating the semantic differences involved were given at (7), (10)–(13).

Verbs from the DECIDING type – *decide (on), determine (on), resolve, choose* – may all take a *that* complement, which can be (a) a judgment about the present, for example *I decided that it was too cold to cycle to work this morning*, or (b) some intention regarding the future, *I decided that I would cycle tomorrow.* Sense (b) of *decide* can alternatively take a 'modal' *to* clause; the complement clause subject is generally not stated and is inferred to be the same as the main-clause subject, for example *I decided to cycle tomorrow.*

The SPEAKING type includes a great number of verbs, some having the addressee as object (e.g. *inform*), many having the topic of discussion as object (e.g. *announce*) and some allowing both possibilities (*tell the news to Mary, tell Mary the news*).

One subtype of SPEAKING verbs refers to a durational activity and is restricted to an *-ing* complement, for example *describe, discuss, refer to*, as in *I described (John's) building the house.* All SPEAKING verbs which may introduce direct speech can, of course, also occur with a *that* clause marking indirect speech, for instance *say, state, announce, remind.* Those SPEAKING verbs whose meanings relate to the future often have a modal in the *that* complement. Corresponding to this, there may be a 'modal' *to* clause; this is used especially when the main-verb subject coincides with complement-clause subject, the latter then being omitted, for example *I proposed/ offered/threatened to go.* There are also some SPEAKING verbs involved in making an assertion, that can take a 'judgment' *to* clause, for instance *I declared that he was stupid, I declared him to be stupid.*

Jussive verbs from the SPEAKING type may have an addressee NP as object followed by a *that* complement clause: *He told the sergeant that his platoon should clean the latrines.* When the addressee coincides with the subject of the complement clause, a *to* construction is often preferred: *He told/ordered the platoon to clean the latrines.* SPEAKING verbs like *order, persuade* and *encourage* show some semantic and syntactic similarities with positive verbs from the MAKING type: *He forced the platoon to clean the latrines.* And there are SPEAKING verbs like *forbid* and *discourage* (negative counterparts of *order* and *encourage*) which, like *stop* and *prevent* from the MAKING type, take *from . . . -ing* complements; compare *Frances encouraged me to apply* and *Frances discouraged me from applying.*

The LIKING type (*like, love, hate, prefer*, etc.) and the ANNOYING type (*annoy, please, excite, satisfy, disappoint* and many others) are syntactic converses in that LIKING verbs may have a complement clause as object and ANNOYING verbs may have one as subject. All the major varieties of complement clause are potentially acceptable and they do, of course, contrast semantically, as in (16):

(16) a. I like it that Mary sings the blues each Friday night (because she goes out, and I get the house to myself that night).
b. I like Mary's singing the blues (and could listen to her all night).

    c. I like Mary to sing the blues (because she is always in such a good mood afterwards).

Sentence (16a) refers to the fact that she does it (I am not interested in the details); (16b) relates to her actual performance (I like listening); and (16c) to a potentiality that I like to see realised.

I have here only highlighted a few of the main points concerning the meanings of complement-clause types in English, and the verbs that they occur with. The reader could consult Dixon (1991: 32–50, 207–66) for a full account of the syntactic possibilities, meanings and semantic co-occurrences.

Before turning to Dyirbal, a language which has no complement clauses *per se*, it will be useful to examine in some detail another language which shows a generous set of complement-clause constructions. Fijian is chosen since it comes from a different language family and a different part of the world (and is a language I have worked on intensively). By comparing English and Fijian we can gain some idea of the semantic tasks Dyirbal could be expected to achieve, by other grammatical means.

3.2 Fijian

Fijian[8] has more speakers than any other language from the Oceanic branch of the Austronesian family (about 300,000). I am here describing the Boumaa dialect, which differs from Standard Fijian perhaps as much as American English does from British English. (A full account, based on fieldwork in a Boumaa village on Taveuni island, is in Dixon, 1988). It will first be useful briefly to outline some basic points in Fijian grammar, which is fairly straightforward. After that I discuss the varieties of complement clauses and their meanings, and then their occurrence with verbs from the various semantic types.

A clause in Fijian normally begins with a predicate; it may consist just of a predicate. The predicate may be intransitive, in which case its head can be a verb (without any suffix), an adjective, a noun or a pronoun. Or it may be transitive, when its head must be a verb bearing a transitive suffix.

The predicate begins with a subject pronoun, for instance:

    (17) au rai 'I am looking.'
    (18) o rai 'you are looking'.
    (19) e rai 'he/she is looking'.
    (20) era rai 'they are looking'.

The reference of this subject pronoun (within the predicate) can optionally be expanded by a subject NP following the predicate, for example:

(21) e rai [a gone] 'The child is looking.'
(22) era rai [a gone] 'The children are looking.'

Note that number is not marked on an NP, but only on cross-referencing pronouns which must be included in the predicate (e.g. third-person singular in (19) and (21), third-person plural in (20) and (22)).

The basic form of a transitive suffix is -*Ci* or -*Ca'ini* (where *C* is a consonant, lexically determined by the choice of verb stem). It is followed by an object pronoun (as part of the predicate):

(23) au rai-ci ira 'I am looking at them.'

A third-person singular object can be specially marked by the pronoun '*ea* following the verb in the predicate (like third-person plural *ira* in (23)); however, the unmarked realisation of third-person singular is to replace the final -*i* of the transitive suffix by -*a*, for example:

(24) au rai-ca 'I am looking at him/her.'

The reference of the object pronoun (within the predicate) can optionally be expanded by an object NP which follows the predicate, for example:

(25) au rai-ca [a qase] 'I am looking at the old person.'
(26) au rai-ci ira [a qase] 'I am looking at the old people.'

Again, number is marked on the object pronoun within the predicate, not on the object NP.

Clauses in Fijian only rather seldom include two explicit NPs, referring to both transitive subject and transitive object. Ambiguity is possible in such sentences; for instance,

(27) e rai-ca [a gone] [a qase]

could mean 'The old person is looking at the child' or 'The child is looking at the old person'. In an actual instance of use, however, any potential ambiguity is likely to be resolved by discourse and/or contextual information.

Many other, optional, elements may occur in a predicate. A tense or aspect marker (e.g. past *aa*, future *na*) or one of a number of grammatical modifiers (including *mai* 'come and', *via* 'want to') come between the pronominal subject and the predicate head, for instance *au na rai-ca* 'I will look at him/her', *au via la'o* 'I want to go.' Following the object pronoun, but still within the predicate, we can get a string of grammatical modifiers, such as *rawa* 'be able to', *ti'o* 'continuous', *be'a* 'perhaps', *mai* 'to here', as in *e na la'o be'a mai* 'He might come here.'

Every predicate, and thus every clause, must include a pronominal marker of the subject (and of the object, if it is transitive). There is no provision for omitting a subject when coreferential with the subject of an earlier clause as there is in English. Thus a 'common subject' must be stated within both main and complement clauses, as in (47) below.

A noun phrase in Fijian begins with what is traditionally called an 'article'. The common article *a∼na* is used if the head of the NP is a common noun and the proper article *o∼ko* is used if the NP head is a proper noun or cardinal (i.e. free) pronoun. Adjectives follow the head. Thus *o Peritaania* 'Britain', *a waqa* 'the/a boat(s)', *a waqa levu* 'the/a big boat(s)'.

The most common possessive construction involves a possessive pronoun, which comes between article and head noun:

(28) a qou waqa 'my boat(s)'
(29) a omu waqa 'your boat(s)'
(30) a ona waqa 'his/her boat(s)'
(31) a odra waqa 'their boat(s)'

The reference of the possessive pronoun can optionally be expanded by a possessive NP, which comes after the head noun (referring to the 'possessed'):

(32) a ona waqa [a cauravou] 'the youth's boat(s)'
(33) a odra waqa [a cauravou] 'the youths' boat(s)'

These are, literally, 'his boat(s), the youth/youths' and 'their boat(s), the youth/youths'.

We can now discuss complement clauses in Fijian, of which there are two broad varieties. The first contains just one type, which I call 'clausal NP'. The second contains five types of complement clause; these can be named after their 'introducer' – *ni*, *se*, *dee*, *me* or *se me*.

Consider the two simple clauses:

(34) o   lesu   mai
     you + SUBJ   return   HERE
     'you return here'

(35) au   aa   rai-ca
     I + SUBJ   PAST   see-TR + 3SG
     'I saw him/her/it'

Now (34) can be embedded into (35), as the object of *rai-ca* 'see, look at'. To achieve this, clause (34) takes on the structure of an NP by (i) including the common article at the beginning; and (ii) substituting the appropriate possessive pronoun in place of the subject pronoun, here *omu* 'your' for *o* 'you'. Then the predicate head, *lesu* 'return' in (34) becomes clausal NP head. Any other components of the predicate naturally carry over into the clausal NP. We now get:

(36) au   aa   rai-ca   [a   omu   lesu   mai]
     I + SUBJ   PAST   see-TR + 3SG   ART   2SG + POSS   return   HERE
     'I saw your returning here.'

Recall that the subject pronoun may be further specified by an NP which follows the predicate, and that the possessive pronoun in an NP may be further specified by an NP which follows the NP head. Thus (37):

(37) era   lesu   mai   a   gone
     they + SUBJ return   HERE   ART   child(ren)
     'The children returned here.'

naturally goes over into the clausal NP which fills the object slot in (38):

(38) au   aa   rai-ca   [a   odra   lesu   mai
     I + SUBJ   PAST   see-TR + 3SG   ART   3PL + POSS   return   HERE

     a   gone]
     ART   child(ren)
     'I saw the children's returning here.'

Clausal NPs in Fijian have – as I shall demonstrate below – a similar meaning to -*ing* complement clauses in English, and are also grammatically similar in that they include the subject in possessive form. A clausal NP has the internal structure of a clause: the predicate head maintains the same form (being now identified as head of the clausal NP) and all predicate modifiers, subject and object NPs and peripheral constituents are preserved unchanged. But it also has a structure very similar to that of a plain NP, with an initial article, and a possessive pronoun (coding the underlying clausal subject). There are differences between plain NPs and clausal NPs: (i) only a plain NP can include a number modifier or *mataqali* 'kind of'; (ii) a possessive pronoun is optional in a plain NP but obligatory in a clausal NP; (iii) a plain NP can have only one post-head embedded NP, expanding a possessor pronoun, as in (32) and (33), whereas a clausal NP may include two, corresponding to underlying subject and object, for example:

(39) au   aa   rai-ca   [a   ona   motu-'a   [a
     I + SUBJ PAST   see-TR + 3SG ART   3SG + POSS   hit-TR + 3SG ART

     pua'a] [a   qase]]
     pig   ART   old person
     'I saw the old person hitting the pig.' (literally: 'I saw [his hitting the pig the
     old person]')

where the complement clause in (39) is based on the transitive simple
sentence:

   (40) e motu-'a [a pua'a] [a qase] 'The old person hit the pig.'

The question of whether 'clausal NPs' in Fijian should be regarded as a
type of NP, or simply as a type of clause, is a tricky one, which could be long
debated. Note that a verb or adjective can only be the head of a clausal NP,
not of a plain NP, so that there is in Fijian no contrast like that exemplified
by (5) and (6) in English. In view of this, the question is scarcely important.

The other variety of complement clause in Fijian is similar to *that*
complements in English in having the structure of a main clause simply
preceded by a complementiser. The complementisers are *ni* 'that', *se*
'whether' and *dee* 'that . . . might'. Both *ni* and *se* can combine with *me*
'should, so that'; *dee* does not combine with *me*, probably because of their
semantic incompatibility. (In a *ni me* construction the *ni* is omittable under
specifiable grammatical conditions.) Like complementisers in English
(except *whether*) and most of those in other languages, all of these
complementisers in Fijian have some other function in the grammar – *ni* can
also introduce 'when' and 'because' clauses; *se* – with the meaning 'or' – can
link constituents of any size; *dee* can have a co-ordinate function 'do X *in
case* Y might happen'; and *me* can link clauses with the meaning 'in order to'
or 'as a result that' (e.g. 'I eat a lot *in order to* be healthy'). The complement-
clause function of these four relations is clearly distinguishable from their
other functions – a complement clause has all the properties of a subject or
object constituent (e.g. a clause in object function can become passive
subject).

We can now consider the meanings of the various kinds of complement
clause. Clausal NPs are semantically very similar to *-ing* clauses in English
and *ni* complements to *that* complements. Parallel to (7a) and (7b) we get
(41a) and (41b):

(41) a. au   aa   rogo-ca   [ni   ra   qaaqaa]
        I   PAST   hear-TR   THAT   THEY   win
        'I heard that they won.'

b. au   aa   rogo-ca   [a   odra   qaaqaa]
   I   PAST   hear-TR   ART   THEIR   win
   'I heard their winning.'

Sentence (41a), with a *ni* complement, states that I became aware of the fact that they had won, whereas (41b), with a clausal NP, implies that I heard a radio commentary on all (or a fair portion) of the match. Clausal NPs refer to some durative activity, focusing on its internal structure. In contrast, a *ni* complement states a fact; in (41a) it treats the 'event' of their winning as a unit.

The *dee* complementiser also refers to an event as a unit and is used (in place of *ni*) if there is any uncertainty involved. Compare:

(42) a. au   'ila-a   [ni   na   mate   [a   qase]]⁹
        I   know-TR   THAT   FUT   die   ART   old-person
        'I know that the old person will die.'
     b. au   'ila-a   [dee   na   mate   [a qase]]
        'I know that the old person may die.'

Complementiser *se* is used in place of *ni* if the complement clause is interrogative; either if it involves an interrogative word, or if it is a polar question, for instance:

(43) au   na   taroga   [se   taalei-ta'ina   [a   dalo]]
     I   FUT   ask-TR   WHETHER   like-TR   ART   taro
     'I will ask whether he likes taro.'

Me, when it occurs in a *ni*-type complement clause, refers to some potentiality and has strong similarities with the 'modal' *to* complementiser in English:

(44) au   vina'a-ta   [mo   laga]
     I   want-TR   SHOULD + 2SG   sing
     'I want you to sing.'

(Note that *me* plus second-person subject pronoun *o* coalesces to *mo*.)

When *me* co-occurs with *se* we get a construction that has some similarities with *wh*-plus *to* in English, as in *He decided who should go*, although the one construction type is only sometimes translatable by the other:

(45) au   va'a-nanu-ma   ti'o   [se   [o   cei]   me   na
     I   think-TR   CONT   COMP   ART   who   SHOULD   FUT

     ca'a-va   [a   ca'aca'a   yai]]
     do-TR   ART   work   THIS
     'I'm thinking about who should do this work.'

We can now survey some of the main semantic types of verb in Fijian that take complement clauses. Note that some of these can be given the same labels as those in English (indeed, it is likely that there are some types which are universal, requiring recognition in every language, such as MOTION, REST, AFFECT, ATTENTION, SPEAKING). There are, however, some differences: for instance Fijian, unlike English, has no MAKING types of verbs (and see the comments below on a MENTAL ATTITUDE type in Fijian).

First of all, we can consider secondary verbs and other realisations of secondary concepts.

NEGATION and MODALS. There is a class of intransitive verbs (that I call 'semi-auxiliaries') which take complement clauses in S function. These include *rawa* 'can, be possible' (which takes a *ni* or *me* complement), *dodonu* 'must, be necessary' (takes only *me*), *bese* 'don't want to' (takes *ni*) as well as the negative used in imperatives *'ua* 'don't' (takes *ni*) and the negative used in non-imperative clauses *sega* 'it is not the case' (takes *ni*).

Rawa and *dodonu* correspond semantically to *can* (in both the 'be able to' and the 'be allowed to' senses) and *must, ought to* in English. Compare *I ought to go* with

(46) e dodonu [me-u la'o]
     literally: 'That I should go is necessary.'

(Note that complementiser *me* and first-person singular subject pronoun *au* reduce to *me-u*.)

Modals in English have no NP arguments independent of those for the verb they occur with. The same applies to *dodonu* and *rawa* (and the other semi-auxiliary verbs) in Fijian; they are intransitives and their subject is a *ni* or *me* complement clause. It is noteworthy that *dodonu* must take a *me* complement; compare this with the *to* of *ought to* in English. *Rawa* may take a *ni* complement clause – the unmarked construction – or a *me* clause, the latter being more positive, implying that the subject is both able and willing to act.

Other modals in English are translated by predicate modifiers in Fijian. Among modifiers that may follow the head are *be'a* 'might' and also a homonymous form *rawa* 'be able to'. (The verb *rawa* tends to be used to describe some general state of affairs, such as 'He can't read', and the modifier *rawa* for some specific instance, like 'I can't read this word'; but there is overlap between them.) Future-tense marker *na*, which precedes the head within the predicate, corresponds to the English modal *will*.

Of the ASPECTUAL verbs *te'evuu(-ni)* 'begin' may take a clausal NP or a *me* complement clause in O function, while *va'a-oti-i* 'finish' is restricted to a clausal NP. This exactly parallels English, where *begin* takes an *-ing* or a *to*, and *finish* only an *-ing* complement. *Tovole-a* can mean 'try' and then takes a *me* complement clause, as in (47), or 'taste, test' and then takes *dee* and *se* complements (e.g. 'I tasted whether it was salty enough').

> (47) au   tovole-a   [me-u   lave-ta   a   vatu]
>   I   try-TR   SHOULD-I   lift-TR   ART   stone
>   'I tried to lift the stone.'

In the WANTING type there is a lexical verb *vina'a-ti* 'want, need, deem good' which has a strong preference for a *me* complement; this is similar to English, where *want* can only occur with a 'modal' *to* complement. Fijian also has a grammatical modifier *via* 'want to' that may be included between the obligatory subject pronoun and the predicate head; it can only be used to translate English sentences where the subject of *want* coincides with the complement-clause subject, whereas the verb *vina'a-ti* may translate any kind of *want* sentence in English – see (44). Another verb from this type, *nui-ta'ini* 'hope for, rely on', generally takes a *ni* complement (*me* may be possible, but *ni* is certainly preferred).

Where English has a semantic type MAKING, including verbs such as *make, force, cause* and *let*, Fijian has a productive derivation involving the verbal prefix *va'a* for forming causatives, e.g. *tu(-ti)* 'stand (on)', *va'a-tu-ri* 'make stand up, put standing up'. Note that corresponding to many *make* constructions in English, a Fijian would specify exactly what was done to bring about the result: for example, instead of just 'I made him go', one would say 'I told him to go' or 'I hit him until he went', etc.[10]

Turning now to Primary-B types, ATTENTION verbs such as *rai(-ci)* 'see, look at', and *rogo(-ci)* 'hear, listen to' may take a clausal NP or a *ni* complement clause in O slot – see (36), (38), (39), (41). Some verbs from the THINKING type – including *va'a-bau-ti* 'believe', *nanu-mi* 'think, remember' and *vaa-'aasama(-ta'ini)* 'think (about)' – may take any kind of complement clause in O slot; this is reminiscent of *remember* in English (see (13)). I recorded *'ila-i* 'know' with all complement types except *me* – see (42). From the DECIDING type, *buci-ni* 'plan' appears to take only *me* complements, while *digi-i* 'choose' may take either a *me* complement (choose to do something) or *se* (choose which one from a number of alternatives).

Verbs from the SPEAKING type, such as *tu'u-ni* 'tell', *talanoa(-ta'ini)* 'recount', *baa(-ta'ini)* 'deny', *buubuli(-ta'ini)* 'swear (e.g. on oath)', *bili-a* 'accuse, blame' and *'udru(-va'ini)* 'grumble (about)' all take a *ni* complement, and most of them also accept clausal NPs, in O function (corresponding roughly to *tell. . . that . . .* and *describe . . . -ing . . .* in English). Some

SPEAKING verbs may take *me* complements. *Bose(-i)* 'confer (over)' takes *ni* when referring to a discussion about something that has happened, but *me* when the discussion is about something that should be done. *Yala-ta'ini* 'promise' can take a *ni* complement in O function when promising that something will happen, for example some duty will be performed, or *me*, which indicates that the person involved thinks it should be done and will do it willingly.

There is no commonly used verb 'order' or 'command' in Fijian. Instead the verb *'ere-i* 'ask/beg for something' is used; this is both extremely polite (in the Fijian cultural context) and also almost mandatory in that the addressee has to do what is asked; *'ere-i* appears to be restricted to a *me* complement. The verb *taro-gi* 'ask (a question)' takes a *se* complement in O slot (see (43)).

Corresponding to the LIKING and ANNOYING verb types and related adjective types in English (Dixon, 1991: 155–65, 78–85), we can recognise a class of MENTAL ATTITUDE verbs in Fijian, which can have a complement clause in O slot. Some, such as *rarawa(-ta'ini)* 'be sad (about)' and *pu'u (-ca'ini)* 'be angry (about)', most commonly take a clausal NP. *'Ila(-va'ini)* 'be scared (of)' may take a clausal NP ('I'm scared of their being drunk') or a *me* clause ('I'm scared that I should see a snake'). *Maarau(-ta'ini)* 'be happy (about)' and *taalei(-ta'ini)* 'like' may take a clausal NP or a *ni* or *me* complement clause in O function.

This has necessarily been a brief survey of complement constructions in Fijian. A full account of their syntax and semantics is in Dixon (1988: 267–94).

In summary, the varieties of complement clauses in Fijian do not have exactly the same meanings as those in English but there are broad similarities – clausal NP with *ing*, *ni* and *dee* with *that*, *se* with *wh*-complements, and *me* with modal 'to' clauses. It will be seen that verbs with similar meanings between the two languages tend to accept complement clauses with similar semantic effects. That is, the choice of complement clause constructions available for any given verb is not arbitrary (simply 'syntactic') but is determined by the meaning of the verb and the meanings of the available complement clauses.

4 Dyirbal

People have occasionally asked why my grammar of Dyirbal (Dixon, 1972)[11] has no mention of complement clauses. The grammar was based on an analysis of Dyirbal texts and describes every grammatical pattern that

Table 10.1 *Systems of case inflections in Dyirbal*

A	ŋaja	ŋinda	-ŋgu	ba-ŋgu-n	ba-ŋgu-l
S			∅	bala-n	bayi
O	ŋaygu-na	ŋinu-na			
DATIVE	ŋaygun-gu	ŋinun-gu	-gu	ba-gu-n	ba-gu-l
GENITIVE	ŋaygu	ŋinu	-ŋu	ba-ŋu-n	ba-ŋu-l
	'I'	'you (sg.)'	case on nouns and adjectives	feminine	masculine
				noun markers	

occurs. Quite simply, there are no complement-clause constructions;[12] that is, Dyirbal does not have clauses filling subject or object slot in a main clause. It does, however, have two 'strategies of complementation', one involving clauses linked at sentence level, and the other a relative-clause construction. Although these are grammatically quite different from complement-clause constructions in English, Fijian and other languages, they do make similar semantic distinctions and effectively achieve the same semantic ends.

It will first of all be necessary briefly to outline some of the relevant points in Dyirbal syntax, in section 4.1, before describing the strategies of complementation, in section 4.2. Then, in section 4.3, we survey Secondary concepts and verbs that correspond to Primary-B verbs in other languages, and their grammatical properties.

4.1 Basic syntax

A noun phrase in Dyirbal can include any combination of (a) pronoun, (b) noun, (c) adjective and (d) noun marker. The latter are determiner-like elements which indicate the location of the reference of the noun ('there' – the unmarked choice – or 'here' or 'not visible'), agree with the noun in case and mark the gender of the noun (masculine, feminine, edible plants or neuter).

It will be useful to work in terms of the three basic syntactic relations S (intransitive subject), A (transitive subject) and O (transitive object). Pronouns inflect on a nominative (SA)/accusative (O) and nouns, adjectives and noun markers on an absolutive (SO)/ergative (A) system. This is illustrated in table 10.1 for two sample pronouns, two noun markers and

the general inflections on nouns and adjectives (ignoring certain allomor-
phic variants). Note that nouns and adjectives take an ergative ending (here
-ŋgu) when in A function but absolutive case (with zero realisation) when in
S or O function. Pronouns, in contrast, have the same form (nominative) in
both S and A functions, but a different form (ending in the accusative suffix
-na) for O function.

Verbs can be classified, on grammatical criteria, as transitive or intransitive. A transitive verb has two core NPs – one in A function (nominative
form for a pronoun, ergative for a noun, etc.) and one in O function
(accusative form for a pronoun, absolutive for a noun, etc.). An intransitive
verb requires one core NP, in S function (nominative form for a pronoun,
absolutive for a noun, etc.). That is, a verb which can occur with a noun,
adjective or noun marker in ergative case, or with a pronoun in accusative
form, is transitive; one that cannot is intransitive.

Each verb in Dyirbal is strictly transitive or intransitive; we do not get the
situation found in English, where some verbs (e.g. *eat*, *break*) can have
either transitivity value. There are productive processes for changing the
transitivity value of a verb, but these are always morphologically marked
(e.g. anti-passive, which is described below). Each verbal stem belongs to
one of two conjugations, whose past-tense inflections are *-n* and *-nyu*
respectively (verbs are quoted here in past-tense form, which is the citation
form). There is one irregular verb, 'to go', whose past-tense form is *yanu*.

We can illustrate the case forms shown in table 10.1, in simple intransitive
and transitive clauses:

(48) [bayi yara]$_S$ yanu 'the man went'
(49) [balan yibi]$_S$ yanu 'the woman went'
(50) [ŋaja]$_S$ yanu 'I went'
(51) [ŋinda]$_S$ yanu 'you went'
(52) [bayi yara]$_O$ [baŋgun yibi-ŋgu]$_A$ buran 'the woman saw the man'
(53) [balan yibi]$_O$ [baŋgul yara-ŋgu]$_A$ buran 'the man saw the woman'
(54) [ŋaja]$_A$ [ŋinu-na]$_O$ buran 'I saw you'
(55) [ŋinda]$_A$ [ŋaygu-na]$_O$ buran 'you saw me'

Pronouns, nouns, adjectives and noun markers can be freely mingled within
a clause, and even within an NP, without any possibility of confusion. Note
that word order is quite free – words can occur not only in any order in an
NP but also in any order within a clause – although an underlying order is
followed in the example sentences here.[13]

Languages differ in the syntactic constraints they impose on co-ordination and embedding, and in related conventions for omitting a repeated NP.
Fijian is almost lacking in constraints of this sort; two clauses can be joined

in a complex sentence construction whether or not they share a common NP, and, if they do, whatever the function of this NP in either clause (Dixon, 1988: 299–301). This is related to the fact that subject and object must be stated within the predicate for each clause, and cannot be omitted.

In English any two clauses may be co-ordinated, and if there is a shared NP it can be replaced by a pronoun whatever the function of the common NP in each clause. But a common NP can only be omitted, from its second occurrence, if it is in subject (S or A) function in each clause; we can say that English operates with an S/A syntactic pivot (Dixon, 1994: 157ff.). Thus, from *John laughed* and *John saw Mary* can be obtained *John laughed and saw Mary* or *John saw Mary and laughed.* If the common NP is in O function in one of the clauses then NP deletion is not possible (we cannot say *John laughed and Mary saw*). One function of passive is to put an underlying O NP into derived S function so that this coreferential deletion can take place, for example *John came and was seen by Mary.*

Although Dyirbal has a mixed morphology – with nouns, adjectives and noun markers inflecting on an ergative, and pronouns on an accusative system – its syntax works entirely in terms of an S/O pivot; that is, it has a strictly ergative syntax. The S/O pivot condition *must* be satisfied if two clauses are to be joined in a co-ordinate construction; it is thus a stronger condition than the S/A pivot in English, which only applies for omission of a repeated NP (co-ordination can take place whatever the syntactic functions of a common NP in the two clauses).

In Dyirbal two clauses may only be joined in a co-ordinate structure if they share an NP which is in S or O function in each clause. The occurrence of the NP in the second clause is then generally omitted (or, just the noun marker element may be retained). Thus, (48) and (52) may be joined together in either order to make one sentence (note that Dyirbal has no overt co-ordinators 'and', 'but', etc.; co-ordination is shown by the whole sentence being assignable to a single intonation unit):

(56) [bayi yara] yanu [baŋgun yibiŋgu]ₐ buran
'The man went and the woman saw him.'

Here *bayi yara* is understood to be in S function for the first verb, *yanu* 'went', and in O function for the second, *buran* 'saw'

In order to co-ordinate two clauses such as (48) and (53), where the common NP 'the man' is in A function in the second clause, an anti-passive syntactic derivation must be applied to (53). This places the underlying A NP into derived S function, marks the underlying O by dative case and places the anti-passive derivational affix -ŋa- ∼ -na- between verb root and inflection, yielding (57), which has essentially the same meaning as (53).

(53) [bala-n   yibi]$_O$ [ba-ŋgu-l   yara-ŋgu]$_A$ bura-n
THERE + ABS-FEM   woman + ABS   THERE-ERG-MASC   man-ERG   see-PAST
'The man saw the woman.'

(57) [bayi   yara]$_S$ bural-ŋa-nyu   [ba-gu-n
THERE + ABS + MASC   MAN   see-ANTIPASS-PAST   THERE-DAT-FEM

yibi-gu]
woman-DAT

Now (48) and (57) can be co-ordinated, giving (58):

(58) [bayi yara] yanu buralŋanyu [bagun yibigu]
'The man went and saw the woman.'

Dyirbal has a type of clause linkage that we can call 'purposive', where the verb of the second clause bears purposive inflection *-li* ~ *-ygu* (the allomorphy being determined by conjugation) in place of a tense choice. Either the activity of the first clause was done *in order that* that of the second should follow, or the activity of the second clause follows *as a natural consequence of* what was described in the first clause. Thus, replacing the past-tense inflection on the verb of the second clause in (56) by purposive, we get:

(59) bayi yara yanu baŋgun yibiŋgu burali
either 'The man went so that the woman should see him'
or 'The man went and as a result the woman saw him.'

Purposive inflection can also appear on the verb of a main clause (although it is found less often in this position than in the second clause of a complex sentence construction such as (59)), for example:

(60) bayi yara yanuli 'The man has to go.'

It is here implied that there is some state of affairs in the light of which the man must go out; for example, his children may be hungry and he may have to go out to hunt. A sentence such as (60) can be translated by 'has to', 'ought to', 'needs to', or even 'wants to' but only when this implies a desire brought on by some external factors, as in (61):

(61) bayi yara miyandaygu
'The man wants to laugh.' (i.e. something has happened to make him want to laugh, and he will have to restrain himself to avoid doing so)

Relative clauses in Dyirbal also work in terms of an S/O pivot. There must be an NP shared between main and relative clauses. It can be in (almost) any function in the main clause, but it must be in S or O function in the relative clause. A relative clause is marked by a special inflection, *-ŋu*, on its verb; this is followed by a case ending agreeing with the case on the common NP in the main clause (absolute is again marked by zero, and ergative by -*rru*). Consider (62):

(62) [bayi yara]ₛ miyanda-nyu 'The man laughed.'

This can be embedded as a relative clause in (48). The NP *bayi yara* 'the man' is in S function in both clauses; the verb *miyanda*- 'laugh' takes relative-clause ending -*ŋu* (plus zero, since the common NP is in S function in the main clause):

(63) [bayi   yara   [miyanda-ŋu]]ₛ   yanu
     THERE + ABS + MASC man + ABS   laugh-REL + ABS go + PAST
     'The man who was laughing went.'

Similarly, from (62) and (52) we can form (64):

(64) [bayi   yara   [miyanda-ŋu]]ₒ   [ba-ŋgu-n
     THERE + ABS + MASC man + ABS   laugh-REL + ABS THERE-ERG-FEM

     yibi-ŋgu]ₐ   bura-n
     woman-ERG   see-PAST
     'The woman saw the man who was laughing.'

If (62) is embedded as a relative clause in (53) then the verb *miyanda*- takes relative-clause inflection -*ŋu* plus ergative -*rru* (because the common NP in the main clause is in A function, ergative case), giving:

(65) [bala-n   yibi]ₒ   [ba-ŋgu-l   yara-ŋgu
     THERE + ABS + FEM woman + ABS   THERE-ERG-MASC   MAN-ERG

     [miyanda-ŋu-rru]]ₐ bura-n
     LAUGH-REL-ERG   SEE-PAST
     'The man who was laughing saw the woman.'

Now suppose that we wish to embed (66) into (48). The common NP is in A function in (66). In order to satisfy the constraint that the common NP must be in S or O function in the relative clause, (66) must be antipassivised, putting the underlying A NP into derived S function, as in (67) (which has essentially the same meaning as (66)).

(66) [bala-n   guda]ₒ   [ba-ŋgu-l   yara-ŋgu]ₐ jilwa-n
     THERE + ABS-FEM   dog + ABS   THERE-ERG-MASC   man-ERG   kick-PAST
     'The man kicked the dog.'

(67) [bayi   yara]ₛ   jilwal-ŋa-nyu   [ba-gu-n
     THERE + ABS + MASC man + ABS   kick-ANTIPASS-PAST THERE-DAT-FEM
     guda-gu]
     dog-DAT

Then we can form a relative clause construction from (48) and (67):

(68) [bayi yara [jilwalŋaɲu [bagun gudagu]]] yanu
'The man who kicked the dog went.'

There is one further topic that should be mentioned in this brief survey of Dyirbal grammar. Just as an adjective, modifying a noun, inflects in exactly the same way as the noun, so Dyirbal has a class of what I call 'adverbals' which modify a verb and agree with it in inflection and also in transitivity. Thus the transitive adverbal *wirrjan* 'do quickly' and the transitive verb *jaŋganyu* 'eat' may be combined into one verb phrase *wirrjan jaŋganyu* 'eat quickly'. (There are a number of derivational processes that form transitive from intransitive verbal stems, and vice versa, and these are used to ensure transitivity agreement.) In Dyirbal, just as an NP can consist of simply an adjective, for instance *bulgan* 'big' (i.e. 'the big one'), so a verb phrase can consist just of an adverbal, the previous discourse or surrounding context making clear what kind of action is being described.

I have recorded about three dozen adverbals, whose meanings include 'do first', 'try to do', 'finish doing', 'do too much', 'do to insufficient degree', 'do too soon', 'pretend to do', 'do again', 'do properly', 'do badly', 'do for no reason', 'do at night', 'do on one's own', 'do like this' and 'do how/what?'

4.2 Strategies of complementation

In section 2.2 we compared the two English sentences:

(1) [The man went] to [bathe]
(2) [The man wanted [to bathe]]

Sentence (1) involves two intransitive clauses linked, through a sentence node, by (*in order*) *to*. In contrast, *want* in (2) is a transitive verb and its O slot is here filled by the complement clause *to bathe*. For both sentences the subject NP of the second clause is omitted under identity with the subject of the first clause.

These sentences would be translated into Dyirbal by (69) and (70),

(69) [bayi yara yanu] [ŋabaygu]
(70) [bayi yara walŋgarranyu] [ŋabaygu]

where the purposive inflection -*ygu* corresponds both to the clause linker (*in order*) *to* and to the complementiser *to*. The important difference between Dyirbal and English is that in Dyirbal (69) and (70) have exactly the same surface structure and underlying structure. Both *yanu* 'go' and *walŋgarra-*

nyu 'want'[14] are intransitive and they are here each linked by the purposive
inflection to another clause; according to the pivot convention, the S NP of
ŋabaygu 'to bathe' is omitted under identity with the S of *yanu* and of
walŋgarranyu. In terms of the grammatical schemes of clause linkage,
presented in section 2.2, (1) is of type (a), with clauses linked at sentence
level, (2) is type (b), with a clause filling object slot, and both (69) and (70)
are of type (a).

Both *yanu* and *walŋgarranyu* are intransitive verbs and they have exactly
the same grammatical possibilities. Sentences (69) and (70) illustrate how a
clause *bayi yara yanu/walŋgarranyu* could be linked to an intransitive
clause, *bayi yara ŋabaygu*. We can also consider how they could be linked to
transitive clauses, such as (52) and (53). Sentence (52) has *bayi yara* as O
NP, satisfying the S/O pivot condition for co-ordination with *bayi yara
yanu/walŋgarranyu*, where *bayi yara* is in S function. We get (59) with *yanu*
and (71) with *walŋgarranyu*:

(71) [bayi   yara]$_S$ walŋgarra-nyu   [ba-ŋgu-n
     THERE + ABS + MASC   man + ABS   want-PAST   THERE-ERG-FEM

     yibi-ŋgu]$_A$ bura-li
     woman-ERG   see-PURP
     'The man wanted the woman to see him' (e.g. while he was 'showing off').

In the case of (53) the NP *bayi yara* is in A function (*ba-ngu-l yara-ŋgu*) and
this sentence must be antipassivised, as (57), to put *bayi yara* into derived S
function in order to satisfy the pivot condition. We can now link *bayi yara
yanu/walŋgarranyu* with (57), giving:

(72) [bayi   yara]$_S$ yanu   bural-ŋa-ygu
     THERE + ABS + MASC   man + ABS   go + PAST   see-ANTIPASS-PURP

     [ba-gu-n   yibi-gu]
     THERE-DAT-FEM   woman-DAT
     'The man went (in order) to see the woman.'

(73) [bayi   yara]$_S$ walŋgarra-nyu   bural-ŋa-ygu
     THERE + ABS + MASC   man + ABS   want-PAST   see-ANTIPASS-PURP

     [ba-gu-n   yibi-gu]
     THERE-DAT-FEM   woman-DAT
     'The man wanted to see the woman' (he might be worried about her).

Discussing (1) and (2), in section 2.2, we pointed out that a user of English
would never have any doubt as to which construction was intended since he
knows that *go* is an intransitive and *want* a transitive verb. In Dyirbal the
same construction type is used for (69) and (70), for (59) and (71) and for

(72) and (73) but the meanings of the verbs carry the same sort of semantic information as the contrasting construction types in English. *Yanu* 'go' is a plain intransitive verb which expects no syntactic accompaniment beyond an S NP; in (69), (59) and (72) it is linked within a purposive construction to *ɲabanyu*, but it need not be. *Walŋgarranyu* 'to want' is also an intransitive verb but one that carries the expectation of a further verb in purposive construction with it, as in (70), (71) and (73). That is, *walŋgarranyu* carries an expectation that it may be linked to another verb by the purposive 'strategy of complementation'.

Want in English takes a *to* complement clause whose subject is most often coreferential with main-clause subject. With *ask*, from the SPEAKING type, the direct object can be followed by a complement clause, for example *I asked John [that his child (should) be quiet]*. Or, there can be a *to* complement clause whose subject is omitted when it is coreferential with the main clause object, as in *I asked him to be quiet*. Now in Dyirbal two co-ordinated clauses must have a common NP which is in a pivot function (S or O) in each clause. Thus we can say (74):

> (74) [[balan yibi]_O [baŋgul yaraŋgu]_A ɲanban] [yanuli]
>   'The man asked the woman to go.'

In (74) *balan yibi* 'the woman' is O of the transitive verb *ɲanban* 'ask' and it is S for *yanu* 'go'.

'Ask' can, of course, be linked to an intransitive or to a transitive verb. In English we can say *I asked the man to give the cigarette to the woman*. The underlying clauses here are *I asked the man* and *The man gave the cigarette to the woman*. These would be translated into Dyirbal by (75) and (76):

> (75) [ŋaja]_A   [bayi   yara]_O   ɲanba-n
>   I + NOM   THERE + ABS + MASC   man + ABS   ask-PAST
>   'I asked the man.'

> (76) [bala-m   jigarrin]_O   [ba-ŋgu-l]   yara-ŋgu]_A
>   THERE + ABS + EDIBLE   cigarette + ABS   THERE-ERG-MASC   man-ERG
>
>   wuga-n   [ba-ɲu-n   yibi-ɲu]
>   give-PAST   THERE-GEN-FEM   woman-GEN
>   'The man gave the cigarette to the woman.'

These two clauses do have a common NP, 'the man', but it is in O function in (75) and in A function in (76). Clause linking is only possible if (76) is first put into anti-passive form, in (77), so that the common NP is now in S function. As before, the anti-passive in (77) has essentially the same meaning as the plain transitive in (76).

(77) [bayi   yara]$_S$ wugal-ŋa-nyu
      THERE + ABS + MASC   man + ABS   give-ANTIPASS-PAST

      [ba-gu-m   jigarrin-gu]   [ba-ŋu-n   yibi-ŋu]
      THERE-DAT-EDIBLE   cigarette-DAT   THERE-GEN-FEM   woman-GEN

Examples (75) and (77) can now be linked, with purposive inflection on the
verb of the second clause, and the second occurrence of the common NP,
bayi yara, omitted:

(78) [[ŋaja]$_A$ [bayi yara]$_O$ ŋanban] [wugalŋaygu [bagum jigarringu] [baŋun
      yibiŋu]]
      'I asked the man to give the cigarette to the woman.'

The verb *yajijarran* 'threaten' is transitive and, like *ŋanban* 'ask', can be
linked to another verb by means of the purposive complementation
strategy, provided that they share an NP which is in S or O function in each
clause. Thus:

(79) [[bayi   yara]$_O$ [ba-ŋgu-n   yibi-ŋgu]$_A$
      THERE + ABS + MASC   man + ABS   THERE-ERG-FEM   woman-ERG

      yajijarra-n]   [baga-li]
      threaten-PAST   spear-PURP
      'The woman threatened to spear the man.'

Here *bayi yara* is O for *yajijarran* 'threaten' and also O for *bagali* 'to spear'.
Since no specific A NP is stated for the transitive verb *bagali* its subject is
understood to be the same as that of *yajijarran*. However, *bagali* could have
a different subject:

(80) [[bayi yara]$_O$ [baŋgun yibiŋgu]$_A$ yajijarran]   [[ba-ŋgu-l
                                                                  THERE-ERG-MASC

      gubi-ŋgu]$_A$ bagali]
      shaman-ERG
      'The woman threatened the man that the shaman would spear him.'

Note that (79) was translatable into English by a *to* complement construction but for (80) we had to use a *that* construction since the syntactic
condition in English on *to* complements with *threaten* (that main-clause
subject should be coreferential with complement-clause subject) is not met.

Let us now consider the transitive verb *ŋuyminyu* 'like (to do)'. This is
commonly joined to another transitive verb within a purposive construction, the two verbs sharing both A and O NPs:

(81) [[ŋaja]$_A$ [bala-m   ŋarrinyji]$_O$ ŋuymi-nyu]] [jaŋga-ygu]
      I + NOM   THERE + ABS + EDIBLE orange + ABS   like-PAST   eat-PURP
      'I like to eat oranges.'

But if the second verb is intransitive, and it describes something that the subject of *ŋuyminyu* (in underlying A function) likes to do, then in order to meet the S/O constraint on coreferentiality, *ŋuyminyu* will have to be made intransitive. This can be done by anti-passive *-ŋa-*, or by adding the derivational suffix *-marri-* (which also has a reflexive function), as in (82):

> (82) ŋaja ŋuymi-marri-nyu ŋaba-ygu 'I like to bathe.'

The verb *ŋuyminyu* can be used with just an O NP and no further verb in purposive construction with it. That is, I was able to elicit (83):

> (83) [ŋaja]ₐ [balam ŋarrinyji]ₒ ŋuyminyu 'I like oranges.'

But informants were not very happy with sentences like (83). They wanted to add a verb in purposive inflection, as in (81), stating *what it is* the subject likes to *do* with the object.

We can see that, corresponding to English verbs such as *want, like, ask* and *threaten*, which take a complement clause in object or post-object slot, Dyirbal has intransitive verbs such as *walŋgarranyu* 'want (to do)' and transitive verbs such as *ŋuyminyu* 'like (to do)', *ŋanban* 'ask' and *yajijarran* 'threaten (to do)' which *expect* to have another clause joined to them through a purposive construction. This is what I call the first strategy of complementation.

The other complementation strategy involves the relative-clause construction. Corresponding to *I described his eating the meat* and *I heard you(r) being chastised* one would say (literally) 'I told about him, who was eating the meat' and 'I heard you, who were being chastised.' That is:

> (84) [ŋaja]ₐ   jinga-nyu   [bayi   yara
>   I-NOM   tell-PAST   THERE + ABS + MASC   man + ABS
>
>   [rubi-ŋu   ba-ŋgu   jalgur-u] ᵣₑₗ]ₒ
>   eat(INTR)-REL + ABS   THERE-INST + NEUT   meat-INST
>   'I told about the man('s) eating the meat.'
>
> (85) [ŋaja]ₐ   ŋamba-n   [ŋinu-na   [milga-ŋu]ᵣₑₗ]ₒ
>   I-NOM   hear-PAST   you-ACC   chastise(TR)-REL + ABS
>   'I heard you(r) being chastised.'

If the common NP is not in S or O function in a putative relative clause then it must be placed in derived S (or O) function by some means like the anti-passive, as in (86) (said by a woman whose promised husband had not claimed her by the appropriate time, and who had to go to claim him):

> (86) [ŋaja]ₛ   ŋurji-nyu   [[ŋanbal-ŋa-ŋu   ba-gu-l
>   I + NOM   be ashamed-PAST   ask-ANTIPASS-REL + ABS   THERE-DAT-MASC

gaŋa-rri-gu]ᵣₑₗ]ₛ

marry-REFL-PURP

'I was ashamed of having had to ask him to get married.' (literally: 'I, who asked him to get married, was ashamed.)'

In section 2.2 I mentioned that the English sentence *I don't like that man painting his front door blue* can be the reduced form of two distinct construction types: a complement-clause construction, in (3) – I do not like what he is doing – and a relative clause construction, in (4) – I do not like that man – with the relative clause simply serving to identify him. No such syntactic distinction is possible in Dyirbal. A sentence like (84) is effectively ambiguous between 'I told that the man was eating the meat' and 'I told something about the man who was eating the meat.' However, the surrounding discourse and/or context would always be likely to resolve any ambiguity.

4.3 Use of complementation strategies

In both English and Fijian some verbs are restricted to one variety of complement clause but many verbs may take several varieties, with appropriate meaning differences. In contrast, most verbs in Dyirbal enter into just one of the complementation strategies. A single verb in my corpus is attested with both strategies; this is the intransitive *ŋarjarrmbanyu* 'feel unsettled in mind, be unable to make up one's mind, try to plan', as in (87) and (88):

(87) [ŋaja]ₛ   ŋarjarrmba-nyu   [[bulgu-ŋgu   galga-ŋu]ᵣₑₗ]ₛ
     I-NOM   feel unsettled-PAST   wife-ERG   leave-REL + ABS
     'I felt restless (couldn't settle to do anything), having been left by my wife.'

(88) [[ŋaja]ₛ ŋarjarrmba-nyu]   [wunyja-rri   yanu-li]
     I-NOM can't decide-PAST   WHERE-TO   go-PURP
     'I couldn't decide where to go.'

There may be a few more verbs of this sort. But certainly most verbs in Dyirbal are restricted to one method of complementation.

We can now survey appropriate semantic types in Dyirbal, following roughly the same headings as English and Fijian, beginning with Secondary concepts.

NEGATION and MODALS. Dyirbal is like English (and unlike Fijian) in showing negation by an uninflecting particle, *gulu*, which can come anywhere before the verb in a clause; there is also a particle *yamba* 'might be'. 'Will' is shown by future-tense inflection and, as mentioned in section

4.1, 'have to', 'ought to', 'need to' (and one sense of 'want to') by purposive inflection on a main-clause verb. There is no form corresponding to the 'be able to' sense of English *can*; speakers might use the generic tense, for example 'I (habitually) swim across the river', or past tense 'I have swum across that river' rather than 'I can swim across that river'. (Interestingly, there are adjectival lexemes *jurun* 'can't swim' and *maymbi* 'can't/never do climb trees'.)

ASPECTUALS. There is a verbal derivational affix *-yarra-* 'start to do', as in *ŋaja yanu-yarra-nyu* 'I started to go'. There are also adverbals such as *ŋunbiran* 'try to do', *jayŋun* 'finish doing' (both transitive), *wudanyu* 'stop doing', *ŋabinyu* 'repeat doing' (both intransitive) which occur in apposition to a main verb and agree with it in transitivity and inflection. Dyirbal also has uninflecting particles *yanda* and *ŋurrma* 'tried to do (but failed)'.

A verb from the WANTING type typically has the same subject as the verb to which it is syntactically linked; for instance, in English a construction like *I want to go* is commoner than one like *I want Mary to go*. This also applies in Dyirbal. Although the subject of a WANTING verb can be coreferential with the O NP of the verb to which it is linked – as in (71) 'The man wanted the woman to see him' – most often the two verbs share the same subject.[15] 'Subject' covers S and A, and Dyirbal works in terms of an S/O syntactic pivot. It is, in view of this, not surprising that verbs of the WANTING type are intransitive in Dyirbal, for instance *walŋgarranyu* 'want to do, choose to do', *garrginyu* 'want to go to a certain place', *nyurrŋinyu* 'be anxious/ready to do something'. These expect a following verb in purposive inflection and it will generally have the same subject as the WANTING verb. The implicated verb may be intransitive, as in (70), or transitive, as in (73), in which case it must be antipassivised to put the subject NP (underlying A) into derived S function, in order to satisfy the S/O constraint.

Thus, Dyirbal operates with both: (a) the universal lexico-semantic expectation that a WANTING verb is most likely to have its subject (underlying S or A) NP coreferential with the subject of the linked verb; and (b) a language-specific syntactic constraint that for two clauses to be coordinated they must share an NP which is in (derived) S or O function in each. It is able to reconcile these through having all its WANTING verbs intransitive. (If they were transitive, they would need to be antipassivised in almost every instance of use, to satisfy the pivot condition.)

Speakers of Dyirbal were hunter–gatherers, living in an egalitarian society which had no chiefs and very little social hierarchy. It is undoubtedly because of this that there are no verbs such as 'order' or 'command' in the SPEAKING type, and there is no MAKING type at all; that is, there are no verbs corresponding to English *make* (*do*), *force, cause* or *prevent* – one must simply specify what is done to make or prevent someone doing something.

In section 1 we said that, in English and in many other languages, Primary verbs can be divided into two sets: Primary-A, which only take NP arguments; and Primary-B, which may take an NP or a complement clause in one argument slot. Since Dyirbal has no complement clauses, the grammatical criterion for such a division of its Primary verbs is not available. However, we can now consider those semantic types in Dyirbal which correspond semantically to Primary-B types in English, Fijian and other languages.

Verbs of the ATTENTION and THINKING types – such as *buran* 'see, look at', *rugan* 'watch (someone) going', *wamin* 'watch (someone) without them knowing they are being watched', *ŋamban* 'hear, listen to, understand, remember' and *yibirranyu* 'dream about' – are all transitive and use the relative-clause strategy of complementation, as exemplified in (85). There is another transitive verb, *ngurrumin* 'think of, imagine, have a premonition about', which must involve thinking of someone else; it takes the same complementation strategy. There is in Dyirbal no verb corresponding to *know* in English.

In common with many other languages in the world,[16] Dyirbal has no grammatical construction of 'indirect speech' (dealt with by *that* clauses in English and *ni* complements in Fijian). A verb like intransitive *wurrbanyu* 'speak, say' or transitive *buwanyu* 'tell' will simply be followed by the quoted direct speech. Other verbs from the SPEAKING type – such as transitive *jinganyu* 'tell about, recount' and *ŋunjanyu* 'blame' – take relative-clause complementation, as exemplified in (84). The intransitive verb *wajin* 'promise to go somewhere' takes the purposive complementation strategy, as does transitive *yajijarran* 'threaten (to do something to someone)', shown in (79) and (80).

Dyirbal has a number of jussive SPEAKING verbs, like *gigan* 'tell to do, let do', *bunman* 'request (someone) to accompany you', *ŋibanyu* 'call (someone) over to do something, or for something to be done to them', and one sense of *ŋanban* 'ask'. These are all transitive and take purposive complementation, as in (74) and (78) and also (89):

(89) [[bala-n   yibi]ₛ   [ba-ŋgu-l   yara-ŋgu]ₐ
     THERE + ABS + FEM   woman + ABS   THERE-ERG-MASC   man-ERG

giga-n]   [yanu-li]
tell to do-PAST   go-PURP
'The man told the woman to go.'

The opposite of *gigan* is *jabin* 'tell not to do, refuse to allow'. This shows the relative-clause method of complementation:

(90) [balan yibi]$_O$ [bangul yarangu]$_A$ jabi-n   [yanu-ŋu]$_O$
                                      stop-PAST   go-REL + ABS
'The man stopped the woman from going.' (by telling her not to)

There is an interesting parallel to English where verbs like *order* and *encourage* take a *to* complement clause whereas their opposites, *forbid* and *discourage*, take a *from* . . . *-ing* complement.

There are a number of MENTAL ATTITUDE verbs. Some, such as *ŋuyminyu* 'like (to do something)' and *jiwan* 'don't like (to do), can't bear', may enter into purposive complementation constructions, as in (81) and (82), and others, including *murrinyu* 'feel ashamed (of having done some wrong)', *ŋurjinyu* 'feel shy (of some new person or place), feel ashamed' and *gayga + gandanyu* 'feel jealous of', can take relative-clause complementation, as in (86) (all of these verbs are intransitive).

5 Summary and conclusion

In section 2.2 three kinds of clause linking were described (see figure 10.1):

(a) Clauses linked under a sentence node, for example [*I ate the bread*] *and* [*Mary drank the wine*], [*I kept the children quiet*] (*in order*) *for* [*Mary to be able to work*]; these can be called co-ordinate/(non-embedded) subordinate constructions.

(b) One clause functioning in subject, object, etc. slot in another, for instance *John knows* [*that Mary drank the wine*], *I want* [*Mary to win*]; these are complement-clause constructions.

(c) One clause filling a modifier slot in a noun phrase which itself fills subject, object, etc. slot in another clause, for example *I shot* [*the man* [*who stole the bread*]]; these are relative-clause constructions.

All languages make a distinction between verbs which in their central meanings can only relate to objects, described by NPs, such as *throw*, *break*, *eat* (Primary-A verbs), and verbs which can relate either just to objects, realised by NPs (e.g. *They discussed the king*), or, alternatively, to an action or event, described by another verb (*They discussed the king's dismissing his jester*) (Primary-B verbs). All languages also have a set of secondary concepts, which must modify a verb; these include all or most of 'not', 'must', 'can', 'begin', 'finish', 'try', 'want', 'make (do)', etc. Secondary concepts can be realised as clause particles, verbal modifiers, verbal affixes or as independent verb lexemes.[17]

There must always be some grammatical means of linking a Primary-B or Secondary verb with another verb. It appears that languages which have in their grammar complement-clause constructions use this device for clause linking. But there are languages, like Dyirbal, which lack (b). We showed how in Dyirbal there are two complementation strategies – one being a variety of (a) sentence-level clause linking, and the other being (c) the relative-clause construction – which achieve the same semantic ends as complement-clause constructions in other languages.

For Panyjima, from Western Australia, Dench (1991: 196–201) describes a situation very similar to that in Dyirbal, with relative-clause constructions used as a complementation strategy for verbs such as 'see' and 'hear', and purposive constructions for 'want', and with 'tell' having available both strategies. There are many other languages that lack complement-clause constructions, but the available grammars say little about complementation strategies.[18] It is likely that a variety of different strategies will be found; some languages may work entirely in terms of (a) sentence-level clause linkages, and others perhaps entirely in terms of (c) relative-clause constructions. There could also be use of nominalisations. Careful grammatical description of such languages should have a high priority in future research.[19]

Typically, markers of complement clauses have some other function in the grammar. Thus, languages with complement clauses are essentially using elements from elsewhere in the grammar to mark the construction types that code the links between a Primary-B or Secondary verb and another verb. Languages without complement clauses use a construction type from elsewhere in the grammar to code such links.

We saw that Dyirbal recognises a smaller number of kinds of interclausal links than do English or Fijian. English (like Fijian) assigns different grammatical structures to [*I went*] to [*bathe*] and [*I wanted* [*to bathe*]], whereas the corresponding Dyirbal sentences have the same structure; we saw that the semantic profiles of the verbs, *go* and *want*, ensure that there could be no ambiguity. However, in the use of the relative-clause construction as a complementation strategy there is grammatical neutralisation, and a consequent possibility of ambiguity. 'They discussed the king who dismissed his jester' and 'They discussed the king's dismissing his jester' have the same form and cannot be grammatically distinguished in Dyirbal.

It appears that there are always at least two types of complement clause or strategy of complementation: one with 'potential' (or 'irrealis') meaning, typically referring to something that has not happened, but which people intend or want should happen ('modal' *to* complements in English, *me* complements in Fijian and purposive constructions in Dyirbal); and one with 'actual' (or 'realis') meaning, typically referring to some existing or certain event or state (the relative-clause strategy in Dyirbal). Many languages make a distinction between at least two 'actual' constructions, one referring to an activity as it extends in time (-*ing* complements in English, clausal NPs in Fijian), and the other simply to the fact of something happening (*that* and *wh*- clauses in English, *ni, se* and *dee* clauses in Fijian). The number of types of complement clauses in a language varies from two in Irish (Stenson, 1981; Noonan, 1985) up to half-a-dozen or more (as in English and Fijian – Dixon, 1991, 1988 provide full accounts). For languages without complement clauses *per se*, the number of different strategies of complementation is also likely to vary – this is a topic for further investigation.

In every language there are similar basic types of Primary-B verb – referring to ATTENTION, THINKING, SPEAKING, etc. – and the same sorts of Secondary concepts, some of which may be expressed as verbs. Semantically similar verbs take semantically similar types of complement clause or complementation strategy across different languages. If there is an indirect speech construction, it will use (one of) the 'actual' variety (or varieties) of complement clause – specifically, the one that refers to the fact of something happening (*that* in English and *ni* in Fijian). However, many languages – including Dyirbal – have no indirect speech mechanism; one must simply quote direct speech. It would be interesting to discover whether there are any languages that lack a complement-clause construction but do have some other means of coding indirect speech.

Verbs of ATTENTION, such as 'see', 'hear', 'notice', 'watch', verbs of THINKING, such as 'think (about)', 'know', and verbs of SPEAKING that make no reference to the future, such as 'describe', 'blame', 'tell' (in the sense of 'inform') will take the 'actual' variety of complement clause or complementation strategy. Verbs such as 'want' and 'like' (sometimes a single lexeme combines these two meanings), 'tell to do' and 'order' will take the 'potential' variety of complement clause or complementation strategy.

There is an important difference between verbs such as 'want' and 'like', on the one hand, and those like 'tell to do', 'order' and 'persuade', on the other. For the former, the subjects of the linked verbs are most likely to be the same (one wants/likes to do something oneself more often than one wants/likes someone else to do something). For the latter the object of the Primary-B or Secondary verb is likely to be coreferential with the subject of the verb it is linked with (one generally orders someone other than oneself to do something). Indeed, Finnish has two distinct infinitive complements –

the 'first infinitive' is used in same-subject constructions (mostly with Secondary verbs such as 'want', 'must', 'try' and 'intend') while the 'second infinitive' is used where main-clause object coincides with complement clause subject (e.g. 'urge') – see Sands (1989).

'Want' is an interesting verb in that many languages employ different grammatical strategies depending on whether the subject of the linked verb is the same as or different from the subject of 'want'. (English is unusual in having the same construction in each instance: *I want to go, I want John to go.*) There are in fact a number of languages where 'want' *must* have the same subject as the verb it relates to (in the same way that 'begin', 'finish', 'must', 'can' and 'not' do).[20] In Fijian, either the verbal modifier *via* 'want to' or the lexical verb *vina'a-ti* 'want, need, deem good' can be used if the subjects are the same, but only the latter for different subjects. Finnish uses the first infinitive for same subjects but a 'that' complement when the subjects differ. Swahili has an infinitive complement for same subject, but a subjunctive complement when the subjects of 'want' and of its linked verb are not the same (Vitale, 1981). Jacaltec, a Mayan language from Guatemala, has an infinitive complement if 'want' relates to a non-stative verb with identical subject but a 'that'-type complement in other circumstances (Craig, 1977).

For the Tupí-Guaraní language Kamaiųrá, spoken in the Upper Xingu region of Brazil, Lucy Seki (personal communication) reports that there is a verb *potat* 'want' which can be compounded with another verb if they share the same subject, for example:

(91) a-maraka-potat
      1SG-sing-want
      'I want to sing.'
(92) ipira   a-ʔu-potat
      fish   1SG-eat-want
      'I want to eat fish.'

If the subjects are not identical, then *potat* must function as an independent verb, with a 'nominalised' clause as object, as in (93):

(93) ne-o-taw-a   a-potat
      2SG-go-NOMINALISER-NP MARKER 1SG-want
      'I want you to go.' (literally: 'I want [your going]')

There is a semantic contrast between 'make (do)' and 'stop (doing)' and between 'order/tell (to do)' and 'forbid/tell not to do'; in view of this, many languages accord them different grammatical treatment. In English, the first member of each pair takes a *to* and the second a *from* . . . *-ing* complement. In Dyirbal *gigan* 'tell to do, let do', takes the purposive complement strategy whereas *jabin* 'tell not to do' takes the relative-clause strategy. In Finnish both 'urge to do' and 'prevent from doing' take the second infinitive, but this is followed by illative case for the first and by elative case for the second verb.

I began this chapter by stating that every language has a similar set of meanings to deal with, but different grammatical means at its disposal. Each construction type has a semantic value, and constructions with similar meanings (even though they may have different grammatical structures) tend to be employed to achieve comparable semantic tasks in different languages. I have attempted to illustrate this principle by reference to complement clauses and complementation strategies.

NOTES

It is a pleasure to offer this to John Lyons, as a small thank-you for the example he has set linguists of how one should integrate syntactic and semantic concerns and criteria when describing a language.

Bill Foley helped me to start thinking on this topic. Kristina Sands allowed me to make use of some of her results – especially concerning 'want' – from Sands (1989). Others who provided data and the most helpful comments on various earlier drafts of this paper are Felix Ameka, Tim Curnow, Des Derbyshire, Lys Ford, Cindi Farr, Charles E. Grimes, Ken Hale, Rodney Huddleston, Ulrike Mosel, Michael Noonan, Lucy Seki, Nancy Stenson, Sandra Thompson, Anna Wierzbicka and especially Tim Shopen.

1 There is a fuller discussion of the notions 'semantic type', 'Primary verb' and 'Secondary verb', with special reference to English, in Dixon (1991: esp. 6ff., 87ff.).

2 Some languages have verbal affixes which indicate whether an action was done while (or after) 'going' or 'coming' (see e.g. Hercus, 1994, on the Australian language Arabana-Wangkangurru). This is the only example I know of a primary verb concept being realised as a verbal affix; it is certainly significant that 'go' and 'come' are shifters (whose meaning varies with the locational focus). And note that such languages do also retain lexemes 'come' and 'go'.

3 As mentioned in section 1 (see Dixon, 1991: 90–3, 172–87) a complement-clause verb – if it is transitive – can often be omitted after *want* under specific circumstances, for example *The man wanted (to get) some fish*. Thus, *want* must be followed either by a full complement clause or by an NP. Of course, a full *want* clause can then be linked to a further clause by (*in order*) *to*: [*The man wanted* [(*to get*) *some fish*]] (*in order*) *to* [*appease his hunger*].

4 In a classic paper, Hale (1976) draws attention to a different type of ambiguity in Warlpiri and other languages; here, a complex sentence construction can be ambiguous between (c) and (a) – that is, a subordinate clause could have the status of a relative clause ('I speared the emu which was drinking water') or of a temporal subordinate clause ('I speared the emu while it was drinking water'). He refers to these as 'adjoined relative clauses', which can have either 'NP-relative' or 'T-relative' interpretations. Tim Shopen (personal communication) has suggested that Warlpiri does not have relative clauses *per se*, but instead uses a 'strategy of relativisation'.

5 There is vast linguistic diversity in South America and although many languages appear not to have complement clauses *per se*, others do show this construction type. See, for instance, Bontkes (1985) on Suruí, a language from the Mondé family within the Tupian stock.

6 Note that *make* and *let* omit the complementiser *to* in the active voice (*they made/let John go*) but that *make* does include it in the passive (*John was made to go*); *let* scarcely occurs in the passive. For a semantic explanation of this see Duffley (1992).

7 In British and Australian – but not in American – English the *from* may be omitted, carrying a meaning difference (see Dixon, 1991: 236–7).

8 The standard Fijian alphabet is used here, with the addition of ' to indicate glottal stop (this occurs in the Boumaa dialect but not in the standard dialect). In addition, I show vowel length (which is contrastive) by doubling the letter; previous grammar books have employed a macron (e.g. *ā*) for length but this is not used in most Fijian literature. The phonemes are, with IPA phonetic values shown in square brackets when these differ from the letter used: bilabial *p*, *b*[ᵐb], *m*, *v*[β]; labio-dental *f*; apico-dental *t*, *d*[ⁿd], *n*, *c*[ð]; apico-alveolar *r*, *dr*[ⁿr], *s*, *j*[tʃ, dʒ], *l*, *y* [j]; dorso-velar *k*, *q* [ᵑg], *g* [ŋ], *w*; glottal ' [ʔ]; vowels *i, e, a, o, u*.

The following abbreviations are used in the glosses of examples in this chapter:

ABS	absolutive	INTR	intransitive
ACC	accusative	MASC	masculine
ANTIPASS	anti-passive	NEUT	neuter
ART	article	NOM	nominative
COMP	complementiser	PL	plural
CONT	continuous	POSS	possessive
DAT	dative	PURP	purposive
ERG	ergative	REFL	reflexive
FEM	feminine	REL	relative
FUT	future	SG	singular
GEN	genitive	SUBJ	subject
INST	instrumental	TR	transitive

9 Note that third-person singular subject pronoun *e* is omitted when it would immediately follow a complementiser *ni, se, dee* or *me*.

10 There is a verb *lai-vi* 'leave' whose meaning may be extended to 'let, allow, permit'. This does not take a complement clause – there is always a plain NP in object slot; however, a *lai-vi* clause can be linked to another clause (at sentence level) by *me* e.g. [*au lai-va a ose*] *me* ['*ana*], '[I left the horse] (in order for [it) to eat].'

11 I use here a practical orthography, which differs at a number of points from the phonetic orthography used in Dixon (1972). The phonemes are (with the 1972 symbols in parentheses, where they differ); bilabial *b, m*; apico-alveolar *d, n, l*; lamino-palatal *j* (ɟ), *ny* (ɲ); dorso-velar *g, ŋ*; rhotic tap or trill *rr* (r), semi-retroflex rhotic continuant *r* (ɽ); semi-vowels *w, y*; vowels *i, a, u*.

12 Note also that Dyirbal lacks any mechanism for deriving nouns from verbs and adjectives (except for a limited agentive suffix '-er'). That is, there are no nominalisations – or abstract nouns – corresponding to *decision, refusal, killing, hatred, size, length, age, colour*, etc.; one simply has to use appropriate verbs and adjectives.

13 There are a number of constituent-order tendencies or preferences; (i) a nominal in absolutive case should precede one in ergative case; (ii) a pronoun in nominative case should precede one in accusative case; (iii) a pronoun should precede a noun; (iv) constituents in S, O or A function should precede the main verb and those in dative inflection should follow it. These may be freely diverged from in spontaneous language use.

14 Although *walŋgarranyu* is here glossed as 'want' it would be used to translate only a small proportion of the instances of *want* from English. *Walŋgarranyu* carries an overtone of strong emotional feeling 'want to do something to satisfy a persistent emotional worry or desire'. The sentence *janyja ŋaja walŋgarranyu mijagu banagaygu*, which occurred in a text, was glossed by the bilingual narrator as 'He worried about to go home' (because he knew he was soon to die, and wanted to return to his own country to die). Sentence (70) might be used if a man wanted to bathe in a water-hole with which he had a religious affiliation.

15 Either the two clauses must share the same subject, or the subject of the WANTING verb must be coreferential with the O NP of the second verb, as in (71). Note that there is no way of translating into Dyirbal, using a WANTING verb, a sentence in which the subject of *want* is not identical to any of S, A or O for the linked verb (e.g. *John wanted Tom to go/to help Mary*). See also note 20.

16 *Pace* Palmer (1986: 164), who suggests that even in languages that have been said not to show indirect speech, this can be recognised, I would maintain that indirect speech, as a grammatical construction type, is absent from a consider-able proportion of the world's languages. However, Palmer's book does contain much valuable discussion relevant to the topic of this paper.

17 Givón (1980, 1990: 515–61) provides a perceptive general survey of a 'semantic hierarchy of "binding" and its syntactic coding' that has some similarities to the discussion here (although Givón works in terms of different kinds of semantic parameters).

18 Grimes (1991: 425–9) gives an explicit account of complementation strategies in
    Buru, an Austronesian language from Indonesia.
19 It would be interesting to investigate whether there is any correlation between
    lack of complement clauses and other aspects of the grammar of a language. We
    noted that Dyirbal has a strong pivot condition – so that deleted material is
    always retrievable by the addressee – whereas Fijian has virtually no pivot, and a
    fair amount of ambiguity. Is this related in any way to the fact that Fijian has a
    rich set of complement clauses while Dyirbal has none? Only detailed syntactic
    studies and comparisons, over a sample of languages from different regions and
    language families, would tell.
20 As pointed out in note 15 above, *walŋgarranyu* in Dyirbal has its S NP either (a)
    coreferential with the S or A of the linked verb, or (b) coreferential with the O NP
    of the linked verb. Thus a WANTING construction in Dyirbal may have different
    subjects for the two verbs only when the second verb is transitive and has its O
    NP coreferential with the S of the WANTING verb (as in (71)). As stated earlier,
    there is no direct translation into Dyirbal of 'I wanted him to go to town'. (When
    I asked how to say this I was given a Dyirbal sentence which is, literally, 'I told
    him to go to town'.)

REFERENCES

Abbott, M. (1991) Macushi. In D. Derbyshire & G. Pullum (eds.) *Handbook of
    Amazonian languages*, vol. III, Berlin: Mouton de Gruyter, 23–160.
Ameka, F. (1991) Ewe, its grammatical constructions and illocutionary devices.
    Ph.D thesis, Australian National University.
Bontkes, C. (1985) Subordinate clauses in Suruí. In D.L. Fortune (ed.) *Porto Velho
    Workpapers*, Brasilia: SIL, 208–30.
Craig, C.C. (1977) *The Structure of Jacaltec*, Austin: University of Texas Press.
Crapo, R.H. & P. Aitken (1986) *Bolivian Quechua Reader and Grammar-dictionary*,
    Ann Arbor, MI: Karoma.
Dench, A. (1991) Panyjima. In R.M.W. Dixon & B.J. Blake (eds.) *Handbook of
    Australian Languages*, vol. IV, Melbourne: Oxford University Press, 124–243.
Derbyshire, D. (1979) *Hixkaryana* (Lingua descriptive series, 1), Amsterdam:
    North-Holland.
    (1985) *Hixkaryana and Linguistic Typology*. Dallas: SIL and University of Texas
    at Arlington.
Dixon, R.M.W. (1972) *The Dyirbal Language of North Queensland*, Cambridge
    University Press.
    (1988) *A Grammar of Boumaa Fijian*, University of Chicago Press.
    (1991) *A New Approach to English Grammar, on Semantic Principles*, Oxford
    University Press.
    (1994) *Ergativity*, Cambridge University Press.

Duffley, P. (1992) *The English Infinitive*, London: Longman.

Foley, W.A. & R. Van Valin (1984) *Functional Syntax and Universal Grammar*, Cambridge University Press.

Gerdts, D.B. (1991) Unaccusative mismatches: Halkomelem Salish. *IJAL* 57: 230–50.

Givón, T. (1980) The binding hierarchy and the typology of complements. *Studies in Language* 4: 333–77.

  (1990) *Syntax, a Functional Typological Introduction*, vol. II, Amsterdam: John Benjamins.

Grimes, C.E. (1991) The Buru language of eastern Indonesia. PhD thesis, Australian National University.

Hale, K.L. (1976) The adjoined relative clause in Australia. In R.M.W. Dixon (ed.) *Grammatical Categories in Australian Languages*, Canberra: Australian Institute of Aboriginal Studies, 78–105.

Hercus, L.A. (1994) *A Grammar of the Arabana-Wangkangurru Language, Lake Eyre Basin, South Australia*, Canberra: Pacific Linguistics.

Jensen, C. (1990) Cross-referencing changes in some Tupí-Guaraní languages. In D.L. Payne (ed.) *Amazonian Linguistics: Studies in Lowland South American Languages*, Austin: University of Texas Press, 117–58.

Karlsson, F. (1983) *Finnish Grammar*, Porvoo: Werner Söderström Osakeyhtiö.

Noonan, M. (1985) Complementation. In T. Shopen (ed.) *Language Typology and Syntactic Description*, vol. II: *Complex Constructions*, Cambridge University Press, 42–140.

Palmer, F.R. (1986) *Mood and Modality*, Cambridge University Press.

Sands, A.K. (1989) A cross-language study of complement clauses (Finnish, Swahili, Mokilese, Jacaltec, Irish). Term paper, Australian National University.

Schachter, P. (1985) Parts-of-speech system. In T. Shopen (ed.) *Language Typology and Syntactic Description*, vol. I: *Clause Structure*, Cambridge University Press, 3–61.

Stenson, N. (1981) *Studies in Irish Syntax*, Tübingen: Narr.

van Driem, G. (1987) *A Grammar of Limbu*, Berlin: Mouton de Gruyter.

Vitale, A.J. (1981) *Swahili Syntax*, Dordrecht: Foris.

11

Grammar and meaning

JOHN LYONS

It is difficult to know quite how to respond to the request to contribute a chapter to a volume that is being published in one's own honour. Should one try to comment in detail on the other contributions? Should one attempt, instead, to provide a more general statement on how one stands now on the issues about which one has written in the past and which are still, or have recently become, prominent in the literature? I have opted for the second of these two possible responses. I will, however, comment selectively, and in some cases very briefly, on relevant points made by the other contributors.

First I must thank those of my colleagues – several of them former students of mine, all of them by now friends of long standing – who have done me the honour of contributing to this volume. I am especially indebted to Frank Palmer for agreeing to act as editor: he was already well established as a leading member of the so-called London School, based at the School of Oriental and African Studies, when I went there as Lecturer in Comparative Linguistics in 1957, and he has continued to be active in research and publication ever since. I will refer to two of his more general, introductory, works presently, when I set the scene for the discussion of grammar and meaning which follows.

I have taken as the title of my article the title of the volume as a whole. My treatment of the topics that it covers, in the present context, will be, inevitably, retrospective and personal. It will also be somewhat autobiographical, but not, I trust, gratuitously or excessively so. Then and now? How did I stand then – when 'then' refers to particular periods in the past marked by the publication of relevant books and articles – and how do I stand now on the still controversial question of the relation between grammar and meaning? That is the subject of my contribution to the present volume. As far as most of the relevant articles of my own are concerned, I can usefully refer to the recently reprinted versions in Lyons (1991a, forthcoming), where they have been contextualised and in some cases supplied with additional, or new, notes and an 'Epilogue'.

Let me begin, however, by establishing a chronological and partly autobiographical framework and noting in relation to it some of the more significant developments that have taken place over the last forty years in what may be referred to (Whiggishly) as mainstream linguistics, in so far as these are relevant to our concerns (see Lyons, 1989b).

I have already mentioned 1957 as the year in which I took up my first university appointment and became a somewhat peripheral member of the (so-called) London School, founded by J. R. Firth (see Lyons, 1991a: ch. 6; forthcoming). It was the year in which Firth himself retired, and it was also the year in which his first definitive, retrospective and synoptic account of the Firthian view of grammar and meaning was published (Firth, 1957b) and his most important earlier articles were reprinted (Firth, 1957a). I will return to the Firthian component in my work towards the end of this article, since it is highly relevant to my view of the relation between grammar and meaning. Let me observe here, however, that the Firthian component in my thinking on this and other issues which were hotly debated at the time did not derive from a direct personal association with Firth himself or, in the first instance, from his writings, but initially from W. Sidney Allen, in Cambridge, and R. H. Robins, in London, my PhD supervisors. This is important in that both of them, whilst being full members (as it were) of the London School, were more receptive to the ideas of other contemporary schools of linguistics and, in particular, were less hostile to Bloomfieldian and post-Bloomfieldian American structuralism than Firth and most of his followers (see Allen, 1957; Robins, 1964). Much of what I now recognise as being an eclectic mixture of the traditional and the modern and, as far as what was regarded in the late 1950s as modern linguistics is concerned, of British, European and American structuralism which is discernible in Lyons (1963) and is set forth explicitly on a broader canvas in Lyons (1968) I owe to the benign and inspiring teaching of Allen and Robins. This was reinforced, as I have mentioned elsewhere, by the influence, subsequently, of the late C. E. Bazell and F. W. Householder, who were similarly eclectic – perhaps I should say catholic – in their evaluation of rival theoretical viewpoints (Lyons, 1968: x). All four of them, incidentally, had read Chomsky's *Syntactic Structures* (1957) more or less as soon as it was published and, unlike many other well-established linguists at that time, on both sides of the Atlantic, were immediately convinced of its significance.

Nowadays, when the year 1957 is referred to by linguists, they tend to think of it as being the year in which linguistic theory was revolutionised by the publication of *Syntactic Structures*, and some accounts of the history of twentieth-century linguistics give the impression that the so-called Chomskyan revolution was theoretically more revolutionary than, in fact, it was in the context of post-Bloomfieldian American linguistics. I would be the last to deny the historic importance, not only of Chomsky's earliest work in transformational-generative grammar, but also of his more recent work on universal grammar and the biological foundations of language (see Lyons, 1991b: 139–53, 154–209). It is important to realise, however, that on everything that concerns us, in the present context, Chomsky's position in *Syntactic Structures* was indistinguishable from that of, say, Harris in *Methods* (1951). This point is established beyond doubt in Matthews (1986, 1993). Chomsky's position was to change later, of course, in what we may now think of as the classical period of generative (or generativist) grammar in the 1960s, when an interpretative semantic component (as well as a phonological component and a separate lexicon) was added to the categorial and transformational subcomponents of the syntax and the lexicon. But by the 1960s, and more obviously in the 1970s, all sorts of other positions were being defended on the relation between grammar and meaning. I will not attempt to deal with these in detail. Some of the more important developments will be mentioned when it is appropriate to do so.

Grammar and meaning. What is grammar? And what is meaning? Volumes could be written on each of these topics – and have been! I will confine myself to making a few general points and saying how I am using the words 'grammar' and 'meaning' in the present context.

The first general point is that the word 'grammar' is ambiguous; it can be used to refer to languages (in whole or in part) or, alternatively, to descriptions of languages. The relation between these two senses can be expressed, of course, by saying that a grammar of a language is a description – more precisely, in my view, a descriptive model – of the grammar of the language in question. The general point I am making is clear enough and uncontroversial, and it is commonly made (and then developed in various ways) in introductory textbooks. (There are other ambiguities deriving from the syntactic ambivalence of 'grammar' and the possibility of using it as one can use 'language', in appropriate contexts, as either a mass noun or a count noun. We may disregard these here.)

The word 'meaning' is not similarly ambiguous. Granted, provisionally, that there is such a thing as meaning (we shall come back to the subtractive fallacy later) and that it is in a language (in some sense of 'in'), we do not use the word 'meaning' to refer both to what is in the language and also to a description of what is in the language. The term that is traditionally employed by linguists in the second sense (and has been since the turn of the century) is, or has been until recently, 'semantics'. As we shall see presently, the coverage of the term 'semantics' – what it is used to refer to by linguists – is nowadays both broader and narrower than it used to be earlier this century and still was, for most linguists, at our *terminus post quem*, the *annus mirabilis* of 1957. Some linguists (including two or three of the contributors to this volume) do of course use 'semantics' (but not 'meaning'), like 'grammar', with what since Chomsky (1965) we have learned to call systematic ambiguity: they talk about the semantics of the language as being something that is in, or expressed by, the language. This is in itself a harmless enough way of talking, but it tends to obscure the difference between the ontological status of grammar and that of meaning, and it may at times be based on a set of genuine and serious theoretical misconceptions. The most serious of these is that meaning exists (albeit inchoate and unstructured) independently of the particular language systems in which it is encoded. But for the moment let us simply note, as my first general point, that the word 'grammar', unlike either 'meaning' or (in the usage of most linguists) 'semantics', is commonly used with systematic ambiguity.

The second general point is also terminological. Since I have made it often enough before, I need not labour it here. The word 'meaning' (in contrast, once again, with 'grammar') is a word of a particular everyday metalanguage, English, which has no fully satisfactory equivalent in many, perhaps most, other natural languages (see Lyons, 1977: 4; 1995: ch. 1). In everything that I have ever written on semantics, or on the relation between grammar and meaning, I have taken the view that we must be careful not to make the assumption that, because there is a noun 'meaning' in English (and more or less semantically equivalent nouns in some, but by no means all, other languages), there is some extralingual substance or entity which it denotes, whatever the ontological status or location of that substance or entity. In taking this view, I have of course been strongly influenced by Quine's criticism of what he called the subtractive fallacy: the fallacy involved in inferring from the true proposition that a linguistic expression has meaning or a meaning, the false proposition that the meaning that it has exists as an identifiable entity or substance, in the mind or wherever (see Quine, 1953: 47–64, 1960: 206; Lyons, 1963: 41; 1995: ch. 8). In effect, Quine is saying (and I think rightly) that the meaning of 'meaning' is syncategorematic. My own structuralist development of this idea in lexical semantics in Lyons (1960/3) was directly inspired by Saussure (1916), but I was also strongly influenced by the relational treatment of abstract properties (and their ontological elimination) by logicians such as Russell (1940) and Reichenbach (1947: 210): see Lyons (1963: 58; 1968: 443–5). When I brought these two notions together in my own work in the late

1950s, I am not sure that they had been previously seen as related. Latterly, I have been suggesting that (if one is using English as one's metalanguage) the word 'meaning' is best kept, and used, by semanticists in the full range of its everyday sense (or senses) and should not be theoretically restricted to what is covered by more technical terms such as 'denotation', 'reference' or 'intension' (see Lyons 1977, forthcoming). This is the view that I am taking here. It does not follow, of course, that I am not in favour of identifying and explicating different kinds of linguistic meaning and supplying ourselves with technical terms in order to refer to them. On the contrary, much of my work has consisted in doing just this and, as Stephen Levinson observes in the first section of his contribution to this volume, supplying myself, if not my colleagues, with more technical terms than most of them judge to be either useful or necessary!

My third, and for the moment final, terminological point has to do with the word 'grammar'. The sense in which I will use it throughout is the sense in which Frank Palmer, writing some twenty-five years ago in his introductory book entitled *Grammar*, said it was 'normally used' by linguists: in contrast, on the one hand, with 'phonology, the study of the sounds of a language', and, on the other hand, with 'semantics, the study of meaning' (Palmer, 1971: 13). This he identified as 'the narrower, or traditional sense'. He noted, however, that there were many linguists who used the term grammar 'in a rather wider sense to include both phonology and semantics'. Whether the term 'grammar' is employed in a wider or narrower sense, with reference either to a language or to a description – or generative model, etc. – of that language is of no consequence, provided that it is clear when it needs to be what is being referred to. One advantage of using it in the narrower sense, in the present context, is that this matches the sense in which 'grammaticality' contrasts with 'semantic well-formedness' (or 'meaningfulness', 'significance', etc.) and 'grammaticalisation' contrasts with 'lexicalisation' (and 'semanticisation'). It is worth noting that in the earliest versions of transformational-generative grammar the term 'grammar' covered neither phonology nor semantics (see Harris, 1952, 1957; Chomsky, 1957). The usage of most generative grammarians since the mid-1960s has of course been different.

As to the difference between one grammatical model or theory of grammatical structure and another, this will not be of concern to us in the present context. What I have to say is intended to be neutral with respect to the difference between generative and non-generative grammars, between word-based and morpheme-based grammars, between grammars formalised as rule systems, and grammars formalised as systems of parameters and principles, between grammars which presuppose, or are integrated with, a richer or a poorer lexicon, between grammars which purport to be models of linguistic competence and those which do not, and so on. Needless to say, this does not imply that I consider these differences to be unimportant. It does mean, however, that what I have to say here will be more or less irrelevant to some of the topics discussed by the other contributors. 'Grammatici certant ...'. The fact that it is possible to talk about grammar and meaning in a theory-neutral way (*pace* Popper and his followers) and to get scholars of different theoretical persuasions to agree that they are talking about the same things is, as I have argued elsewhere, evidence for the validity of so-called autonomous linguistics, of which autonomous linguistic semantics is a part (see Lyons, 1991a: ch. 2).

I have referred to 1957 as an *annus mirabilis* and have noted that it was the year in which, not only Chomsky's *Syntactic Structures*, but also Firth's *Papers* and 'Synopsis', were published (the latter in *Studies in Linguistic Analysis*, the Special Volume of the Philological Society which contains many other now classic articles of the London School). It was also the year in which, on the one hand, the first edition of Joos' *Readings* and, on the other, the second edition of Ullmann's *Principles of Semantics* appeared. But one must not make too much of the coincidence of the actual year of publication of historically significant works. It is not so much the year 1957 that is important for present purposes as the mid-to-late 1950s, a period for which 1957 serves as a conveniently central focal point. This was a period both of consolidation and of ferment. On the one hand, recognisably distinct schools of structural linguistics were taking stock and establishing their position *vis-à-vis* one another (sometimes uncharitably and uncomprehendingly); on the other, much of the isolationism which had developed during the Second World War and which continued into the 1950s was beginning to break down. It was also a period during which semantics – initially in the narrower sense of lexical semantics – began to be the object of serious theoretical enquiry and speculation.

It may well be that my own reaction to some of the issues which divided one school from another in the mid-to-late 1950s when I came into linguistics (from classical philology) was also, in many respects, uncomprehending. I had by then read the first edition of Ullmann's *Principles* (1952), as well as Guiraud (1955) and one or two other works, which had introduced me to post-Saussurean structural semantics and more especially to Trier's (1931, 1934) notion of lexical (or semantic) fields ('Wortfelder', 'Sinnfelder'). Under the influence of Sidney Allen, I then read, not only the relevant major articles by Firth and works by his followers which illustrated the London School approach, notably Mitchell (1957b), but also a good deal of American work, including Harris (1951, 1952, 1954) – whose distributionalism I initially tried to marry with Firth's contextualism (and, more particularly, with his collocational approach to what the neo-Firthians subsequently called lexis) – and, at the other extreme, as it were, Goodenough (1956) and Lounsbury (1956).

The work of Goodenough and Lounsbury (and of others in the same tradition) exemplified another major trend in mainstream American linguistics, stemming from Boas and Sapir, rather than Bloomfield: a trend that was cultural–anthropological, rather than text-based and distribution-alist, and was much closer in its philosophical underpinning to the various European schools of structural linguistics. The two articles by Goode-nough and Lounsbury that I have just mentioned introduced me to the distinctively American version of structural semantics – componential analysis – which was to be taken up enthusiastically in the 1960s (without the original cultural–anthropological influence which had initially made it so attractive to me some years earlier) in the context of what we have now learned to call the generative enterprise. (Componential analysis had its antecedents in European structural linguistics; but it was the American version with which I first became familiar.) By the end of the 1950s, on the basis of my experience of analysing the vocabulary of knowledge and understanding in Platonic Greek, I had myself become sceptical about the possibility of extending the principles of componential analysis to all lexical fields in the vocabulary of all languages. When I came to write Lyons (1968), componential analysis (coupled with universalism) was part and parcel of the current orthodoxy in generative grammar (to whose original aims, as I understood them, I was of course – and still am – fully committed), and I felt it necessary to draw the attention of students to what I took to be the facile and uncritical presentations of componential analysis that were by then commonly found in textbooks.

My scepticism in respect of componential analysis is noted by Adam Kilgarriff and Gerald Gazdar, in their contribution to this volume, with particular reference to the traditional distinction between polysemy and homonymy and the possibility of explicating what, following Apresjan, they call (with justifiable reservations about the implications of the term) regular polysemy. It is perhaps incumbent on me to respond; and it is convenient to do so at this point. First of all, I would agree that 'once we have a fully developed theory of subregularity, it is unlikely that a distinction between "irregular polysemy" and "homonymy" would serve any purpose in a synchronic description of the lexicon', since, on the assumption that every kind of synchronically determinable relatedness of meaning is accounted for in the fully developed theory, 'homonymy' becomes the name 'for whatever same-form/multiple-sense cases remain'. The terminological point is worth making. But nothing of importance, it seems to me, turns on it. Presumably, nonce cases of what are intuitively or experimentally determined as cases of relatedness of meaning are seen as regular and represented in the model as cases which fall within the scope of a rule of maximally limited applicability. The important question is whether the distinction between homonymy and polysemy is a question of fact or simply the product of where and how one draws the boundary between grammar and lexicon. And this, as we shall see presently, is one part of a much more general question. Kilgarriff & Gazdar appear to draw the boundary, for English at least, more or less where it is traditionally drawn (though the model with which they are operating represents the information associated with lexemes in what is, at first sight, an unfamiliar format). Taking them on their own terms, I certainly agree with the view they adopt in respect of so-called regular polysemy.

I also agree that they are right to say that, not only metaphor, but other kinds of relatedness of meaning too, especially metonymy (which plays a major role in the description of the lexical field that they use for purposes of exemplification), are involved in what is traditionally regarded as polysemy. The passage that they quote from Lyons (1981: 47) is quite clearly misleading in this respect. So too are any of the passages in my work which can be construed as implying that a componential analysis of lexical meaning is in principle incapable of representing polysemy. The notorious case of the English word *bachelor* (independently of how many senses we assign to it synchronically) demonstrates the contrary. This, then, is not the issue. What is at issue, in what I have written on componential analysis, is whether (a) it can be used to describe all areas of the vocabulary satisfactorily and (b) the components are universal, rather than language-specific. Componential analysis can certainly handle some part of the meaning of some lexemes and some of the sense relations among (and within) lexemes. So too, however, can meaning-postulates. At the end of the day it may well be simply a question of notational variation and the historical provenance of what are often presented as alternative and conflicting ways of handling the data. Kilgarriff & Gazdar are especially concerned to construct a computationally tractable model of the language system.

Among the issues which divided one school from another, and sometimes one group from another within the same school in the 1950s, I would list the following as being especially relevant to the topics dealt with in the present volume. Is the grammatical (and phonological) structure of natural languages determined by meaning (and, if so, how and to what degree)? Is semantics a separate level of analysis on a par with grammar and phonology? Is the structure (grammatical, phonological, semantic) which linguists claim to be describing really part of the language or is it an artefact of their theoretical and methodological decisions? As I have said elsewhere, 'a superficial reading of the recent history of linguistics might suggest [wrongly] that, because linguists no longer engage, at least overtly, in the disputes, which bear [the labels that they bore at the time] or use the same, rather quaint terminology, the underlying issues have been resolved' (Lyons, 1991a: 107).

Before saying how I stood then and how I stand now on the three issues that I have singled out as being especially relevant in the present context, let me pick up and develop the point I made earlier about changes in the interpretation of the term 'semantics' in the intervening years: I said that its coverage nowadays is both broader and narrower than it was earlier. It is broader in that it is no longer restricted, as it used to be, to what is now called lexical semantics. It is narrower in that these days many, if not all, linguists would reject the once standard definition of 'semantics' as 'the study of meaning': they would say that some part of the study of meaning falls within the more recently established level of linguistic analysis (if 'level' is the right term) known as pragmatics. Coupled with this re-interpretation of the term 'semantics', and causally connected with it, there has developed among linguists a greater sensitivity to the difference between grammatical and semantic well-formedness, on the one hand, and between each of these and acceptability, on the other. None of us can afford to be as exuberant and as carefree – not to say as irresponsible – in our 'arguments from asterisks' as we were twenty or thirty years ago (see Householder, 1973; Lyons, 1991a: 139). The point that I have just made is relevant to much of my own earlier work (including Lyons, 1963, 1968): I would now less readily classify as ungrammatical (or indeed as semantically ill-formed) actual or potential utterances which, though unacceptable in most normal contexts, could be motivated, and then seen as acceptable, with at times minimal adjustment of our normal ontological assumptions. This change in my (and others') view of grammaticality and semantic well-formedness (which is already evident in Lyons, 1981, and is even more marked in several of the chapters in 1991 and forthcoming) reflects an increased philosophical sophistication among linguists these days, which is very much to be welcomed.

It is gratifying, in this connection, to have in the present volume a broad-ranging article written jointly by a linguist and a philosopher, Adrienne Lehrer and Keith Lehrer. It is all the more gratifying in that I find myself wholly sympathetic to its aims and in full agreement with all the points of substance that are made in it. I cannot comment on the technicalities of the model they are proposing, but what they refer to as 'the metaphor of vectors' has an intuitive plausibility and is clearly worth developing further.

Let me return now to the more general point relating to the re-interpretation of the term 'semantics' that has taken place in recent years. This is conveniently illustrated by referring to the difference between the first and the second editions of Frank Palmer's *Semantics* (1976 and 1981): the second edition devotes much more space (including additional chapters) to non-lexical semantics and pragmatics. Evidence for the general acceptance by linguists of the legitimacy of the recently adopted (if not newly born) term 'pragmatics' is provided by the appearance at the beginning of the 1980s of the interestingly complementary textbooks by Leech (1981) and Levinson (1983), which used it in their title; Gazdar's somewhat earlier *Pragmatics* (1979), which did much to clarify the issues in part of the emergent field, was of course a monograph, rather than an introductory textbook. As we shall see presently, most of the contributors to this volume draw a distinction between semantics and pragmatics; and I comment on the use that some of them make of this below.

What I have said about changes that have taken place in the use of the term 'semantics' in mainstream linguistics – or at least in mainstream Anglo-American linguistics – in the last twenty-five years or so is consistent with what Peter Matthews says (with supporting quotations and references) in his chapter on 'Syntax, semantics, pragmatics' in this volume. Matthews also notes, correctly, in his historical survey of Bloomfieldian and post-Bloomfieldian usage that one reason why the term 'semantics' was restricted, in an earlier period, to the study of lexical meaning was that 'grammar', and more especially 'syntax', had been traditionally understood to include the study of non-lexical meaning (as well as lexical meaning in so far as this was held to determine the combinability of words in well-formed sentences). He further notes: (i) that it was some of Bloomfield's followers (whom we now refer to as post-Bloomfieldians) rather than Bloomfield himself who, by methodological fiat, sought to make grammar (and phonology) independent of meaning; (ii) that this methodological decision was associated with the general principle that the so-called levels of analysis should be kept separate and should be ordered ('hierarchically') in such a way that, in the description of a language, phonology should precede (and not presuppose or draw upon the findings of) morphology (or any higher level), that morphology should precede syntax, that syntax should precede semantics (for those post-Bloomfieldians who considered that semantics is, or should be, a proper part of the description of languages) and (when pragmatics was institutionalised as the study of non-semantic$_2$ meaning) that semantics (in the narrowed sense of 'semantics$_2$') should precede pragmatics; and (iii) that, nowadays, the post-Bloomfieldian anathematisation of what used to be called the mixing of levels (together with the attempt to formulate discovery procedures for the determination of the structure of languages) has been generally abandoned.

The central question that Matthews addresses (which 'originally owed more to methodology than to fact') is whether the 'institutionalised divisions' between syntax and semantics, on the one hand, and between semantics (i.e. semantics$_2$) and pragmatics, on the other, are methodologically necessary, or even desirable. Whether I am in full agreement with Matthews in the answer that he gives to this question I am not sure. I certainly agree that the separation of levels, and in particular the separation of grammar from semantics (whether semantics$_1$ or semantics$_2$) and of semantics$_2$ from pragmatics (however we draw the distinction between semantics$_1$ and semantics$_2$), is the product of the methodological decisions taken by certain linguists and does not necessarily reflect psychological (or any other kind of) reality. But relatively little is known so far about the structure of language systems from a psychological (or cognitive) point of view; and I do not think that descriptive linguistics should be seriously constrained, in this respect, by considerations of psychological, or cognitive, reality. Hence my continued commitment to (so-called) autonomous linguistics (Lyons, 1991a: ch. 2).

The separation of levels (to use this term) may not be methodologically necessary; but I would say that it is methodologically justifiable on the grounds that it makes for a more systematic and more elegant account of the linguist's data. I realise that this may sound like a very old-fashioned response to the question. But it follows directly from the answers that I would give to the three questions that I listed earlier as being questions which were hotly debated in the mid-1950s. I think it is fair to say that my views have not changed significantly, over the years, on any of the three issues I have identified: whether the grammatical structure of (so-called) natural languages is determined by meaning, whether semantics is (or ought to be) a separate level of analysis, whether the phonological, grammatical and lexical structure which linguists claim to be describing is really part of the language or an artefact of their theoretical and methodological decisions. However, I hope I have become clearer in my mind recently, if not always in what I have written, about the implications of the views I formed and expressed in earlier work.

I have always taken the view that, although meaning does, as a matter of fact, determine grammatical structure to some considerable degree (and, as Bob Dixon puts it at the very beginning of his chapter, can be said to be its very *raison d'être*), it is demonstrably the case that the grammatical structure of (so-called) natural languages is not fully determined by meaning. This being so, it seems to me that the arguments that were deployed by the post-Bloomfieldians (including Chomsky in 1957) to the effect that grammaticality cannot be equated with meaningfulness have lost none of their validity with the passage of time. The main difference between my present view and the view I expressed in such earlier publications as Lyons (1963, 1968) is that I would now subsume much of the semantic determination of grammatical structure – especially categorial structure – under ontology (filtered, of course, in reality by perception and cognition) and I would draw heavily on the notion of possible worlds in the explication of what I have recently been calling categorial incongruity, as a particularly interesting kind of unacceptability. Much of what I have just summarised here is spelled out in greater detail in the 'Epilogue' to my (1966) parts-of-speech article in Lyons (1991a: 137–45).

This is an important difference; and it reflects, I trust, my own assimilation of some of the philosophically more sophisticated ideas now current in linguistics to which I referred earlier. But I would still subscribe to the quotation that I put at the beginning of chapter 2 of Lyons (1960; cf. 1963: 10): 'We should like the syntactic framework of the language that is isolated and exhibited by the grammar [sc. the linguist's model of the language-system, J. L.] to support semantic description and we shall naturally rate more highly a theory of formal structure that leads to grammars which meet this requirement more fully' (Chomsky, 1957: 102). As I understand the principle that is expressed here, it implies that, in practice, when it comes to the evaluation of so-called weakly equivalent grammars of the same language goodness of fit between syntax and semantics will be a powerful criterion motivating one's choice between them. Much of the descriptive work that has been done on English and other well-studied languages since, and even before, the mid-to-late 1950s has, I believe, confirmed the heuristic validity of trying to interrelate grammar (and more particularly syntax) and semantics in the description of particular languages without, however, accepting that either is fully determined by the other. I think that it is also true to say that work which is presented as having been carried out 'on semantic principles' (such as Dixon's analysis of complement clauses in English, Dyirbal and Fijian in chapter 10) need not be seen as undermining the methodological validity of the post-Bloomfieldian principle of the separation of levels. What Firth and his followers used to refer to as the (partial) congruence of levels that exists (presumably) in all natural languages, coupled with the acceptance of the principle of rough justice (see below), ensures that, in the main, analyses of the grammatical structure of a language that are based on semantic principles and grammatical analyses of the same language that are based on the principle of the separation of levels will be interconvertible.

Having said this, I must then go on to say that I would no longer subscribe to the view held by many post-Bloomfieldian linguists that semantic analysis must necessarily follow a prior (and in the ideal complete) grammatical analysis of the language carried out without regard to semantic considerations. I did of course explicitly take this view in Lyons (1960), even though I equally explicitly accepted Chomsky's (and the Firthians') rejection of the post-Bloomfieldian goal of formulating algorithmic discovery procedures for grammatical (and phonological) analysis. But, of course, I did not in fact carry out the prior grammatical analysis of Platonic Greek myself; I simply took it for granted that a purely formal (i.e. non-semantic) transformational-generative grammar could be constructed and would validate essentially the same categories and constructions as a traditional, non-formal, grammar. To the best of my knowledge this was, and still is, a valid assumption. The reason why it is a valid assumption is precisely because the grammatical structure and semantic structure of Ancient Greek are, to a considerable degree, congruent and, in so far as they are determinate, independently determinable. It may be worth mentioning at this point that much that Dixon says about the interpenetration of grammar and meaning and exemplifies from the three typologically different languages, Dyirbal, English and Fijian, could also be illustrated from Ancient Greek, as is indeed made explicit at times in Lyons (1960/3). But I will come back to this later.

I think it is also true to say that the results of my semantic analysis of the words for knowledge and understanding in Platonic Greek (which was probably the first work in semantics, theoretical or descriptive, to be based overtly on the principles of generative grammar) would not be affected by the adoption of any of the later models of generative grammar, Chomskyan or non-Chomskyan, that have been developed since the early 1960s. It is worth noting, in particular, that it would be relatively easy to reformulate these results in terms of either a categorial or a dependency grammar associated with a slightly non-standard version of modern formal semantics. Although I did not realise this at the time, it has become clear to me over the years that my analysis was, in effect, both compositional and truth-functional (though neither of these two terms figures anywhere in Lyons, 1960/3).

This is not to say, of course, that I think that linguistic semantics should be restricted to truth-conditionally explicable (i.e. propositional) meaning. It so happens that the lexical field which, following Trier, I selected for analysis and the texts that I used as my primary data made it reasonable to adopt for the analysis itself what was in effect a truth-conditional approach. I have long held the view that linguistic semantics should deal with both propositional and non-propositional (especially socio-expressive) meaning in so far as this is encoded in the lexical and grammatical structure of particular language systems. This is quite clearly one of the issues on which contributors to this volume are divided and one of the ways in which they are representative of the whole community of linguists working in the field of semantics.

What is not so clear, however, is whether this difference of opinion is as serious as it might appear to be at first sight. Few, if any, of the contributors say how they stand on the third of the three questions that I listed above: is the structure that linguists claim to be describing (and for which they may be claiming descriptive adequacy) really part of the language system that is stored (presumably) as competence in the brains of the members of a particular language community? Many of them, no doubt, like most linguists these days, would indeed claim to be describing the linguistic competence of native speakers. But what does this mean? And what practical effect does it have on the analysis? Granted that descriptive linguistics is not all 'hocus pocus' (and did anyone ever believe that it was in the 1950s, when the issue was debated in these terms?), is it a matter of 'God's truth' or 'rough justice' (see Lyons, 1991a: 221)?

As will be clear from what I have said above (and at greater length elsewhere), I would opt for the latter. That being so, I can as readily accept what Ruth Kempson has to say in her overtly 'God's truth' contribution to this volume as I can accept what Matthews and other contributors (who are either agnostic or less definitely committed in this respect) say in theirs. I would, however, wish to reformulate the first paragraph (and especially the opening sentence) of Kempson's chapter and invite her to be rather more explicit than she is about sentences, expressions, denotational (as distinct from referential) ambiguity, etc., and about the difference between intrinsically encoded information (in contrast with the information that is conveyed by the use of an expression on particular occasions of utterance). I would also wish to take issue with her, of course, on her implicit restriction of linguistic semantics to the work of what has been, historically, only one school or movement: high-profile and justifiably influential, no doubt, but none the less only one school among several. The main point I wish to make here, however, is the more general one: that, because much of what linguists present as fact (in both semantics and grammar) can, and in my view should, be re-interpreted as fiction (i.e. as rough-justice model-construction), it is quite possible to reject an author's premises and yet to accept his or her conclusions.

Most of the contributors to this volume operate explicitly or implicitly with a distinction between semantics and pragmatics, though none of them apart from Stephen Levinson tells us explicitly how they draw the distinction and whether it is for them a matter of fact or of methodological commitment. I am myself committed, methodologically, to the view that, if one draws a terminological distinction between semantics and pragmatics, it is most profitably drawn in terms of a distinction between the meaning (non-propositional as well as propositional) that is encoded in sentences (and other expressions of the language system) and the meaning that is conveyed in utterance-tokens that are the product of the use of sentences (and other expressions) in particular contexts of situation (see Lyons, 1981, 1995, forthcoming). This is essentially how Levinson draws the distinction.

It is interesting to look now at Miller's chapter in the light of this distinction, given that he deliberately declines to avail himself of the terminological distinction that most of the others draw between semantics and pragmatics (though he does draw a clear distinction – clearer than do many of the other contributors – between expressions of the language system and units of text that are the product of the utterance of such expressions).

Miller's argument that clauses, rather than sentences, are the basic units of syntax (and especially of government and dependency) is, I think, irrefutable, if language systems are considered independently of the medium in which the forms of the language (i.e. the forms of expressions) are realised; and I now think that there is good reason to treat language systems in this way. I would also now agree with Miller that (if one retains the traditional concept of the sentence) sentences are best defined in terms of clauses, rather than conversely. Some of the reasons for taking this view – including the difficulty of establishing compound (in contrast with complex) sentences and the fact that syntactic dependencies can run over 'a sequence of what would normally be regarded as separate sentences' – were actually given in Lyons (1968: 170ff.); I did not, however, draw from this evidence the conclusions that, arguably, I should have done.

Apart from other considerations and independently of the generality and validity of his main thesis, Miller usefully reminds us of the powerful influence that has been, and still is, exerted on linguistic theory by the normative and literary prejudices of traditional grammar. He also makes it clear that theoretically minded linguists should once again take more seriously than many of them have done since the pendulum-swing from relativism to universalism in the 1960s the possibility that such concepts as word and sentence (as they are commonly defined) are relevant in the description of some, but not all, languages and may also be, to some degree, medium-dependent and style-dependent. Having said this, however, I would not too swiftly accept his (apparent) conclusion, that, because 'there is very little evidence to support either text-sentences or system-sentences in spontaneous spoken language' (in respect of the languages he refers to), there is no reason to postulate sentences as theoretical constructs in an overall medium-neutral and style-neutral description of some, if not all, language systems. I still incline to the view that the system-sentence (consisting of a single clause or a clause-complex) is justifiable in these terms for English and German, and perhaps also for Russian. The status of compound sentences is, I agree, much more dubious in a medium-independent description of these languages. (Dixon notes that compound sentences in Dyirbal are defined in terms of their intonational contour; this is perhaps tantamount to saying that they are not rightly regarded as grammatically definable units of the language system.)

I have just declared my commitment to the sentence (i.e. the system-sentence) as a theoretical construct for the description of certain languages. In doing so, I should emphasise in this more specific instance a point made more generally above: it must not be assumed that, because sentences are useful theoretical constructs (if they are) for the description of this or that language system, they have any psychological reality or play any part in the production and interpretation of utterances in this or that language. The linguist's model of the language system is inevitably idealised and, in the present state of the art, cannot be assumed to reflect users' competence or performance point for point. It may very well be the case, however, that a model which takes the clause, rather than the sentence, as basic is psycholinguistically more realistic. (Clauses correspond more closely to simple propositions than do simple – that is, non-composite – sentences (see Lyons, 1995: ch. 6).)

What I said earlier about resting the distinction between semantics and pragmatics on the distinction between sentence-meaning and utterance-meaning can of course be reformulated without difficulty with reference to clauses (and clause-complexes). The really basic distinction, anyway, is between expressions of the system and products of the use of the system in performance. The prominence that the notion of sentence-meaning has acquired in recent semantic theory is the product of a too ready acceptance in formal semantics of the priority of sentence-meaning over what is loosely called word-meaning, on the one hand, and, on the other, of an equally ready acceptance of what the experience of empirically grounded work in descriptive linguistics over the last half-century has shown to be the naive and theoretically indefensible view that actual text – the product of either speech or writing – is normally made up of sentences (in the sense of system-sentences).

It would be impossible in the space available to pick up and to comment upon the many points that Levinson makes in his contribution to the present volume. I will restrict myself to the use that he makes of the distinction between utterance-types and utterance-tokens. I should begin, however, by making explicit what should perhaps be evident to all readers: though Levinson operates with a distinction between sentence-meaning and utterance-meaning and makes this the basis of his distinction between semantics and pragmatics, everything that he says in this connection could also be reformulated without making the sentence a basic unit in all (or any) language systems.

At first sight, the use that Levinson makes of the type–token distinction in relation to (the product of) utterances is very different from the use that I make of it in Lyons (1977) and more especially in Lyons (1991a; cf. 1995). But, unless I am mistaken, his use and mine turn out to be fully compatible. I exploit the distinction between utterance-tokens and utterance-types primarily to demonstrate that sentences cannot be satisfactorily defined (as they often have been) as type–token classes of (the products of) utterances on particular occasions and then to show how tokens of the same utterance-type (e.g. *Not if you don't want to*) can be derived (by decontextualisation) from indefinitely many different system-sentences. (Incidentally, I never apply the type–token distinction to system-sentences, though I have often been misunderstood as having done so: it applies only to forms, and system-sentences are expressions, with both meaning and form; they are not forms, not even meaningful forms.) In showing that this is the case, I point out (operating with the notion of the sentence) that, paradoxically perhaps, the product of the utterance of a (system-)sentence, an utterance-token, in one sense is never a sentence (i.e. a system-sentence) and in another sense may be, but in conversation usually is not, a sentence (i.e. a text-sentence). The paradox is resolved, of course, by recognising, first of all, that the English verb *to utter* (like many other transitive verbs in English) can take two kinds of direct object, a normal object of affect and an object of effect, and, then, by noting a correlated ambiguity or equivocation in the use of the term 'sentence' (and 'clause', 'phrase', 'word', etc.) in both traditional grammar and modern linguistics.

What Levinson is suggesting (reformulated within this framework) is that there is frequently an intermediate level in the production and interpretation of utterances at which the general frequency of occurrence of tokens of a particular utterance-type with a particular meaning is so greatly preponderant (or, I would add, the contextual determination of the meaning of an utterance is so strong) that this meaning can be assigned by default, without the need for reconstruction (by decontextualisation) of a particular sentence from which the utterance-token can be said to be derived (as a perhaps elliptical or otherwise highly context-dependent form of the sentence). This seems to me eminently plausible. Indeed, it has always seemed to me more or less self-evident that what I have here (and elsewhere) referred to as the reconstruction of sentences as part of the process of interpretation is only rarely a matter of real-time reconstruction (I have said that sentences should not be assumed to have any cognitive existence), but, to use Levinson's term, of logical reconstruction. Levinson further proposes that over time the assignment of a default interpretation to utterance-types may result in the development of what are in effect new lexicalised or idiomatic expressions. Once again, this seems eminently plausible; and, as Levinson notes, in particular cases there is sound diachronic evidence to support the proposal.

Many of the resultant expressions (e.g. *Bless you!*) are what Saussure called 'ready-made expressions' ('locutions toutes faites', 1916: 238), which are usually produced and interpreted as unanalysable wholes, though, on reflection ('à la réflexion') they can sometimes be at least partially analysed and given a so-called literal interpretation. But the reconstructed literal interpretation will often be irrelevant. Consider, for example, the irrelevance, in practice, of the literal interpretation of tokens of *Don't mention it* after the utterance of tokens of *Thank you*. *Don't mention it* is at least interpretable compositionally in terms of the synchronic structure of Contemporary Standard English. But what is the synchronically determinable literal meaning of *Thank you* and *Bless you*? Are they, synchronically, second-person imperative utterances? If not, why not? And, if they are, how can one get any kind of relevant compositional meaning out of them? Levinson's thesis applies admirably to such utterances. It is, to me, all the more acceptable in that he makes it clear that, in his view, there is no sharp discontinuity between the level of utterance-type meaning and either (semantic) sentence-meaning or (pragmatic) utterance-token meaning. This implies, I take it, that it is, for Levinson as for me, a matter of rough justice where – and indeed whether – one draws the two boundaries which establish, by methodological decision, the additional level of utterance-type meaning. The alternative, presumably, is the more traditional one of putting what one judges to be fully lexicalised, compositionally unanalysable, utterance-types in the lexicon as idiomatic and formally invariant expressions. In this connection, one might refer to the lexically simple, idiomatic, expression 'red herring' in comparison with the lexically and syntactically composite, and compositionally interpretable, 'red herring', which share the common form *red herring*. (My notation is different from Levinson's, but this illustration should demonstrate the interconvertibility of the two systems, as well as the importance of the difference between expressions and forms.)

There is one point that Levinson does not make explicit – and may not accept. This is that, in the limiting case of the complete predictability of a token of a particular utterance-type in a given context, the utterance-token in question will have no specifiable utterance-meaning. To invoke the information-theoretic principle that cries out to be invoked at this point: 'Meaningfulness implies choice' (Lyons, 1968: 413). Although Levinson does not make these connections explicit, he is clearly aware that his work, like much current work in the field of Gricean and neo-Gricean pragmatics, is relatable to the information-theoretic studies of communication that flourished in the 1950s. It is also relatable to Firthian work in semantics: for example, to Mitchell's classic (1957b) study of the language of buying and selling in Cyrenaican Arabic. I will come back presently to the Firthian connection. What is original of course in Levinson's work and in that of others who adopt the same paradigm is its philosophical sophistication and its potentially greater explanatory adequacy.

It is interesting to read Trudgill's contribution in the light of Levinson's (and conversely), even though they are operating, *prima facie*, in two different branches of linguistics and in two quite different paradigms. Or are they? They are both concerned with (amongst other things) the way in which expressions (or rather, one or more of their forms) can be grammaticalised (and in the limit desemanticised) diachronically as a result of contextually determined, and thus predictable, use. And they both pray in aid in their explanation of their, *prima facie*, very different data, the same kind of cybernetic, or information-theoretic, notions as were more generally invoked by linguists in the 1950s. (I have noted above that such notions figure once again in current work in Gricean and neo-Gricean pragmatics.)

Trudgill explicitly refers to Martinet (1962); he might also have referred, of course, to Zipf (1949) or indeed to Hockett (1955) or Joos (1950). These notions went out of fashion in theoretical linguistics – and I think this is the right way to put it – when Chomsky (1956, 1959, etc.) criticised (correctly) their association with radical, *tabula rasa*, behaviourism and finite-state models of language acquisition and of grammaticality. Their rehabilitation within the framework of more satisfactory models of the structure and use of language is very much to be welcomed.

That what is technically referred to as redundancy plays an important role in the communicative use of language is all but self-evident (see Lyons, 1977: 41–50). The institutionalisation of fast-speech, or allegro, phenomena (which can be accounted for in terms of this concept) has, of course, commonly been seen as the explanation of the origin of such forms as *Goodbye* in English or the Modern Greek future particle *tha* (*thelo na* 'I wish to/will' > *thena* > *tha*). The latter case is not strikingly different from those discussed by Trudgill in respect of the hypothesised delexicalisation of certain expressions in East Anglian English and their grammaticalisation (more precisely, the grammaticalisation of their allegro forms) or from some of the cases discussed by Levinson.

Another of the contributors who operates (in this case explicitly) with a distinction between semantics and pragmatics is Bernard Comrie in his discussion of the German Perfect and the Simple Past (or Preterite). I cannot comment on the data; but I certainly agree with Comrie's methodological commitment to the principle of going as far as one can with system-valid notions of Gesamtbedeutung and markedness and, by throwing the burden of accounting for context-dependent interpretations on to pragmatic notions such as relevance, avoiding the multiplication of meanings assigned to particular tenses and aspects. Personally, I would also have welcomed the introduction into the discussion of the possibility that subjectivity, or experientiality, also plays a role in the interpretation of utterances containing perfect or past-tense forms. But my King Charles' head is bound to rear itself at times! And it may be that considerations of this kind would be judged by Comrie to fall within the scope of pragmatics and be handled differently. I take the view that some kinds of subjectivity are encoded, in some languages, in the grammatical and lexical structure of the language-system (see Lyons, 1995: chs. 5, 10; forthcoming).

John Anderson has for many years now – ever since he was a graduate student – been pursuing his own individual research programme, informed by a rare understanding both of traditional dependency grammar (as explicated and, up to a point, formalised by Tesnière and Hjelmslev) and of modern generative grammar and by a sound training in philology. His contribution to the present volume is but one of the many products of that programme which challenges apparently well-established principles. All I can say in response to it (whilst acknowledging that his conclusions are indeed challenging) is that, given that he is concentrating on (so-called) possessive constructions to illustrate the possibility of a contradiction, or conflict of directionality, between concord and rection (or government), I find it surprising that he says nothing in this connection about the localist analysis of possessives and, within this framework, about the development of 'have'-constructions out of (or into) adnominal locatives, which may then coexist in the same language with what are more exclusively possessives (in the traditionally broad sense of this term). Intuitively, there is an evident conflict (or ambivalence?) of dependency in structures in which a locative can be taken as either a subject or a predicate (see Lyons, 1977: 475ff.). To make contact more directly with cases discussed by Anderson: is the directionality of dependency the same for the adnominal dative–locative as it is for the possessive adjective in the French phrase *mon livre à moi*? And, in Latin, is it the same for the dative *mihi* in *Mihi est liber* as it is for the nominative *ego* in *(Ego) habeo librum*? I may be wrong, but I think that these cases are relevant to Anderson's thesis.

I have now referred, though in some instances all too briefly, to each of the other contributions to this volume in the light of general developments in linguistic semantics (in the broad sense) since the mid-to-late 1950s and of my own reaction to them. It remains to say something about my indebtedness to Firthian semantics, in connection with the relation between meaning and grammar and, then, to pick up and develop, in my own terms, one or two of the points Dixon makes in his chapter.

Firth always maintained of course that, unlike the post-Bloomfieldian (self-styled) structuralists, he took meaning into account at all levels of analysis. But Firth's notion of meaning was widely regarded as idiosyncratic, if not perverse. So too was his insistence on the relevance, at all levels, of what he called the context of situation.

In Lyons (1960/3), I tried to combine post-Bloomfieldian (and Chomskyan) distributionalism with Firthian contextualism, on the one hand, and with post-Saussurean structural semantics, on the other, first of all by drawing a distinction between environment and context and then by drawing a distinction between what was in effect the Firthian notion of having meaning (or being meaningful) and the notion of having (such-and-such) a meaning (the word 'meaning' being syncategorematic in both cases, though I did not make the point in these terms at the time). The context of a unit was so defined that it included both the co-text (or environment) in which the unit occurred and the relevant features of the situation in which the utterance containing the unit occurred. Units of whatever level were said to have meaning (in a given context) if and only if their occurrence (in the given context) was not wholly determined by context (and was therefore predictable). Only if a unit had meaning (in this syncategorematic sense of 'meaning') could one go on to ask what meaning it had; and the answer (when the question was pertinent) would be formulated, first of all, in terms of the structuralist notions of equivalence and contrast (sameness and difference) and, then, more interestingly, as far as lexical meaning was concerned, in terms of other paradigmatic relations of sense (hyponymy, antonymy, etc.), on the one hand, and of a variety of syntagmatic relations, on the other. So far (except for my subsequent development of sense relations in what were in effect truth-conditional terms), the theory of semantics that I adumbrated in my earliest work was thoroughly Firthian. And so far, apart from making certain minor terminological adjustments, I would not wish to change anything.

There is no need to go further into the details, since these are given, not only in Lyons (1960/3; cf. forthcoming), but also with no essential differences in Lyons (1968: 412–20). As to Firth's contextual theory of meaning, independently of my own adoption of some of his ideas, this is discussed somewhat critically in Lyons (1966a) and more sympathetically in Lyons (1977: 607–13). What I wish to concentrate upon here is my use of what I said was an essentially Firthian notion of having meaning (in the context of situation) and the structuralist notion of contrast (in the text and in the system). It was the coincidence between these two notions in what I described as the limiting case which, I said, provided the bridge between semantics and grammar: the limiting case was described as one in which there was nothing in the context of utterance to increase an expression's probability of occurrence (and hence its predictability) beyond its probability of occurrence for the particular environment (cf. Lyons, 1963: 26; forthcoming). This is still my view. I would now formulate it, however, as I did not earlier, on the basis of a prior distinction between (context-independent) sentence-meaning and (context-dependent) utterance-meaning and without invoking the statistical notion of probability of occurrence.

Thus reformulated, the principle should not be as controversial as it undoubtedly is. What it says, in effect, is that, generally speaking, expressions (e.g. morphemes or words) which are in grammatical contrast (i.e. which are intersubstitutable *salva grammaticalitate*) in some larger expression (phrase, clause, sentence) will have a meaning assigned to them in the language system because, even if they are totally predictable in that environment in some (or even most) contexts of the utterance of the larger expression, there will be at least one context of utterance in which they can be replaced in that environment by an expression (or, in the limit, by zero or the absence of an expression) which can be shown to have either the same meaning or a different meaning. There are two points to be noticed about this rather cumbersome statement of the principle. First, it avoids the subtractive fallacy by making an expression's sameness and difference of meaning with that of other expressions logically prior to the meaning that it has. Second, there is a sense in which it makes utterance-meaning methodologically, if not logically, prior to sentence-meaning; and this second feature of the formulation of the principle that I have just given makes it, at first sight at least, controversial. But it should not be. The only access that one has to sentence-meaning, which, as I mentioned earlier, is a theoretical construct, is via utterance-meaning; and sentence-meaning has no role to play, ultimately, other than the role that is assigned to it in the linguist's model of the production and interpretation of utterances. I will not go further into this question here. I will simply note that, although the principle that I have been expounding is essentially the one that I adopted in my earlier work, I have extended its application considerably in more recent publications, especially in Lyons (1995), where I have given far more attention to grammatical meaning, both categorial and structural, than I did before.

Earlier in this chapter, when I was discussing the view that I took of grammar and meaning in my analysis in the late 1950s of the vocabulary of Plato, I said that many of the points relating to what Dixon calls complementation strategies and illustrates from English, Fijian and Dyirbal could also be exemplified from Ancient Greek. They could equally well be exemplified from Latin, which, in respect of its grammatical structure, is of course typologically very similar to Ancient Greek. But there are interesting differences between the two languages as far as their complementation strategies are concerned: they both exhibit the three kinds of clause linking that Dixon mentions; they both have fully developed processes for syntactic and lexical nominalisation; and (unlike certain languages – I am inclined to agree with Dixon here) they both make available to their users clearly identifiable indirect-discourse constructions governed by what he calls Primary-B verbs. But Greek has a much wider range of constructions than Latin had for the complements of particular subsets of Primary-B verbs. Up to a point, some of these differences correlate with independently identifiable differences of lexical meaning between one subset of Primary-B verbs and another: for example, the difference between the complements of verbs of saying, thinking, etc., and the complements of verbs of sensation and perception, etc. Other differences also correlate, again up to a point, with differences in the propositional or non-propositional meaning of the complement as a whole: for instance, the difference between accusative-and-infinitive and nominative-and-infinitive constructions; between full-clause complements (with alternative complementisers) and either infinitival or participial complements; between an indicative and an optative clausal complement; etc. I will not go into the details, since they are readily accessible in any standard reference grammar of Greek and Latin.

What I will do here is use one of these differences between Ancient Greek and Latin (more precisely, Classical Latin) in order to make explicit a point that is not usually made explicit in standard grammars of these languages. It is a point that is relevant to Dixon's thesis about the interdependence of the grammatical and semantic structure of natural languages. It is also a point that can be invoked to demonstrate, with sound empirical evidence for it, the fact that the logical form of natural languages – contrary to what appears to be the view of most formal semanticists and many theoretically minded grammarians these days – is non-universal. The point is that the propositions expressed by indirect-statement complements in Latin are necessarily tenseless (as are infinitival, but not full-clause, indirect-discourse complements in Ancient Greek). The logical status of tensed propositions is, of course, controversial in formal semantics (see Lyons, 1977: 809ff.; 1995: ch. 6).

In conclusion, let me generalise the point I have just made about the non-universality of logical form in natural languages by relating Dixon's identification of the complement of Primary-B verbs to my own distinction between first-order and second-order referring expressions, on the one hand, and extensional and intensional referring expressions, on the other. (In earlier work, I operated with what was, *prima facie*, a one-dimensional three-way distinction (see Lyons, 1977: 441ff.; 1978: 170–5). I now think it is theoretically more satisfactory and makes for a more perspicuous set of terms if what I previously called third-order expressions – and entities – are reclassified as second-order intensional expressions – and entities – and what I previously called simply second-order expressions as second-order extensional expressions (see Lyons, 1989a, 1995). Indeed, this two-dimensional reclassification is implicit in my discussion of the ontological basis of the grammatical structure in Lyons (1977) and in the use that is made of this at various points elsewhere in that book and subsequent publications. The principal difference between the earlier and the later nomenclature – and the only one of substance – is the introduction of first-order intensional expressions – and entities – to handle what some formal semanticists call individual concepts. But this does not concern us in the present context.)

In terms of this two-dimensional classification, what Dixon calls Primary-A verbs take first-order-extensional referring expressions both as subjects and (where relevant) as objects. What he calls Primary-B verbs (in those languages which have such verbs) take second-order referring expressions in object position (and perhaps derivatively in subject position). But they subdivide semantically and perhaps also grammatically – and this is the crucial point – into those which take extensionally referring objects and those which take intensionally referring objects: that is, those which refer to situations (activities, states of affairs, etc.) in an extensional world (whether actual or potential), on the one hand, and, on the other, those which refer to propositions – propositions being the intensional correlates of situations, as truth is the intensional correlate of (extensional, spatio-temporal) reality (see Lyons, 1978, 1979a, 1989a, 1995). In many familiar languages that have Primary-B verbs, including English, there is of course class-cleavage (to use Bloomfield's term), notably with the verb 'to see', which is also a Primary-A verb and as a Primary-B verb can take either an extensionally or an intensionally referring object. Interestingly enough, in some cases, including that of *to see* in English, the object-expression can have double (or combined) second-order reference: for instance, *John saw that it was raining* (see Lyons, 1987: 175; 1989: 177).

I will not go further into the details of how this two-dimensional classification relates to the grammatical and semantic structure of particular languages. How it relates to Dixon's discussion of Primary-B verbs and their complements will be clear, I trust, from a consideration of his (7a) and (7b), where the former has an intensionally referring *that*-clause (which is characteristically the case in English) and the latter an intensionally referring participial/gerundival complement. (There is, of course, the additional possibility of a perfective complement without an *-ing*-form: *I heard (saw) America beat France.*) The difference between extensional and intensional reference is again quite clear in (13a) and (13b) – to which we should add the interestingly bifocal *The doctor remembered himself examining Mary Brown*, which differs semantically from *The doctor remembered examining Mary Brown* in the way that *The doctor remembered Professor Smith examining Mary Brown* does (see Lyons, 1989: 175) – and, once again, it correlates with a clear difference in the grammatical structure of the complements.

I cannot but echo Dixon's plea that 'careful grammatical description of [languages that lack complement clause constructions] should have a high priority in future research'; but I would seek to broaden the scope of that research and to make it semantically (and philosophically) more sophisticated. Not only do 'the available grammars [of such languages] say little about complementation strategies', but, like the available grammars of most languages, including English, they have little or nothing to say about what I have elsewhere referred to as 'a neglected aspect of syntactic typology' and have related to Quine's (1960) notion of 'semantic ascent' (see Lyons, 1989a).

It would appear that many of the languages of the world do not lexicalise, and (though this is less clear) that some do not grammaticalise, the traditional notion of 'abstract noun (or NP)'. It is impossible to discover from most existing accounts whether and to what degree a particular language has extensionally referring and intensionally referring abstract nouns and NPs. I have conjectured, in the article to which I have just referred, that some natural languages are ontologically richer than others – richer in their expressive power (to use the terminology of formal semantics) – because they encode (and make exploitable for scientific and philosophical purposes) 'this or that kind of distinction between concrete and abstract expressions'. I do not wish to develop this conjecture, or hypothesis, here. Still less do I wish to defend, in the present context, an updated, and more respectable, version of the once widely held view, based on highly suspect 'accounts of the languages of barbarous races', that 'the more advanced a language is, the more developed is its power of expression of abstract or general ideas' (Jespersen, 1922: 429). This, too, I will do elsewhere (Lyons, forthcoming). But I do wish to insist upon the fact that, despite the undoubted advances that have been made in the study of grammar and meaning in the last forty years or so, we are still not in a position to give a properly informed answer to the question whether 'ontology recapitulates philology' (see Quine, 1960; Lyons, 1989a). And it is, after all, a question that is, or ought to be, at the very heart of linguistics as a theoretically driven empirical discipline. Most linguists will, of course, almost automatically answer this question in the negative. But I am unaware of any reliable empirical evidence from linguistics or psychology that can be advanced in favour of the negative response; I am similarly unaware of any valid theoretical argument, supporting this negative response and it may be, historically, no more than a product of linguists' eminently justifiable negative reaction towards 'the classical fallacy' (Lyons, 1968: 9).

REFERENCES

Allen, J. Patrick B. & S. P. Corder (eds.) (1973) *Readings for Applied Linguistics* (The Edinburgh Course in Applied Linguistics, 1), Oxford University Press.

Allen, W. Sidney (1957) *On the Linguistic Study of Language: an Inaugural Lecture*. Cambridge University Press. (Reprinted, with 'Author's note [1965]', in Strevens (ed.), 1966: 3–26; and (without notes or references), with '[Author's] Foreword [1971]', in Allen & Corder (eds.) 1973: 147–61.)

Allerton, David J., E. Carney & D. Holdcroft (eds.) (1979) *Function and Context in Linguistic Analysis*, Cambridge University Press.

Arnold, Douglas G., M. Atkinson, J. Durand, C. Grover & L. Sadler (eds.) (1989) *Essays on Grammatical Theory and Universal Grammar*, Oxford University Press.

Bazell, Charles E. (1949a) Syntactic relations and linguistic typology. *Cahiers Ferdinand de Saussure* 8: 5–20.

(1949b). On the problem of the morpheme. *Archivum Linguisticum* 1: 1–15. (Reprinted in Eric P. Hamp, F. W. Householder & R. Austerlitz (eds.) *Readings in Linguistics*, vol. II, Chicago University Press, 1966, 216–26.)

Bazell, Charles E., J. C. Catford, M. A. K. Halliday & R. H. Robins (eds.) (1966) *In Memory of J. R. Firth*, London: Longman.

Chomsky, Noam (1956) Three models for the description of language. *IRE Transactions on Information Theory* IT-2. 113–24. (Reprinted, with corrections, in Luce, Bush and Galanter (eds.) 1963: 105–24.)

(1957) *Syntactic Structures*, The Hague: Mouton.

(1959) On certain formal properties of grammars. *Information and Control* 2: 137–67. (Reprinted in Luce, Bush and Galanter (eds.) 1963: 125–55.)

(1965) *Aspects of the Theory of Syntax*, Cambridge, MA: MIT Press.

Firth, John R. (1957a) *Papers in Linguistics, 1934–1951*, Oxford University Press.

(1957b) A synopsis of linguistic theory, 1930–1955. *Studies in Linguistic Analysis* 1–32. (Reprinted in Firth, 1968:168–205; extract in Kühlwein (ed.) 1973: 24–7.)

(1968) *Selected Papers of J. R. Firth 1952–1959*, ed. F. R. Palmer, London: Longman.

Fodor, Jeremy A. & J. J. Katz (eds.) (1964) *The Structure of Language: Readings in the Philosophy of Language*, Englewood Cliffs, NJ: Prentice Hall.

Gazdar, Gerald (1979) *Pragmatics*, London and New York: Academic Press.

Goodenough, Ward H. (1956) Componential analysis and the study of meaning. *Language* 32: 195–216.

Guiraud, Pierre (1955) *La Sémantique*. Paris: Presses Universitaires de France.

Harris, Zellig S. (1951) *Methods in Structural Linguistics*, University of Chicago Press. (Republished as *Structural Linguistics*, 1961.)

(1952) Discourse analysis. *Language* 28: 1–30.

(1954) Distributional structure. *Word* 10: 775–93. (Reprinted in Fodor & Katz (eds.) 1964: 33–49; Harris, 1970: 775–94; Katz, 1985: 26–47.)

(1957) Co-occurrence and transformation in linguistic structure. *Language* 33: 283–340. (Reprinted in Householder (ed.) 1972: 15–185.)

(1970) *Papers in Structural and Transformational Linguistics*, Dordrecht: Reidel.

Hockett, Charles F. (1955) *A Manual of Phonology*, Bloomington: Indiana University Press.

Householder, Fred W. (1957) Rough justice in linguistics. *Georgetown University Round Table on Language and Linguistics 1957*. Washington, DC: Georgetown University Press, 157–71.

(ed.) (1972) *Syntactic Theory*, vol. I: *Structuralism*, Harmondsworth: Penguin.

(1973) On arguments from asterisks. *Foundations of Language* 10: 365–76.

Jespersen, Otto (1922) *Language: its Nature, Development and Origin*, London: Allen and Unwin.

Joos, Martin (1950) Description of language design. *Journal of the Acoustical Society of America* 22: 701–8. (Reprinted in Joos (ed.) 1957: 349–56.)

(ed.) (1957) *Readings in Linguistics*, Washington, DC: American Council of Learned Societies. (Republished as *Readings in Linguistics 1*, Chicago University Press, 1966.)

Katz, Jerrold J. (ed.) (1985) *The Philosophy of Linguistics*, London: Oxford University Press.

Kühlwein, Wolfgang (ed.) (1973) *Linguistics in Great Britain*, II: *Contemporary Linguistics*, Tübingen: Niemeyer.

Leech, Geoffrey N. (1981) *Principles of Pragmatics*, London: Longman.

Levinson, Stephen (1983) *Pragmatics*, Cambridge University Press.

Lounsbury, Floyd, L. (1956). A semantic analysis of the Pawnee kinship usage. *Language* 32. 158–94.

Luce, R. Duncan, R. R. Bush & E. Galanter (eds.) (1963) *Handbook of Mathematical Psychology*, vol. II, New York and London: John Wiley.

Lyons, John (1960) A structural theory of semantics and its application to some lexical subsystems in the vocabulary of Plato. PhD dissertation, University of Cambridge (see Lyons, 1963).

(1963) *Structural Semantics* (Publications of the Philological Society, 20), Oxford: Blackwell. (Revised version of Lyons, 1960.)

(1966a) Firth's theory of meaning. In Bazell *et al.* (eds.) 1966: 288–302.

(1966b) Towards a 'notional' theory of the 'parts of speech'. *Journal of Linguistics* 2: 209–36. (Reprinted with new notes and 'Epilogue' in Lyons, 1991a: 110–45.)

(1968) *Introduction to Theoretical Linguistics*, Cambridge University Press.

(1977) *Semantics*, 2 vols., Cambridge University Press.

(1978) Deixis and anaphora. In Myers (1978: 88–103). (To be reprinted in Lyons, forthcoming.)

(1979) Knowledge and truth: a localistic approach. In Allerton *et al.* (eds.) (1979: 111–41. (To be reprinted in Lyons, forthcoming.)

(1981) *Language, Meaning and Context*, London: Fontana/Collins.

(1987) Semantics. In Lyons *et al.* (eds.) *New Horizons in Linguistics*, vol. II, London: Penguin, 152–78.

(1988a) Semantic ascent: a neglected aspect of syntactic typology. In Arnold *et al.*

(eds.) 153–86.

(1989b) The last forty years: real progress or not? *Georgetown University Round Table on Languages and Linguistics 1989*. Washington, DC: Georgetown University Press, 13–18.

(1991a) *Natural Language and Universal Grammar: Essays in Linguistic Theory*, vol. I, Cambridge University Press.

(1991b) *Chomsky*, 3rd (revised and expanded) edn, London: HarperCollins.

(1995) *Linguistic Semantics*, Cambridge University Press.

(forthcoming) *Semantics, Subjectivity and Localism: Essays in Linguistic Theory*, Cambridge University Press.

Martinet, André (1962) *A Functional View of Language* (The Waynflete Lectures, 1961), Oxford: Clarendon Press.

Matthews, Peter H. (1986) Distributional syntax. In Theodora Bynon & F. R. Palmer (eds.) *Studies in the History of Western Linguistics Theory: in Honour of R. H. Robins*, Cambridge University Press, 245–77.

(1993) *Grammatical Theory in the United States*, Cambridge University Press.

Mitchell, Terence F. (1957a) Long consonants in phonology and phonetics. *Studies in Linguistic Analysis* 182–205.

(1957b) The language of buying and selling in Cyrenaica: a situational statement. *Hesperis* 44: 31–71. (Reprinted in Mitchell, 1975: 167–200.)

(1975) *Principles of Firthian Linguistics*, London: Longman.

Myers, Terry (ed.) (1978) *The Development of Conversation and Discourse*, Edinburgh University Press.

Palmer, Frank R. (1971) *Grammar*, Harmondsworth: Penguin.

(1976) *Semantics: a New Outline*, Cambridge University Press (2nd edn, 1981).

Quine, Willard V. (1953) *From a Logical Point of View*, Cambridge, MA: Harvard University Press (2nd edn, 1961).

(1960) *Word and Object*, Cambridge, MA: MIT Press.

Reichenbach, Hans (1947) *Elements of Symbolic Logic*, London: Macmillan.

Robins, Robert H. (1964) *General Linguistics: an Introductory Survey*, London: Longman (3rd edn, 1979).

Russell, B. (1940) *An Inquiry into Meaning and Truth*, London: Allen and Unwin.

Saussure, Ferdinand de (1916) *Cours de linguistique générale*, ed. Charles Bally & Albert Séchehaye, Paris: Payot.

Strevens, Peter (ed.) (1966) *Five Inaugural Lectures*, Oxford University Press.

Studies in Linguistic Analysis (1962) (Special volume of the Philological Society), Oxford: Blackwell.

Trier, Jost (1931) *Der Deutsche Wortschatz im Sinnbezirk des Verstandes*, Heidelberg: Carl Winter.

(1934) Das sprachliche Feld: eine Auseinandersetzung. *Neue Jahrbücher für Wissenschaft und Jugendbildung* 10: 428–49.

Ullmann, Stephen (1957) *The Principles of Semantics*, 2nd edn, Glasgow: Jackson, and Oxford: Blackwell (1st edn, 1952).

Zipf, G. K. (1949) *Human Behaviour and the Principle of Least Effort*, Cambridge, MA: Addison-Wesley.

John Lyons: publications

Books

1963 *Structural Semantics*, Oxford: Blackwell.

1966 with R. J. Wales (eds.) *Psycholinguistics Papers*, Edinburgh University Press.

1968 *Introduction to Theoretical Linguistics*, London and New York: Cambridge University Press; foreign editions include: French (Larousse, 1970), German (Beck, 1971), Italian (Laterza, 1971), Spanish (Teide, 1971), Japanese (Taishukan, 1973), Polish (Państwowe Wydawnictwo Naukowe, 1975), Russian (Progress, 1979), Portuguese (Companhia Editora Nacional, 1979), Turkish (Olgac Basimevi, 1983), Malaysian (DBP, 1994), Indonesian (Gramedia, forthcoming), Romanian (Editura Stiintifica, forthcoming).

1970 *Chomsky*, London: Fontana, and *Noam Chomsky*, New York: Viking; foreign editions include: (DRV, 1971), Danish (Blyndendal, 1971), French (Seghers, 1971), Portuguese (Cultrix, 1972), Polish (Wiedza Powszechna, 1972), Japanese (1973), Dutch (Meulenhoff, 1973), Spanish (Grijalbo, 1974).

1970 (ed.) *New Horizons in Linguistics*, Harmondsworth: Penguin; foreign editions include: Japanese (1973), Swedish (Wahlström and Widstrand, 1973), German (Rowohlt, 1975), Italian (Einaudi), Portuguese (Cultrix, 1975), Spanish (Alianza, 1975.)

1977 *Chomsky*, 2nd, revised and expanded edn, London: Fontana, and New York: Viking/Penguin; foreign editions include: Japanese (1980).

1977 *Semantics*, 2 vols., London and New York: Cambridge University Press; foreign editions include: French (Larousse, 1978 and 1980), German (Beck, 1980 and 1983), Spanish (Teide, 1981), Italian (Laterza, 1980), Portuguese (Editorial Presenca, 1980), Polish (Państwowe Wydawnictwo Naukowe, 1984 and 1990).

1981 *Language and Linguistics*, London and New York: Cambridge University Press; foreign editions include: German (Beck, 1983), Italian (Laterza, 1981), Portuguese (Editora Guanabara Koogan, 1982), Spanish (Teide, 1984), Japanese (Hori, 1987), Malaysian (DBP, 1992), Greek (Patakis, 1995).

1981 *Language, Meaning and Context*, London: Collins/Fontana; foreign editions include: Spanish (1983).

250

1987 *New Horizons in Linguistics 2* (ed. with R. Coates, M. Deuchar and G. Gazdar), Harmondsworth: Penguin.

1991 *Chomsky*, 3rd, revised and expanded edn, London: HarperCollins.

1991 *Natural Language and Universal Grammar: Essays in Linguistic Theory*, vol. I, London and New York: Cambridge University Press; foreign editions include: Malaysian (DBP, forthcoming).

1995 *Linguistic Semantics: an Introduction*, London and New York: Cambridge University Press.

forthcoming *Semantics, Subjectivity and Localism: Essays in Linguistic Theory*, vol. II, London and New York: Cambridge University Press.

Articles

1962 Phonemic and non-phonemic phonology. *International Journal of American Linguistics* 28: 127–33. (Repr. in W. E. Jones & J. Laver (eds.) *Phonetics in Linguistics*, London: Longman, 1973, 229–39.)

1963 Coding the Russian alphabet for the purpose of machine translation. *Mechanical Translation* 7: 43–6.

1965 The scientific study of language. University of Edinburgh Inaugural Lectures, 24.

1966 Firth's theory of meaning. In C. E. Bazell, J. C. Catford, M. A. K. Halliday & H. R. Robins (eds.), *In Memory of J. R. Firth*, London: Longman, 288–302.

1966 Towards a 'notional' theory of the 'parts of speech'. *Journal of Linguistics* 2: 209–36.

1966 Intervention in discussion. In Lyons & Wales, *Psycholinguistics Papers*, 129–32.

1967 A note on possessive, existential and locative sentences. *Foundations of Language* 4: 290–406. (Repr. in French in *Langages*, 34 (1974): 390–6.)

1968 Existence, location, possession and transitivity. In B. Van Rootselaar & J. F. Staal (eds.) *Logic, Methodology and Philosophy of Science*, vol. III, Amsterdam: North Holland, 495–504.

1969 Intervention in 'Formal logic and natural languages'. *Foundations of Language* 5: 269.

1970 Generative syntax. In Lyons (ed.), *New Horizons in Linguistics*, 115–39.

1970 The meaning of meaning. *Times Literary Supplement*, 23 July 1970, 795–7.

1971 Grammar. In N. Minnis (ed.), *Linguistics at Large*. London: Gollancz, 55–74.

1971 Human language. In R. A. Hinde (ed.) *Non-Verbal Communication*. Cambridge University Press, 49–85.

1973 Structuralism and linguistics. In D. Robey (ed.) *Structuralism: an Introduction*, Oxford: Clarendon Press, 5–19.

1974 Linguistics. *Encyclopaedia Britannica*, 15th edn, 912–1012.

1975 The use of models in linguistics. In L. Collins (ed.) *The Use of Models in the Social Sciences*, London: Tavistock, 173–88.

1975 Deixis as the source of reference. In E. L. Keenan (ed.) *Formal Semantics of*

Natural Language, Cambridge University Press, 61–83.

1977 Statements, questions and commands. In A. Zampolli (ed.) *Linguistic Structures Processing*. Amsterdam, New York and Oxford: North Holland, 255–80.

1978 Foreword to William Labov, *Sociolinguistic Patterns*, Oxford: Blackwell, xi–xviii.

1978 Deixis and anaphora. In T. Myers (ed.) *The Development of Conversation and Discourse*, Edinburgh University Press, 88–103.

1978 The basic problems of semantics. In W. Dressler (ed.) *Proceedings of the Twelfth International Congress of Linguistics* (Innsbrucker Beiträge zur Sprachwissenschaft), Innsbruck: Institut für Sprachwissenschaft der Universität, 13–21.

1980 Pronouns of address in *Anna Karenina*: the stylistics of bilingualism and the impossibility of translation. In G. Leech & S. Greenbaum (eds.) *Studies in English Linguistics*, London: Longman, 235–49.

1980 Knowledge and truth: a localistic approach. In D. Allerton, E. Carney & D. Holdcroft (eds.) *Context and Function*, Cambridge University Press, 111–41.

1981 *Structural Semantics* in retrospect. In T. E. Hope, T. B. W. Reid, R. Harris & G. Price (eds.) *Language, Meaning and Style*. Leeds University Press, 73–90.

1981 Language and speech. In H. C. Longuet-Higgins, J. Lyons & D. E. Broadbent (eds.) *The Psychological Mechanisms of Language* (Philosophical Transactions of the Royal Society, London B295), London: Royal Society and British Academy, 215–22.

1982 Deixis and subjectivity: *Loquor, ergo sum?* In R. J. Jarvella & W. Klein (eds.) *Speech, Place and Action*, London and New York: John Wiley, 101–24.

1983 Modern languages and modern linguistics. *Modern Languages* 64: 87–94.

1983 Deixis and modality. *Sophia Linguistica* 12: 77–117.

1983 Current issues in semantics. *Sophia Linguistica* 12: 118–33.

1983 Subjectivity and objectivity as reflected in language. *Sophia Linguistica* 12: 134–46.

1983 Language and culture. *Sophia Linguistica* 12: 147–62.

1984 La subjectivité dans le langage et dans les langues. In G. Serbat (ed.) *E. Benveniste aujourd'hui*, vol. I, Paris: Société pour l'information grammaticale, 131–9.

1987 Origins of language. In Andrew Fabian (ed.) *Origins*, Cambridge University Press, 141–66.

1987 Introduction. In Lyons *et al.* (eds.) *New Horizons in Linguistics 2*, 1–29.

1987 Semantics. In Lyons *et al.* (eds.) *New Horizons in Linguistics 2*, 152–78.

1988 Theoretical semiotics and theoretical semantics. In Michael Herzfeld & Lucio Malazzo (eds.) *Semiotic Theory and Semiotic Practice*, Berlin: Mouton de Gruyter, 672–88.

1989 Semantic ascent: a neglected aspect of syntactic typology. In Douglas G. Arnold, R. M. Atkinson, J. Durand, J. Grover & L. Sadler (eds.) *Essays on*

Grammatical Theory and Universal Grammar, Oxford: Clarendon Press, 153–86.

1989 The last forty years: real progress or not? *Georgetown University Round Table on Language and Linguistics 1989*, Washington, DC: Georgetown University Press, 13–38.

1990 Linguistics: theory, practice and research. *Georgetown University Round Table on Language and Linguistics 1990*, Washington DC: Georgetown University Press, 11–30.

1991 Linguistics and law: the legacy of Sir Henry Maine. In Alan Diamond (ed.) *The Victorian Achievement of Henry Maine*, Cambridge University Press, 294–350.

1994 Subjecthood and subjectivity. In Marina Yaguello (ed.) *Subjecthood and Subjectivity: the Status of the Subject in Linguistic Theory*, Paris: Ophrys, 9–17.

1995 Colour in language. In Trevor Lamb and Janine Bourriau (eds.), *Colour: Art and Science*, Cambridge University Press, 194–224.

1995 Performance and competence and related notions. In Gillian Brown, K. Malmkjær & J. Williams (eds.) *Performance and Competence in Second Language Acquisition*, Cambridge University Press.

Reviews

1958 N. Chomsky, *Syntactic Structures*. *Litera* 5: 109–15.

1960 H. M. Hoenigswald, *Language Change and Linguistic Reconstruction*. *Bulletin of the School of Oriental and African Studies* 27: 621–2.

1961 K. J. Dover, *Greek Word Order*. *Classical Journal* 57: 274–7.

1962 C. Mohrman, A. Sommerfelt & J. Whatmough (eds.) *Trends in European and American Linguistics*. *American Anthropologist* 64: 1117–24.

1963 P. Ziff, *Semantic Analysis*. *International Journal of American Linguistics* 29: 82–7.

1963 A. Martinet, *A Functional View of Language*. *Nature* 197: 734–5.

1963 R. M. W. Dixon, *Linguistic Science and Logic*. *Lingua* 12: 431–44.

1964 O. S. Akhmanova, I. A. Mel'chuk, R. M. Frumkina & E. V. Padučeva, *Exact Methods in Linguistic Research*, and P. Garvin, *Natural Language and the Computer*. *New Scientist* 23: 286–7.

1964 S. Ullmann, *Language and Style*. *British Book News* 288 (August), 580.

1965 C. Mohrman *et al.*, *Trends in Modern Linguistics*. *Journal of Linguistics* 1: 87–92.

1966 J. Katz & P. Postal, *An Integrated Theory of Linguistic Description*. *Journal of Linguistics* 2: 119–26.

1966 N. Chomsky, *Aspects of the Theory of Syntax*. *Philosophical Quarterly* 16: 393–5.

1967 A. Martinet, *Elements of General Linguistics*. *Archivum Linguisticum* 17: 187–90.

1967 V. G. Admoni, *Osnovy Teorii Grammatiki*. *Archivum Linguisticum* 17: 183–7.

1969 N. Ruwet, *Introduction à la grammaire générative*. *Journal of Linguistics* 5: 189–90.

1969 M. Ivić, *Trends in Linguistics*. *Lingua* 22: 278–86.

1969 T. Langendoen, *The London School of Linguistics*. *American Anthropologist* 71: 713–14.

1969 M. Leroy, *Main Trends in Modern Linguistics*. *Language* 45: 105–8.

1971 W. C. Chafe, *Meaning and the Structure of Language*. *Times Literary Supplement* (9 July): 810.

1972 Yorick Wilks, *Grammar, Meaning and the Machine Analysis of Language*. *Modern Language Review* 67: 859–60.

1972 R. A. Wisbey (ed.), *The Computer in Literary and Linguistic Research*. *Modern Language Review* 68: 858–60.

1973 D. D. Steinberg & L. A. Jakobovits (eds.) *Semantics*. *Modern Language Review* 68: 619–21.

1973 Roy Harris, *Synonymy and Linguistic Analysis*. *Times Literary Supplement* (25 May): 591.

1973 R. S. Jackendoff, *Semantic Interpretation in Generative Grammar*. *Times Literary Supplement* (5 October): 1181.

1974 R. A. Hall *An Essay on Language*. *International Journal of American Linguistics* 40: 152–5.

1975 G. Lepschy, *A Survey of Structural Linguistics*. *Modern Language Review* 70: 840–1.

1976 N. Chomsky, *Reflections on Language*. *New Society* 35: 677–8.

1977 G. Harman (ed.) On *Noam Chomsky*. *Modern Language Review* 72: 137–9.

1977 Ian Robinson, *The New Grammarians' Funeral*. *Modern Language Review* 72: 131–2.

1977 J. D. Fodor, *Semantics*. *Times Literary Supplement* (8 July): 827.

1977 D. M. Rumbaugh (ed.) *Language Learning by a Chimpanzee: the LANA Project*. *Nature* 267: 731–2.

1978 C. F. Hockett, *The View from Language*. *Journal of Linguistics* 13: 323–8.

1979 Roger W. Cole (ed.) *Current Issues in Linguistic Theory*. *Quinquereme* 2: 290–2.

1979 Robert Martin, *French Contribution to Modern Linguistics*. *Etudes Anglaises* 32: 220–2.

1979 Robert Martin (ed.) *Modèles logiques et niveaux d'analyse linguistique*. *Etudes Anglaises* 32: 222–4.

1980 Josette Rey-Debove, *Le Métalangage*. *Journal of Linguistics* 16: 292–300.

1990 Roy Harris (ed.) *Linguistic Thought in England 1914–1945*. *Albion* 23: 165–8.

1990 Johannes P. Louw & E. A. Nida (eds.) *Greek–English Lexicon of the New Testament Based on Semantic Domains*. *International Journal of Lexicography* 3: 204–11.

1992 Jerrold J. Katz, *The Metaphysics of Meaning*. *Times Literary Supplement* (3 January): 24.

Index

Abbott, M., 178
abstract expressions, 40, 224, 246
acceptability, 229
adjacency, 168
adjectives
    context-dependency of interpretation, 63
    semantic types, 175–6
'adverbals', in Dyirbal, 204
adverbial clauses, 118, 129, 132
adverbs, context-dependency of
    interpretation, 63
African languages, 179, 183
Aitken, P., 178
Algeo, J., 36
Algonquian languages, 163, 169
algorithms, 233
Allan, K., 51, 53, 54–5
Allen, W. Sidney, 222, 226
alternation relations, 11–21
ambiguity
    between complement clause and relative
      clause meaning, 182–3, 217n
    denotational, 234
    lexical, 45n
    non-syntactic, 56
    problem in the truth-theoretic paradigm,
      62–70
Ameka, F., 179
American English, 160n
American structural linguistics, 222, 227
analytic–synthetic distinction, 34
anaphoric dependencies, 62–3, 64–7, 107
    local coreference, 102
Anderson, John M., 162–74
    Lyons on, 240–1
Anderson, S.R., 163, 164, 166, 169
antonymy, 35, 40, 242
Apollonius Dyscolus, 52
Apresjan, Ju. D., 2, 227

Arabana-Wangkangurru 216n
Arabic, 184
    Cyrenaican, 239
    Lebanese, 171–2
articulation process, speed of, 95–6, 110,
    111n, 143–4
aspectual verbs, 187, 196–7, 210
assimilation, 143–4
association, 36
Athabaskan, 169
Atlas, J.D., 93, 101, 106, 110n, 111n
Austin, J.L., 91, 94
Australian languages, 108, 183, 213
Austronesian languages, 108, 190, 219n
autonomous linguistics, 226, 231

Bach, K., 28
Bamberg, Michael, 149, 154–5
Bantu languages, 178
Barwise, J., 64, 86, 95, 100, 111n
Bazell, C.E., 222
behaviourism, 240
Belfast, 142
belief shifts, and semantic change, 32–3
Bernstein, B., 143, 144
Biber, D., 118
binding, semantic hierarchy of (Givón),
    218n
binding theory, see Government–Binding
    theory
biological foundations of language, 223
Bloomfield, L., 127, 222, 245
    on assumption of constant and specific
      meaning, 58–9
    on semantics and linguistic meaning, 48,
      49, 50, 58
    on syntax and semantics, 51, 53
Boas, F., 227
Bontkes, C., 217n